ARCTIC OCEAN

Severnaia
Zemilia

LAPTEV SEA

BERING SEA

EASTERN
SIBERIA

Lena R.

KAMCHATKA

Okhotsk

Petropavlovsk-
Kamchatskiy

Nizhnyia Tunguska R.

Aldan R.

SEA OF OKHOTSK

Lena R.

Amur R.

Lake Baikal

Irkutsk

Transiberian Railroad

MANCHURIA

Ulan Bator

Vladivostok

SEA OF JAPAN

Tokyo

CHINA

Port Arthur

KOREA

JAPAN

Peking

Pacific Ocean

For Carlotta, Malda and Peggy

This book would never have been produced had it not been for one invaluable Russian lady, Natasha Krupina. After she visited an exhibition in Moscow about the last Tsar of Russia, she telephoned us in London, strongly urging us to make a visit ourselves as she had found it so fascinating. After many delays and telephone conversations we reached Moscow the day the exhibition was to be dismantled. One of the directors of the exhibition, Mikhail Agroskin, kindly kept it open so that we could have a private viewing. Since that day we were determined to make use of this captivating material, and we spent many days and weeks at the State Archives of the Russian Federation, researching the contents of their files on the Romanovs. These were the humble beginnings of our project "*The Romanovs: Love, power & tragedy*." Originally we intended to make this book into a photo album; however the subject demanded a more complex approach. Therefore we commissioned various Russian scholars to contribute. The chapter, "Alix's Childhood", is the work of Dr. Manfred Knodt, who has written much on the history of the Dukes of Hesse-Darmstadt. We wish to express our gratitude to him and to Lyudmila Xenofontova who not only translated this book for us but also put her heart and soul into it with extensive research and tolerating telephone calls in the middle of the night; Gui Kai for all his photographic work; Charlie Knight and Craig Adelman for their dark room labours, Sandra for her picture research; Igor Petrushevski and Tanja Houston, students in Moscow at the time as our "unofficial" interpreters; Angela van Ness for her beautiful artwork; Marco Houston for assisting Lyudmila; Father John Helm of St Edward The Confessor, Golders Green; Paul Marsh, Anne-Marie Bucknall, Kelly Punter, Fiona Florence, Angela Macdonald, Deborah Crane. Our deepest gratitude also to Tatiana Pavlova and the late B I Kaptelov, Archive Director when the project began ; to Bob Houston for designing this book; and, finally, to Sergei Mironenko for his assistance and advice.

Judy Pederneski-Widmann

FIRST PUBLISHED IN THE UNITED KINGDOM 1993. © LEPPI PUBLICATIONS
BRITISH LIBRARY CATALOGUING IN PUBLICATION DATA
Leppi Publications
The Romanovs, Love, power & tragedy
I. Title
ISBN 0-9521644-0-X

CAPTION COMPILATION © JUDY WIDMANN-PEDERNESKI
PHOTOGRAPH CREDITS:
ALL PHOTOGRAPHS SUPPLIED BY THE STATE ARCHIVES OF THE RUSSIAN FEDERATION

ALIX CHAPTER: PHOTOGRAPHS THE PRIVATE COLLECTION OF DR. MANFRED KNODT.

Extracts from "The World Crisis" by Sir Winston Churchill reproduced with permission of Curtis Brown Ltd., London, on behalf of the Estate of Sir Winston S Churchill. Copyright the Estate of Sir Winston S Churchill.

LEPPI
PUBLICATIONS

The Romanovs
Love, power & tragedy

Alexander Bokhanov

Dr Manfred Knodt

Vladimir Oustimenko

Zinaida Peregudova

Lyubov Tyutyunnik

TRANSLATION
Lyudmila Xenofontova

LEPPI
PUBLICATIONS

AFTER SEVEN DECADES, A TRUE IMAGE OF THE LAST ROMANOVS

The State Archives of the Russian Federation is the repository and guardian of unique, priceless riches, access to which was blocked for many decades after 1917. Not only foreigners, but even our own countrymen were denied any opportunity to work with authentic documents relating to the most crucial events in the country's history. For a long period the life of the last Russian Tsar, Nikolai II, was one of these restricted zones. This can be easily accounted for as the topic was rather sensitive for the new regime. Given the vexatious persistence with which they tried to obscure the real image of the Tsar, it seems quite incredible that all his documents, as well as those belonging to his family, have not been destroyed. More than that, they have been meticulously collected and carefully preserved.

Only two days after the execution of the Tsar's Family in Yekaterinburg, Yakov Yurovskiy, the commander of the executioners, left for Moscow carrying all valuables and documents which had belonged to the Family. For a time, the Tsar's archive was kept in the Kremlin, in the premises of the All-Russia Central Executive Committee of the Workers', Peasants' and Soldiers' Deputies. Later, the documents were handed over to the State Archives where they have been kept intact till this day. The collection was replenished with new acquisitions from palaces and estates which had formerly belonged to the members of the Imperial Family. Thus, in 1919, the so-called Novoromanovskiy Archive (The New Romanov Archive) was set up, and also included manuscripts from the libraries of the Winter Palace and the palaces of Tsarskoye Selo, the entire collection comprising over fifty archives totalling more than forty thousand files.

The Tsar's documents, their destiny and utilisation, have lived through various periods. For long years they lay buried under seven seals, and only official publications intended to compromise the last Russian sovereign gave evidence that such documents existed, that they had not been destroyed "for lack of historical value". During the "thaws" of liberal times, access to the documents became less restricted, but their publication was deemed "inexpedient". Only with the arrival of *perestroika,* and, finally, after the failed coup of August 1991, did access to them become totally unrestricted. The archive of the Tsar's Family is a rich, varied collection, and, undoubtedly, of paramount importance for the understanding of Russian history. Unless all these documents are given due consideration, it is impossible to decipher the real implications of the events which took place in Russia in 1917, and which proved pivotal for the entire world historical process.

The State Archives of Russia holds the collection of Nikolai II's diaries, in which the Tsar methodically kept a daily record of his life, the diaries of Tsarina Alexandra Feodorovna, the Family's correspondence with representatives of the European reigning dynasties, exercise-books of Nikolai II and his children as pupils, their drawings, paintings, and photographs. One fascinating document is the questionnaire of the First General Census of the Population of Russia of 1897 (illustrated on this page) filled in by the hand of Nikolai II, in which the Tsar indicated his "occupation" – "the Master of the Russian Land", and he described his wife as "the Mistress of the Russian Land".

The correspondence of Nikolai II and his wife and volumes of their private letters give a genuine portrait of the Tsar's personality, revealing his warm-heartedness and subtlety. These letters are witness to their amazing love story, a twenty-four year-long honeymoon of a marriage. And they are also a documented account of their tragedy as, step by step, they approached the fatal abyss which emerged with the destruction of their world.

The real pearls of this collection are the Family's albums of photographs. There are more than a hundred of these albums, each containing 150-300 pictures, to say nothing of individual photos kept in separate files. Many of them were taken by Nikolai II, the passionate photographer.

It will not take the reader long to grasp the value of this book, an illustrated chronicle of the life of the last Tsar's Family. I remember my own reaction when I saw these albums for the first time. They had an astonishing and staggering impact on me. They profoundly altered my understanding of Nikolai II. Only a man for whom his family was so important would strive to get a memorable imprint of every moment of their lives. Neither the lustre of the Russian throne, nor the omnipotence of absolute power in a vast country outweighed the family circle so dear to his heart, the core of his inner world.

Take an unhurried look at these photographs, study these documents carefully . . . and you will come to the same conclusion.

Sergei V. Mironenko
Professor of History,
Director,
State Archives of the Russian Federation

Contents

The Romanovs

THE CAST
OF
CHARACTERS
IN THE
TRAGEDY

NiIKOLAI II, TSAR OF RUSSIA, 1894-1917
Before 1894, Cesarevitch Nikolai Alexandrovitch

ALEXANDRA FEODOROVNA, TSARINA OF RUSSIA
Born Princess Alix of Hesse-Darmastadt

ALEXEI NIKOLAYEVITCH
Heir Cesarevitch Nikolai II's son
OLGA NIKOLAYEVNA
Grand Duchess
TATIANA NIKOLAYEVNA
Grand Duchess
MARIA NIKOLAYEVNA
Grand Duchess
ANASTASIA NIKOLAYEVNA
Grand Duchess

GEORGIY ALEXANDROVITCH
Grand Duke, Nikolai II's brother, Heir Cesarevitch (since 1894)
MIKHAIL ALEXANDROVITCH (Misha)
Grand Duke, Nikolai II's youngest brother, Cesarevitch 1894-1904
XENIA ALEXANDROVNA
Nikolai II's sister
OLGA ALEXANDROVNA
Grand Duchess, Nikolai II's sister

IRINA
daughter of Grand Duke Alexander Mikhailovitch and Grand Duchess Xenia Alexandrovna, wife of Prince Felix Yusupov
ALEXANDER MIKHAILOVITCH (Sandro)
Grand Duke, Nikolai I's grandson, Nikolai II's brother-in-law
ALEXEI ALEXANDROVITCH
Grand Duke, Alexander II's son, Nikolai II's uncle
SERGEI ALEXANDROVITCH (uncle Gega)
Grand Duke, Nikolai II's uncle, Governor-General of Moscow, married to Yelizaveta Feodorovna
PAVEL ALEXANDROVITCH
Grand Duke, Nikolai II's uncle
VLADIMIR ALEXANDROVITCH
Grand Duke, Nikolai II's uncle
BORIS VLADIMIROVITCH
Grand Duke

KIRILL VLADIMIROVITCH
Grand Duke; in 1924, in Paris, proclaimed himself Tsar

DMITRIY PAVLOVITCH
Grand Duke, Nikolai II's cousin, who took part in Rasputin's assassination
ANDREI
Grand Duke

ALEXANDER II NIKOLAYEVITCH
Tsar of Russia, Nikolai II's grandfather
ALEXANDER III ALEXANDROVITCH
Tsar of Russia, Nikolai II's father
MARIA FEODOROVNA (Minnie)
Alexander III's wife, Empress of Russia, Nikolai II's mother, born Princess Sophia Frederica Dagmar of Denmark
MIKHAIL FEODOROVITCH ROMANOV
the first Tsar of the Romanov Dinasty (1613)

ALEXEYEV MIKHAIL VASILYEVITCH
Adjutant-General, Chief of Staff of the Supreme Commander-in-Chief (since August 1915), after the February revolution Commander-in-Chief
BENCKENDORF, ALEXANDER KONSTANTINOVITCH
Count, Hofmeister, Russian Ambassador Extraordinnaire and Plenipotentiary in Great Britan in 1903-1916
BENCKENDORF, PAVEL KONSTANTINOVTICH
1853-1921 Count, Chief Hofmeister

BUBLIKOV, ALEXANDER ALEXANDROVITCH
Commissar of the Provisional Government
BUCHANAN, Sir George William
British Ambassador in Russia in 1910-1918

KERENSKIY, ALEXANDER FEODOROVITCH
Minister-Chairman of the Provisional Government
KOKOVTSOV, VLADIMIR NIKOLAYEVITCH
Count, Minister of Finance, Chairman of the Council of Minister
KORNILOV, LAVR GEORGIEVITCH
Infantry General, Supreme Commander-in-Chief in July-August 1917
LENIN, VLADIMIR ILYICH
Born Ulanov, leader of Bolsheviks who led coup in October 1917
PLEHVE, VYASHESLAV KONSTANTINOVITCH
Minister of the Interior (1902-1904)
PROTOPOPOV, ALEXEI DIMTRIEVITCH (Kalinin)
Minister of the Interior
RODZIANKO, MIKHAIL VLADIMIROVITCH
Commander-in-Chief of the North-Western and Northern Fronts (1916)
RUZSKIY, NIKOLAI VLADIMIROVITCH
Commander-in-Chief of the North-Western and Northern Fronts (1916)
SHULGIN, VASILY VITALYEVITCH
member of the Interim Committee of the State Duma
STOLYPIN, PYOTR ARKADYEVITCH
Minister of the Interior and Chairman of the Council of Ministers (from1906)
TATISCHEV, ILYA LEONIDOVITCH
Count, Adjuntant-General Lieutenant-General, Nikolai II's personal representative at Wilhelm II's (1905-1914)
TROTSKY, LEV DAVIDOVITCH
Lenin's lieutenant
WITTE, SERGEI YULYEVITCH
Count, Chairman of the Council of Minister (1903-1906) and the Committee of Finance (1906-1915)
GUCHKOV, ALEXANDER IVANOVITCH
member of the Provisional Government (March-April 1917)
AVDEYEV, ALEXANDER DMITRIEVITCH
Superintendent of the "House of Special Purpose" in Yekaterinburg
KOBYLINSKIY, YEVGENIY STEPANOVITCH
Colonel, Commander of Tsarskoye Selo garrison
SVERDLOV YAKOV MIKHAILOVITCH
Chairman of the AIII-Russian Central Executive Committee
YAKOVLEV VASILIY (Konstantin Alexeyevitch Myachin)
Soviet Commissar
YUROVSKIY, YAKOV MIKHAILOVITCH
Superintendent of the "House of the Special Purpose" in Yekaterinburg
GOLOSCHEKIN, PHILIPE ISAYEVITCH (Shaya)
military commissar of the Ural region

DOLGORUKOV, VASILIY ALEXANDROVITCH (Valya)
Prince,Stepson of Count P.K. Benckendorf
FREDERICKS, VLADIMIR BORISOVITCH
Count, Minister of the Imperial Court
VOYEIKOV, VLADIMIR NIKOLAYEVITCH
Major-General of the Suite, the Palace Superintendent
DEMIDOVA, ANNA STEPANOVNA (Nyuta)
Tsarina Alexandra Feodorovna's maid
SEDNEV, IVAN DMITRIEVITCH
footman of the Tsar's family
SEDNEV, LEONID (Leonka)
kitchen boy, nephew of Sednev the footman
TETERYATNIKOV, N. K.
Nikolai II's valet
TRUPP, ALEXEI YEGOROVITCH
Nikolai II's footman
VOLKOV, ALEXANDER ALEXANDROVITCH
Tsarina Alexandra Feodorovna's valet
CHEMUDOROV, TERENTIY IVANOVITCH
NIkolai II' s valet

GIBBS, GEORGE SYDNEY
tutor of the Tsar's children
GILLIARD, PIERRE
tutor of the Tsar's children
PETROV, PYOTR VASILYEVITCH
tutor of the Tsar's children
VASILYEV, ALEXANDER PETROVITCH
priest, religious instructor of the Tsar's children, confessor of the Tsar's family (1914-1917)
YANISHEV, IOANN
archpriest of the Court Cathedrals, Nikolai II's confessor

BOTKIN, YEVGENIY SERGEYEVITCH
Physician
DEREVENKO, VLADIMIR NIKOLAYEVITCH
Surgeon
FEODOROV, SERGEI PETROVITCH
Professor, Surgeon
VYRUBOVA, ANNA ALEXANDROVNA (Anya, Ania)
Tsarina Alerxandra Feodorovna's Maid of honour and close friend
BUXHOEVEDEN, SOPHIA KARLOVNA (Isa)
Baroness, Tsarina Alexandra Feodorovna's Maid of honour
DEHN, JULIA ALEXANDROVNA (Lili)
Tsarina Alexandra Feodorovna's friend
GENDRIKOVA, ANASTASIA VASILYEVNA (Nastia)
Countess, Tsarina Alexandra Feodorovna Maid of honour
SCHNEIDER, CATHERINE (Yekaterina Adolfovna)
tutor who taught Tsarina Alexandra the Russian language

ALICE
daughter of Queen Victoria, Grand Duchess of Hesse- Darmstadt, wife of Louis the IV, Alexandra Feodorovna's mother
QUEEN VICTORIA
Queen of Great Britain, Alexandra Feodorovna's grandmother
VICTORIA, ALEXANDRA OLGA MARY ("Tora, Toria")
Queen Victoria's grand-daughter,Nikolai II's and Alexandra's cousin.
VICTORIA FEODOROVNA ("Ducky")
born Princess Victoria Melita of Saxe-Coburg-Gotha, wife of Ernst Ludwig of Hesse-Darmastadt; after divorce, wife of Grand Duke Kirill Vladimirovitch)

VISHNYAKOVA, MARIA IVANOVNA
Cesarevitch Alexei's nurse
NAGORNY, KLEMENTIY GRIGORYEVITCH
sailor on the Imperial yacht Standard Cesarevitch Alexei's attendant
DEREVENKO, ANDREI YEREMEYEVITCH
Bo'sun, Cesarevitcvh Alexei's attendant

FRANZ-FERDINAND
Archduke of Austria
WILHELM II (Willy)
German Kaiser (1888-1918)
ERNST LUDWIG (Ernie)
Grand Duke of Hesse-Darmstadt, Tsarina Alexandra Feodorovna's brother
YELIZAVETA FEODOROVNA ("Ella")
born Princess Elizabeth Alexandra Louise Alice of Hesse-Darmstadt, Tsarina Alexandra Feodorovna's sister, wife of Grand Duke Sergei Alexandrovitch
KSCHESSINSKA, MATHILDE
famous ballerina, romantically linked to Cesarevitch Nikolai Alexandrovitch before his marriage to Alexandra Feodorovna
BRASOVA, NATALIA SERGEYEVNA
wife of Grand Duke Mikail Alexandrovitch in morganatic marriage
RASPUTIN, GRIGORIY YEFIMOVITCH
Siberian holy man –"starets" – murdered in 1916
PURISHKEVITCH, VLADIMIR MITROFANOVITCH
one of Rasputin's assassins
YUSUPOV, FELIX FELIXOVITCH
Prince, Count Sumarokov-Elston, one of the Rasputin"s assassins.
JOHNSON, BRIAN
Grand Duke Mikhail Alexandrovitch's secretary
SABLIN, NOKOLAI PAVLOVITCH
senior officer (1911-1915) and commander (1916) of the Imperial yacht Standard

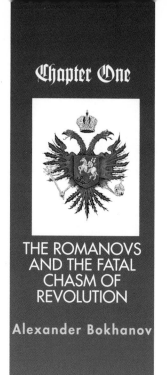
THE LAST TSAR, ADRIFT ON A SHIP OF STATE, HEADING FOR THE ROCKS

The pages of the world chronicles of the outgoing century are permeated with an amazing pathos and incredible dramatic sense. They are pierced with pain and suffering, hopes and disappointments, and imbued with the gains of entire nations as well as that of individuals. This is the century of Adolf Hitler and Joseph Stalin, Bertrand Russell and Andrei Sakharov, GULAG and the Universal Declaration of Human Rights. What is the great secret that time has concealed? How can the tangle of the thorny paths of humanity be unravelled? Much can be accounted for by history. However, hardly anybody would take the risk to assert that he has discerned the absolute truth of human history and its fateful purport. Yet there are certain tenets which cannot be denied, one of them being the tremendous influence of Russia on the destiny of Europe and, therefore, on the destiny of the whole world – and this influence has been particularly marked in the 20th century.

The disaster which overtook Russia in 1917 represented not only the triumph of ruthless left-wing radicalism in the biggest empire of the world – the Russian revolution of 1917 also represents the fatal chasm of the twentieth century. The red totalitarianism in many respects prompted the patterns of the world's political developments, resulting in a series of social conflicts and wars, systematically waged. There is no denying that the "red threat" was pre-empted by the "brown threat" in Germany, thus countenancing the Nazi's rise to power. But the sternest price was paid by Russia, which was to go through the crucible of protracted and unsavoury social experimentation.

The date when the country embarked upon its Way of the Cross can be pinpointed precisely – March 2 (15), 1917. That day, at a small provincial station, the last Russian Tsar, Nikolai II, abdicated the throne. The millennium-long history of the thrones and crowns of Russia was over, the natural course of events disrupted, and the country's Book of Fate deflected for recording new chapters, whose savageness – hidden for decades from the world's scrutiny – reached unimaginable proportions.

Why did the collapse come about? Was it remorseless fate or a tragic contingency, or was it a malicious intent of some universal force? The answers might be numerous and divergent. In a cacophony of contradictory estimations and judgements, one will find it too difficult to distinguish between right and wrong. For the depth and intensity of its impact, this grandiose catastrophe can be compared with the collapse of the Roman Empire. But while the fall of Great Rome has been a subject of extensive historical research, profound and impartial, the factors which caused the Tsarist Empire to vanish have not been studied coherently enough. As a matter of fact, it is not the number of treatises on a subject that actually count, but the ideological prejudice which leads investigation astray; whereas the way to perceive the truth can be paved only through overcoming ideological stereotypes, through a new approach in comprehending familiar facts.

The life of every society and the destiny of every country is affected by many circumstances, but in an authoritarian system, such as the Russian autocracy was, the personality of those empowered with supreme authority played a decisive role. However, the latter presumption has not always been given due consideration. As for Nikolai II, his portrait appeared plain and pellucid. At fate's haphazard decree, a mediocre, narrow-minded man turned out to be the one on the throne; he surrounded himself with primitive and sometimes abnormal people, hindered the progressive development of the country; and, as a logical result, fell victim to the "onward march of history." All the "t's" were crossed, all the "i's" dotted. History's harsh verdict had been passed, once and for all.

Reality, though, cannot be trammelled by shallow, stereotyped patterns, and in full measure this applies to the main characters of the pathetic drama of the Russian monarchy. Nikolai II ascended the throne after the death of his father, Emperor Alexander III, on October 20, 1894, and for over 22 years he personified supreme power in the vast empire which stretched from the banks of the Vistula in the west to the Aleutian Isles in the east. He had not sought to become a monarch – the lot fell to him as the Tsar's son. But along with the burden of unlimited power, the Tsar was to assume the load of moral and political responsibility for the course of affairs in the country. Public

and state governmental foundations (the parliament, the independent court, the free press, etc.) emerged in Russia only after the revolution of 1905, and the nascent institutions never matured into efficient instruments of control and power.

After the legislative reforms of 1905-1906, the system gradually acquired a new character: the State Duma was convened and the Tsar was supposed to rule in accordance with the will of the people's elected representatives. However, Russia failed to become a constitutional monarchy in the true sense of the word, and the Tsar's actions were to be modified by liberal public opinion rather than by definite legal regulations.

Only the first few years after Nikolai II's ascension to the throne were relatively peaceful. The major part of his reign was an incessant chain of upheavals, tumults and wars. For various reasons, the rumblings of discontent affected the new strata of society, and, as the Empire of the two-headed eagle irreversibly headed towards ruin, the malcontent comprised an overwhelming majority of Russia's politically conscious population. The sentiments that the methods of governing Russia were "all wrong", that "things could not be worse" and that people "could not go on living like that", became stale.

At the turn of the century, Russia was like a huge ship drifting without direction, captured by unpredictable currents, the unwieldy state hierarchical machine often

Pyotr Stolypin (above) was born in 1863 into the rural nobility. At the height of the revolution in 1905 he was Governor of Saratov province. In 1906 he became Minister of Interior and was asked by Nikolai II to succeed Witte as Chairman of the Council of Ministers. A much admired statesman, simple and straight forward, he attempted to restructure the absolutist system of governing and responded to the popular will. Attempts on his life were made in 1907 when his daughter and son were injured. He was assassinated in September 1911 when he attended a performance of Rimsky-Korsakov's "Tsar Sultan", when the Imperial Family was in attendance. (Left) Sergei Yulevich Witte was born in Tiflis, Georgia. His father was of Dutch origin, his mother Russian. He entered government office in 1889 as Director of the Department of Railway Affairs. In 1893 he was appointed Minister of Finance by Alexander III, and subsequently Chairman of the Council of Ministers. Witte proved himself one of the finest brains in government, striving to turn Russia into a first division industrial power. He fell from grace in 1903, a victim of political intrigue, but after skilfully negotiating peace with Japan in 1905 he was given the title of count by Nikolai II. He became Head of government during the 1905 revolution. In 1906 Witte, again dogged by plots and intrigues, asked to be relieved of office.

(Facing page) The first Duma was convened on April 27, 1906 in St Petersburg. Nikolai II was accompanied at the ceremonial opening by Dowager Empress Maria Feodorovna and the Tsarina. (Above) 1906. St. Petersburg. Members of the first Duma in the Tavrichesky Palace. The first Duma was dissolved by the Tsar on July 8, 1906, amidst acrimonious disputes over land reform. (Right) The second Duma in session. Convened on February 20, 1907 under Stolypin, it was dissolved on June 2. Stolypin created a third Duma, November 1, 1907, which gave more power to the country gentry. The fourth Duma was convened on November 15, 1912 and survived till February 27, 1917, when the Interim Committee of the State Duma was formed.
(Facing page) A welcome to the Tsar and the Tsarina from the "Incorporated Chamber of Commerce Liverpool (Great Britain) ". "May it please your Majesty we representatives of. . . desire to join most heartily in welcoming Your Majesty and the Empress on your arrival in this country, to which both are so closely allied by ties of blood. It has lately been the privilege of this Chamber to receive and entertain at Liverpool Members of the Russian Duma and representatives of the Russian Nation, and it is hoped that the visit of both Rulers and subjects may tend to promote feelings of friendship and confidence between Powers governing worldwide territories. . .We have the honour to be Your Majesty's most Faithful Servants". August 5, 1909.

merely idling. At the close of the 19th century the symptoms of what is called "crisis of power" were evident, and a monarch – independent of his personal qualities – could only aggravate or ease the tension, but he had no chance of controlling it. This is fundamental and indispensable for a sound analysis of the social and political situation faced by the historical power at that time.

Autocracy had existed in Russia for centuries and it had facilitated the establishment and consolidation of the empire. This model of governing met the requirements of the time when society was rather simple and its advancement could be guided by instructions and directives from the centre. But as the internal structure of society became more and more complicated, there arose the need for a switch from autocratic methods of governing to democratic ones, so that power and responsibility could be delegated to polycentric authorities. But then it became obvious that the traditional, evolutionary way trod by European countries was no good for Russia. Authoritarian power was the basic cement of the Russian system, and its dilution or rejection inevitably led to weakening and even the disintegration of the Empire, which had managed to combine its incompatibilities to the degree that colonies and the centre developed within an integral territory. Thus, in Russia,

the latest achievements of civilisation kept company with ignorance and backwardness, and opulence and refinement were mixed with destitution and barbarism.

It is apparent from historical experience that the Russian monarchy may have had a chance to survive if social and economic institutions and structures had been reformed, as advocated by Stolypin, Chairman of the Council of Ministers and Minister of the Interior. But the policy suggested by the "strong Premier" – and approved by Nikolai II – was attacked not only by radical and liberal circles; it also met the antagonism of those close to the throne. The remnants of the Russian gentry, lofty and obstinate, were reluctant to give up any of their privileges – minor and illusory as they often were – and opposed all change. And without change, there could be no progress. The half-measures and palliatives in which the history of the last reign abounded, reflected the futile attempts to reach a compromise between habitual existence and common sense.

Historically, the power of the Tsar was based on the charismatic 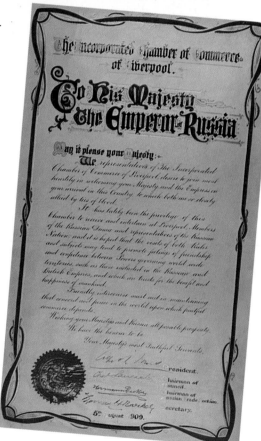 principle. The subjects were to fulfil the will of His Majesty, who was vested with a Divine gift. The monarch was responsible not to the constitution and the parliament, but to the Most High, which was deemed by believers to be the supreme form of responsibility. In 1906, in a letter to Stolypin, the Tsar asserted: *"For all the powers that I have appointed I bear a terrible responsibility to God, and at any time I am ready to give my account to Him"*.

The autocrat's decisions came more and more into conflict with new historical realities and new conditions of social life. Before, it was only in a small world of *beau monde* salons or in very few circles of left-wing radicals that state policy could be criticised; during the reign of Nikolai II all that changed. The social and economic modernization of the country, launched in the middle of the 19th century, gave an impetus to the formation of new social groups which, gaining weight and autonomy from the state, strove to participate in state decisions, and thus attempted to plant European rules of the political game in the Russian soil. The Russian educated society, satiated with universal humanist values, professed ideas of parliamentarianism and clamoured for accountability of power. But it was Fate's bitter irony that the liberal opponents of autocracy, who undertook to speak on behalf of the entire Russia, proved to have expressed the aspirations and attitudes of a very limited strata.

Vladimir Illyich Lenin and his lieutenants, leaders of the "St. Petersburg Union of Struggle for the Liberation of the Working Class". Left to right: (seated) V.V. Starkov, G.M. Krzhizhanovskiy, Lenin, Y.O. Martov; (standing) A Malcenko, P.K. Zaporozhets and A.A. Vanyev. During the purges of the 1930's Malcenko was executed on Stalin's order.

The peasants, who constituted 85 percent of the population, were far from understanding the meaning of European parliamentary models. Suffering from lack of land and indigence, Russian "Ivans" dreamt of greater plots of land and cared not for reconstruction of the political system. They believed in God, revered the Tsar, trembled before local authorities and knew nothing about constitutions. Political agitation in the capital, anti-government tirades of the Duma orators, passionate articles in liberal publications never reached the minds of the majority of the population.

The fiasco of liberalism manifested itself soon after the collapse of the monarchy, at the first free elections to the Constituent Assembly in November 1917. The overwhelming majority of votes were won by radical demagogues who had promised land to the peasants, while the parties of "Russian Europeans and gentlemen" received less than 10 percent of the votes between them.

Tsar Nikolai was aware of the growing discord between power and society. The revolution of 1905 ruthlessly exposed all contradictions and conflicts which had been stealthily smouldering hitherto, and so the Tsar had to face the grave dilemma of how to carry out radical reforms without injuring the core of the state system – autocracy. Seeking a compromise, the Tsar issued the Manifesto of October 17, 1905, which proclaimed political freedom and the elections to the national assembly – the State Duma. At Nikolai II's initiative, the government set about solving the most acute social problem – land reform. Constitutional reforms and political transformations were scheduled for the long term, but History decreed that no time would be given for them to be implemented.

God, Russia and Family were the vital values for Tsar Nikolai. Since his youth he had been convinced that the power of the Tsar was for the good of the country, and the monarch's historical predestination was to reign according to his will and sense, in agree-

(Left) Vladimir Illyich Lenin, photographed for the Tsarist police files. The young Lenin was involved in radical student politics and was expelled from the University of Kazan. Lenin's eldest brother, Alexander Illyich Yulianov, was a medical student. At the age of twenty-one he became involved in a plot to murder Alexander III. He was executed by hanging in 1887.

ment with God's will, for the welfare of his subjects. In his opinion, autocracy and Russia were indissoluble. This fundamental ideological principle had been ingrained in his consciousness since early childhood, and the Tsar remained faithful to it throughout his life. Nikolai II appeared to be a captive of the principles he had inherited, and he regarded the slightest digression from them as a betrayal of Russia's interests, and a challenge to the sacred fundamentals bequeathed to him by his ancestors. He was never tempted by a lust for power, nor was he ambitious. He really cared for the future of the country, and he bore responsibility for it to God and to his beloved son, Alexei.

(Above) False identification papers from 1913 for Yuli Osipovitch Martov, who shared Siberian exile with Lenin. By then, the division of the socialist revolutionaries into "Bolshevik" (majority) and "Menshevik" (minority) had taken place and Martov became the official leader of the Mensheviks. He was opposed to the Bolshevik *coup d'état* in October 1917. When he voiced opposition, he was told by Leon Trotsky: *"Go where you belong – into the dustbin of history"*.

The Tsar never doubted that it had been Divine Providence that had appointed him to this high post so that he could reign for the strengthening and prosperity of the empire. He had his own view of Russia's well-being, derived from his ideas of the past in which he had always taken an ingenuous interest. Besides his father, Nikolai II held in special veneration Tsar Alexei Mikhailovitch ("The Most Placid"), the second Tsar of the Romanov dynasty, and his reign appeared to Nikolai to have been Russia's "golden age". Nikolai sympathised with the idea of the "people's realm", which proved to be no more than a utopian dream. In Russia, this vast country eroded with absurdity and contrasts, the internal contradictions were so deep and acute and had such a long history that the creation of a society of universal prosperity under the sovereign's sceptre was but another hopeless illusion – and Tsar Nikolai was to pay a very high price for it. Till the very end, until the last day of his life on earth, despite all realities and folly of the world surrounding him, Nikolai preserved an unshakable faith in the "God-bearing people", and he prayed for the well-being of the Motherland he fervently loved. He abdicated the throne only because those surrounding him persuaded the physically and morally exhausted Tsar that such a step was essential for Russia's happiness.

The history of the last Romanovs is inseparable from the history of Russia, the bitter experience of the past, its delusions, disappointments and hopes that lit its path in the 20th century.

"WHAT IS GOING TO HAPPEN TO RUSSIA? I AM NOT READY TO BE A TSAR . . ."

n July 27, 1867, the 22 year-old Cesarevitch Alexander Alexandrovitch, who was to be Tsar Alexander III from 1881 till 1894, began a new diary. The first entry read: *"God grant that this journal be filled with felicitous moments of my life and of my wife's. My only concern and prayer is that God gives us children, and how happy I would be if already at the end of this journal I could be writing as a father of a family, or at least could be sure of this"*. His wish came true. In this very notebook he wrote on May 6/18, 1868, underlining the heading for emphasis: *"The birth of our son Nikolai"*. He described in details the throes his wife suffered, and the moment of birth: *". . . The pangs were stronger and stronger, and Minnie [Maria Feodorovna] suffered a lot. Papa . . . helped me to hold my darling all the time. At last, at half past two, came the last minute and all the suffering stopped at once. God sent us a son whom we gave the name of Nikolai. What joy it was, it is not to be described. I rushed to embrace my darling wife who cheered up at once and was terrifically happy. I was crying like a baby . . . We embraced with Papa and Mama wholeheartedly . . . We drank tea and talked with Minnie till 11, and I went several times to admire our little angel, and they took him to Minnie, too"*.

Amid the universal joy nobody took note that Nikolai's birthday fell on the day set aside in the Russian Orthodox calendar for the martyr St. Job. Only much later, when misfortune would start haunting the last Russian Tsar, would he associate his failure with the fatal coincidence. The father of little Nikolai, Grand Duke Alexander Alexandrovitch, became heir to the throne in April 1865, after the death of his elder brother, Cesarevitch Nikolai Alexandrovitch. Several months later the Danish Princess Louise Sophia Frederica Dagmar, accepted the proposal of the new Cesarevitch. The wedding took place in October 1866 and the nuptial ceremonies were magnificent. Alexander, who adored his charming, cheerful little wife, proved a good husband and a good father.

Their second baby, Alexander, born May 20, 1869, did not see his first birthday, dying on April 20, 1870. Four more children would join Alexander Alexandrovitch and Maria Feodorovna: Georgiy, born on April 27, 1871; Xenia, March 25, 1875; Mikhail, November 22, 1878; and Olga, June 1, 1882. Nikolai's closest companions in games were brother Georgiy and sister Xenia.

Grand Duke Georgiy Alexandrovitch (1871-1899) was Heir to the Russian throne for nearly five years, from Nikolai's ascension to the throne in 1894 till 1899. He was a weak child and often suffered headaches, nose bleeds and other ailments. Later he would develop tuberculosis. He joined his elder brother in the cruise of 1890/91 which his parents hoped would ease his condition. But due to his health he had to leave Nikolai in India. He spent the last years of his life in Abbas Tuman in the Caucasus, where he died of consumption in June 1899.

Grand Duchess Xenia Alexandrovna (1875-1960) lived a long life and died in London. She was the first of Alexander III's children to marry. Her husband, Grand Duke Alexander Mikhailovitch, was her second uncle. They had one daughter, Irina (1895-1970), and six sons: Andrei (1897-1981), Feodor (1898-1968), Nikita (1900-1974), Dmitriy (1901-1980), Rostislav (1902-1978) and Vasiliy (1907-1989). Irina married Prince Yusupov, Rasputin's future assassin. After the revolution, Xenia Alexandrovna managed to escape in 1919 together with her mother and husband, rescued on the British battleship *Marlborough.*

Grand Duke Mikhail Alexandrovitch (1878-1918) after Georgiy's death became the Heir to the Russian throne and he bore the title till 1904, when Nikolai's son Alexei was born. In 1912 he secretly entered into a morganatic marriage to the twice-divorced, born Sheremetevskaya, Mamontova in her first marriage, Wulfert in her second. The marriage took place in Vienna and was sternly disapproved of by Nikolai II. Mikhail was pronounced incapable of handling his own affairs, and his property and personal transactions were taken over by Nikolai. Mikhail Alexandrovitch was forbidden to return to Russia, dismissed from service and deprived of the rank of Aide-de-Camp to the Tsar. He returned to Russia in 1915. The wardship was lifted, his rank of Aide-de-Camp restored, his marriage acknowledged, and his wife was given the surname of Brasova, after the name of Mikhail's estate in the Oryol province. They had one son, Georgiy. Mikhail Alexandrovitch Romanov was the first of the Romanov martyrs to be murdered by the Bolsheviks in Perm, one month before Nikolai.

Grand Duchess Olga Alexandrovna (1882-1960) was the only child born to Alexander III after his ascension to the throne. Only thirteen years older than Nikolai II's eldest daughter Olga, the young "auntie" was the best friend and benefactress of the last Tsar's daughters. Outings together with their aunt were the favourite pastime for the Grand Duchesses. She first married Prince Pyotr Alexandrovitch of Oldenburg in 1901. She divorced him in 1916 because of his inability to have full marital relations. She entered into a morganatic marriage with her first husband's Aide-de-Camp, captain of the Life-Guards Cuirassier regiment, Nikolai Alexandrovitch Kulikovskiy, bearing him two sons. In 1919, she escaped from the Bolsheviks on board a British battleship and, till 1948, lived in Denmark. She settled in Canada and died in November 1960, seven months after her sister.

Relations between the parents and children were warm and touching. Nikolai's attitude to his parents is an example of sincere filial love, the intensity of the feeling appearing very rare in a nature of little emotion. Nicky would always perpetuate the blessed remembrance of Papa and he tenderly revered Mama. In his life there were very few objects of lasting adoration: wife, children and, of course, his mother. "My dear darling Mama" and "Ever loving you Nicky" – the opening and closing words of his numerous letters to Empress Maria Feodorovna – were not just conventional polite expressions. His mother was his "nearest and dearest", his reliable adviser, and there was utter mutual understanding between them. However, later there appeared a topic closed for discussion: Rasputin, but it came at the very end . . .

(Above) Maria Alexandrovna and Alexander II, Nikolai's grandparents. Alexander II was assassinated by terrorists in 1881.
(Facing page) Nikolai at the age of three with his mother, Maria Feodorovna.

As a rule in the family of a Tsar, the best education was given to the heir of the throne. Alexander III had learned a serious lesson from his experience. The lack of this special training made him, as an adult and a father of a family, resume his education to make up the deficiency. Now he saw to it that all his children were given an equally good education. Nikolai and Georgiy were taught by the same tutors, but their classes were individual, even in separate classrooms. The tutors were highly professional, among them outstanding Russian scholars and statesman: the chemist and physicist N.N. Beketov;

General N.N. Obruchev; the economist N.C. Bunge; the lawyer and eminent statesman K.P. Pobedonostsev. The outstanding historian V.O. Klyuchevskiy was for a short period Nikolai's history tutor.

The programme for the children's education was meticulously worked out over a thirteen-year period. The first eight years were to cover the school curriculum, and then their education was to cope with the course of the Academy of the General Staff. Their father personally supervised his children's education. Adjutant-General Danilovitch, the mathematics master, was responsible for the professional staff and compiled the timetable which he was to submit to Alexander Alexandrovitch for approval. The staff of tutors for Mikhail was different, but they were equally efficient.

During the first years of their schooling the children learned Russian, English, French, German, religion and natural history. They had classes in calligraphy, drawing and music. Later, the curriculum became more complicated to include chemistry, physics, geography, biology and fundamentals of mineralogy. They were also trained in fencing and riding. Foreign languages were given special attention. Every other day, the English and French tutors took turns spending the whole day with the children and, from 8 a.m. till 7 p.m., they spoke only English or French. Thanks to such intensive practice, Nikolai spoke fluent English and French. His German was passable, and he could speak some Danish.

A.P. Ollengrain, the first governess of Grand Duke Nikolai Alexandrovitch, remembers the rigorous instructions given by Cesarevitch Alexander Alexandrovitch to the tutors: *"Neither I, nor the Grand Duchess, are going to make green-house flowers out of them. They must pray well to the Lord, learn, play, and prank within reason . . . teach them well, don't let them get out of hand, take special care to discourage idleness . . . I repeat, I do not need porcelain, I want normal, healthy Russian children. If they fight – let them. But the sneak will get the first whip. This is my very first requirement".*

"Pray well to the Lord" – that was one of the most important precepts in the Imperial Family which observed all religious rites, fasting and feast days and were regular church-goers. Their favourite holiday was Easter, when the children delighted in helping the adults to colour eggs. In a letter to his sister Xenia (April 8, 1884) Nicky wrote: *". . . After dinner we worked colouring eggs together with Mr. Heath and [we] got rather stained . . . Yesterday we were at the Winter Palace for matins which lasted two hours. A lot of people exchanged triple kisses with Papa and Mama in the church".* The Imperial couple exchanged traditional Easter salutations with their kin and friends, and also, with their servants and guards. Nikolai maintained the tradition.

Alexander III's children were brought up in spartan simplicity. They slept on simple army cots with hard mats and pillows. Training in sports and active, outdoor games were an indispensable part of their everyday life. The children were given birds, rabbits and bear-cubs as presents, and they took care of their pets themselves. The children had their

(Top) Olga Alexandrovna and Mikhail Alexandrovitch, Nikolai's brother and sister. (Above) Olga as a toddler. (Facing page) An 1889 portrait of Nikolai, taken in St Petersburg, and (insets) his Russian history exercise book and an entry in his diary *"My Diary. I began my records on January 1, 1882 . . . in the morning we drank chocolate . . ."*

Nikolai's aunts and uncles: (above) Heir to the throne Cesarevitch Nikolai Alexandrovitch, born 1843, who died in 1865. (Right) Grand Duchess Maria, Alexander II's favourite child, and Grand Duke Vladimir Alexandrovitch. (Below) Grand Duke Alexei, fourth child of Alexander II, who died in 1908. (Below right) in classical poses, Grand Duke Sergei and his brother Grand Duke Pavel. Sergei Alexandrovitch, the second youngest, later married to the Tsarina's sister Ella and was murdered in 1905 by terrorists, and Pavel Alexandrovitch, the youngest son, escaped the Bolsheviks and lived in exile. Facing Page: with parents Cesarevitch Alexander and Maria Feodorovna, Nikolai poses with sister Xenia on her father's lap, and Grand Duke Georgiy who died of tuberculosis in 1899, aged 28. (Inset) The coat of arms, intertwining "A" and "M" devised to commemorate the couple's 25th wedding anniversary.

Alexander III and his family all enjoyed painting and above is a pencil drawing by Nikolai with the autograph *"Nicky, Feb 26, 1882."*
(Left) Alexander III's undated watercolour of a medieval castle.
Facing page: (top) Grand Duke Georgiy's watercolour, with the inscription *"In Fredensborg, August 30, 1883, from Georgiy"* Very often the pupils were assisted by their tutors in their efforts.
(Middle) Nikolai's charcoal drawing from 1886.
(Bottom left) Watercolour by his mother, Maria Feodorovna, inexplicably in the corner she wrote: "Cottage 1868".
(Bottom right) Plan of travelling to the Finnish skerries, July 16-29, 1884, outlined by Cesarevitch Nikolai in coloured pencil.

Гельзенборгъ 30 Августа 1883. отъ Жороль.

Або.
Сандестрёмъ.
Жнесъ. Гельсингф. р. Кимень.
Гакгутъ. Барзундъ. Ловиза. Борненсельмъ. Выборгъ.
финскій заливъ. Трангзундъ.
Кронштадтъ. Біорквэу.
Петергофъ.

Поѣздка въ шкеры съ 16го по 29го
Іюня 1884 г. на яхтѣ „Царевна."

Puppy love and an enchanted summer holiday in Denmark

Nearly every summer the grown-up children of King Christian IX and Queen Louise of Denmark visited their father and mother. They came together with their families, and the old castle Fredensborg was crowded with the King's and Queen's English, Greek and Russian grand-children. Those visits brightened up the life of the elderly royal couple. The holidays of 1883 were very special for the fifteen year old Cesarevitch Nikolai – he fell in love.

Curious, with a new, unusual interest, Nicky looked at his cousin, an old companion in children's games – the British Princess Victoria. He saw a tall, svelte adolescent whom he found entertaining and charming. The Cesarevitch would entrust his amorous avowals to his diary: *"I am in love with Victoria, and she seems to be with me, but I don't care. Yes, it is still more pleasant if she loves me . . ."*

They had their Danish lessons together, sketched or went for walks. They sat next to each other at meals. *"Awfully enjoy being with her"*, he continued, *"and I feel dull without her."* Practically every day he would mention the name of "Tora", "Toria" in his diary. The entry of August 25: *"My evening game with Victoria is that she hides and I seek. When I find her too soon, she gets cross and starts chasing me. If she catches me, she tries to knock me down, but she fails. Then she beats me with her fists, and I bear it as the Lamb of God."* (August 25/September 6).

The new emotion had come all of a sudden and completely engulfed the youngster. The attention of the young lady gave a fascinating feeling, and he described the development of their relations with winsome ingenuousness: *"It seemed to me that Victoria despised me, but luckily I was very much mistaken. The less I cared for her, the more she followed me, and I secretly rejoiced. In the evening I tried to be alone with her and kiss her: she is so lovely."* (August 27/September 8).

Next day their roles changed: *"The more Victoria torments and teases her prey, the more the prey loves her. This prey is ME".*

The daily entries featured their enjoyment of their life in Denmark – journeys to Copenhagen, yachting, meetings and parties. The youngsters had a lovely time

together, romping and making fun *"in a small corner room"*, or playing hide-and-seek, or chasing each other in the galleries of the palace, or going out for a walk to the forest. *"Papa, Aunt Olga [Queen of Greece, née Grand Duchess Olga Konstantinovna], Victoria and I went for a walk; in the forest we cito! cito!!! And Papa wrote that [we] smoked."* (September 18/30); *"After dinner Victoria and Alix [Princess Alexandra of Greece] tickled and chased me."* (September 19/October 1); *"In the evening the English Louise and Christian were hiding, and we were seeking. Victoria and I went around together all the time, pretending that we were seeking them"* (September 26/October 8).

The day of departure came too soon. *"Still more and more I love Victoria, awfully sorry we'll have to leave soon. There'll be no playing and romping with her in the small corner room."* (September 27/October 9). They promised to come back to Denmark every other year, and they would miss each other. *"I cannot say how much I miss Victoria, I am waiting for letters to come from her"*, Nicky admitted in his diary, October 3/15. Letters sped to and from Britain and Russia. In the evenings he would take them out, spread them on the desk, rereading those nice billets-doux and admiring the photos.

The holidays in Denmark, 1883, were memorable for both of them. The lovely childish affection was not to grow into a serious feeling, but their tender, romantic relations survived in the diaries, letters and in kind memory, and they prepared Nicky's heart for his great, strong love for Alix.

Victoria lived till 1935, through the reigns of her father King Edward VII and her brother George V. She never married, though, and it was felt that her wit and sharp tongue may have scared off potential suitors . . . or perhaps she never found the man of her dreams after that teenage crush in Denmark.

A Merry Christmas 1894   Victoria.

For my darling
"Old Nick."

Health,
Prosperity
and a
Happy Christmas
to you.

Maria.

1894.

Pictures taken during Nikolai's journey to the Far East.
(Above) Nikolai, fourth from left in the second row with the officers and sailors of the cruiser *Pamyati Azova*.
(Right) Nikolai in India.
(Below) Nikolai's' cabin on the *Pamyati Azova*.
(Below right) The ranks and sailors of cruiser *Pamyati Azova* (commemorating the siege of Azov).
Facing page: (top left) Nikolai, Crown Prince George of Greece (standing) and friends in Ceylon in 1891.
(Top right) A photograph given to Nikolai with an inscription by Emperor Yakihito of Japan.
(Bottom) Nikolai in India with friends and officers.

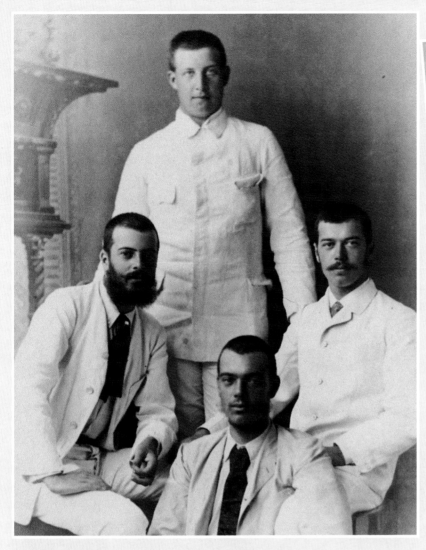

Takeshita. 18th May 2551.

Malabar Point. 11 Декабрь 1890.

31

(Top) Nikolai and a companion enjoy a trip by
rickshaw in Japan.
(Above) Heir Cesarevitch Nikolai Alexandrovitch (in the centre). To his right, Crown
Prince George of Grece; To the Cesarevitch's left, Prince Vladimir Baryatinskiy; far right to Nikolai
is Prince Victor Kochubey and to his far left is Colonel Gerard (a British officer).

(Left) Nikolai's arrival in Japan and (above) the Russian cemetery in Nagasaki with Nikolai's inscription: *"Russian Cemetery in the village of Inasa."*
(Below) Another exotic experience; sharing a pipe in Cairo with Nikolai are Prince George of Greece, to his left and brother Georgiy, third to his left.
Nikolai was to write to his father: *"At three o'clock we went to visit the Khedive* [Egypt's ruler]. *There we were all seated on a sofa and had a 'chibouque' with excellent tobacco shoved in our mouths and were treated to coffee."* Prince George, nicknamed "The Athlete" for his outstanding strength and powerful build, rescued Nikolai from an assassination attempt by a fanatic in Otsu, Japan.

happiest times when they left the city for the Imperial estate in Gatchina. There, with their parents and other adults, they worked in the garden, clearing up old twigs and branches, and potatoes baked outdoors in hot cinders seemed the most delectable dish to them. Winter was a pretty good time, too, with skiing or sleighing down the hills. They enjoyed riding down a hill on a piece of board – an unpretentious sport borrowed from local children. Their mother, Empress Maria Feodorovna, often joined in the fun.

Cesarevitch Nikolai started keeping his diary at the age of thirteen. The first entry is dated Friday, January 1/13, 1882. He wrote: *"In the morning drank chocolate; tried on the Life Guard Reserve full-dress uniform . . . went to the garden with Papa and made a great fire. Went to sleep about half past nine"*. The boy's diary entries were naive and sincere; they reveal his interests and thoughts, and describe his everyday activities – *"had classes"*, *"cleaned the parrots and canaries"*, *"my bullfinch came out of its cage and ate from my hands"*, *"worked in the green-house"*; *"worked in the zoo"*. The usual pastime of an evening was a family reading: *"Papa read 'Viy'* [by Gogol] *and Mr. Heath read* [Shakespeare's] *'Merchant of Venice' "*.

Nicky was rather well-read. His reading included not only Russian authors, but English and French as well, and he read them in the original. As Nikolai II, he was to build a unique library which was kept in the Winter Palace. Part of it is now property of the Library of the US Congress, and it is noteworthy that the purchase of 318 works in 757 volumes cost only 3,131 US dollars.

There were many family traditions and shared pastimes. For birthdays, the children used to prepare presents in secret, usually pictures. Nicky wrote about the watercolours which he presented to Papa and Mama. One of the children's hobbies was to take clippings from magazines, often English and French,

34

The two year-old Nikolai and a lock of his hair kept by his wife, Alix. This piece of hair is being used in the attempt to identify the last Tsar's remains.

(Above left) A young Nikolai on his horse, and (left) his father Alexander III, in a similar pose. A powerfully built man, Alexander was an outstanding horseman.

Facing page: (top) Tsarskoye Selo, 1890. In the foreground Grand Dukes Pavel and Vladimir Alexandrovitch, Nikolai's uncles, with relatives and guests at the lake in the beautiful grounds.

Nikolai's brothers: (inset) Grand Duke Georgiy Alexandrovitch and (bottom) Grand Duke Mikhail Alexandrovitch.

and to paste them on the walls in the dining-room, corridors and even living-rooms. The pictures featured famous people, ceremonies and monuments. The French tutor, Lanson, author of the *"History of French Literature"*, was to recollect: *"They* [Alexander III's children] *were fond of laying the table, packing their cases before journeys and unpacking upon arrival, putting each thing into its right place".* This diligence and exactitude which Nikolai had developed since childhood, was to prove very helpful later. The Tsar managed without a private secretary, read all the correspondence he received, replied personally, and even sealed them in envelopes himself.

The young Nicky had a propensity for humour and mischief. The children's pranks, however, were not always innocent. A diary entry in 1882 narrates: *"Between lessons and before dinner* [we] *shot peas at Hisytch* [the nickname of the English tutor Mr Heath, a distorted Russian pronunciation of his name] *out of pea-shooters, and he beat us with his walking stick".* But, surely, on both sides it was all in fun, for there were plenty of entries to show that relations between the tutor and his charges were quite friendly. Nikolai mentioned "Hisytch" very fondly in his diaries, and later he would use every occasion to send him his best regards.

The family were passionate theatre-goers. They were also fond of the circus, and Nicky wrote about his impressions, March 19, 1884: *"After breakfast went to Ciniselli's* [circus] *and watched the clowns' various performances . . . Everything was excellent; the clowns made us laugh terrifically".* But the theatre held special fascination: *". . . Went to the Bolshoi Theatre where Tchaikovsky's opera 'Mazepa' was on . . . I liked it terrifically, the cast was superb".* Several days later Nicky would mention the opera again. He admired ballet and in his description of a production of *Don Quixote*, he wrote: *"The choreography was very beautiful".* It is interesting to note that starring as Don Quixote was his dancing tutor, Timofey Stukolkin.

All the males of the Romanov Family served in the army – it was a duty and a privilege of the reigning house – and military training was an important part of their versatile education. Nikolai was most enthusiastic about it. Like all boys, he was fond of war games. On June 12, 1883, he would report: *"Today was a march to the fortress. Sergei, Georgiy and I were with guns, the rest without. Both watch-teams behaved perfectly,*

disorder happened in the non-combatant team, but given time it will improve. Please send me: a book of soldiers' songs, a fortress flag and a fife. For munitions supplies I shall order to make a trail. Please, come to us next Sunday, June 19, to the fortress near the farm. Your lieutenant, commander of the Alexander team, Nikolai Romanov".

Military parades and music were a special attraction for the young princes. Recollecting his childhood Nikolai wrote to Alix, May 16/28, 1894: "*. . . That puts me in mind of old days: when we used to have lessons (thank goodness that is finished and for ever) and heard music and drums in the street; we had such a terrible wish to scramble off the window and have a look at the soldiers, but alas were seldom allowed to do that! The masters even used to scold us, they said we saw soldiers enough, only babies and the common people like to look on at such things! That made us frantic and of course made us feel quite the contrary towards military service in the end!!".*

The military training curriculum included tactics, military topography, navigation, artillery, military administration, military law and strategy. Nikolai began learning these subjects at the age of fourteen, and he was nineteen when he went to his first military camp. He served two years in the Preobrazhenskiy Regiment as a subaltern and then as a company commander. Then he spent two seasons with a Hussar regiment as a platoon officer and, later, as a squadron commander. His next military posting was with an artillery regiment.

The year of 1890 was a turning-point in Nikolai's life: "*Today I finished definitely and forever my classes*", he commented in his diary in May. His education was concluded by a nine-month cruise. In October of that year Nikolai, together with his brother Georgiy and friends, left St. Petersburg. The itinerary included Austria, Greece, Trieste, Egypt, India, Siam, China and Japan. The 35,000 mile-long tour abruptly ended in Otsu, Japan. Walking in the street, the Cesarevitch was suddenly attacked by a Japanese who tried to hit him with a sword. Prince George of Greece, one of their party, knocked the assailant off his feet and the assassin failed to wound the Cesarevitch seriously. But Nikolai was to bear the mark of the assault, a scar on his skull, for the rest of his life, and recurring pains in his head would remind him of the incident time and again.

The way home lay across Siberia. In Vladivostok, he took part in a religious service dedicated to initiating the construction work on the Trans-Siberian Railway. Sergei Witte, then Finance Minister, recollected that he suggested to Alexander III that Cesarevitch Nikolai be appointed chairman of the Committee for Construction of the Great Siberian Railroad. "But he is absolutely a child", was Alexander III's response. "He has the judgement of a child – how would he be able to be chairman of the committee?" But after some deliberation, the Tsar agreed to the appointment. As a matter of fact, the Cesarevitch took his new responsibilities very seriously, and he coped with them well. "The child" was twenty-four then, and a year and half later he would become Emperor of all Russia.

Alexander III died at the age of forty-nine. He never cared much for his health, nor was he serious about being treated when he fell ill. Nobody ever heard him complain about being unwell. He had been Cesarevitch for nearly fourteen years before coming to the throne at the age of thirty-six. He had never been specially trained to be Tsar, but he had time enough to prepare before he assumed the supreme responsibility. Being quite sure that Nikolai still had plenty of time to prepare for the task, Alexander III was rather reluctant to entrust his son with any serious tasks that required independent judgement. Not until 1889 was Nikolai invited to attend sittings of the State Council and of the Committee of the Council of Ministers. Therefore Nikolai was to take on his great responsibilities ill-equipped.

His father's death crushed him. His uncle, Grand Duke Alexander Mikhailovitch, the "Sandro" of his childhood, who was with Nikolai II at the dreadful moment, recalled the new Tsar muttering: "*What is going to happen to Russia? I am not ready to be a Tsar. I cannot rule the Empire. I have no idea of even how to talk to the ministers*".

Portrait of Cesarevitch Nikolai Alexandrovitch taken in 1890

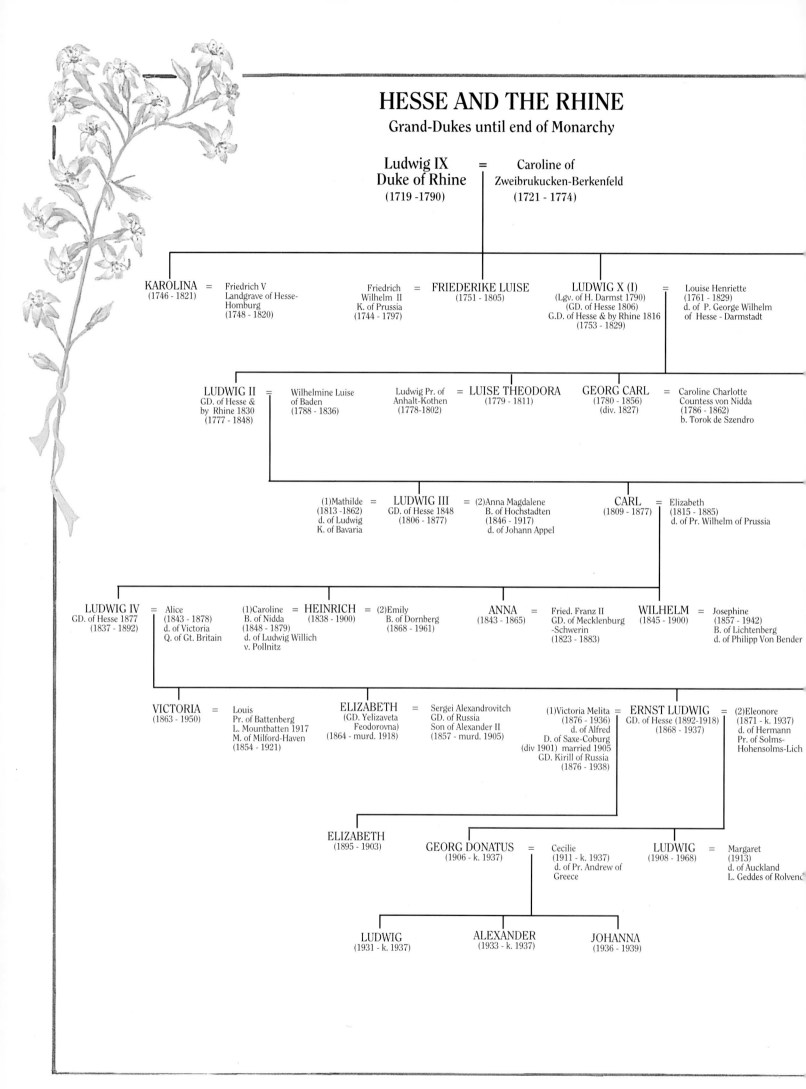

HESSE AND THE RHINE

Grand-Dukes until end of Monarchy

Ludwig IX
Duke of Rhine
(1719 -1790)
=
Caroline of
Zweibrukucken-Berkenfeld
(1721 - 1774)

KAROLINA
(1746 - 1821)
=
Friedrich V
Landgrave of Hesse-
Homburg
(1748 - 1820)

Friedrich
Wilhelm II
K. of Prussia
(1744 - 1797)
=
FRIEDERIKE LUISE
(1751 - 1805)

LUDWIG X (I)
(Lgv. of H. Darmst 1790)
(GD. of Hesse 1806)
G.D. of Hesse & by Rhine 1816
(1753 - 1829)
=
Louise Henriette
(1761 - 1829)
d. of P. George Wilhelm
of Hesse - Darmstadt

LUDWIG II
GD. of Hesse &
by Rhine 1830
(1777 - 1848)
=
Wilhelmine Luise
of Baden
(1788 - 1836)

Ludwig Pr. of
Anhalt-Kothen
(1778-1802)
=
LUISE THEODORA
(1779 - 1811)

GEORG CARL
(1780 - 1856)
(div. 1827)
=
Caroline Charlotte
Countess von Nidda
(1786 - 1862)
b. Torok de Szendro

(1)Mathilde
(1813 -1862)
d. of Ludwig
K. of Bavaria
=
LUDWIG III
GD. of Hesse 1848
(1806 - 1877)
=
(2)Anna Magdalene
B. of Hochstadten
(1846 - 1917)
d. of Johann Appel

CARL
(1809 - 1877)
=
Elizabeth
(1815 - 1885)
d. of Pr. Wilhelm of Prussia

LUDWIG IV
GD. of Hesse 1877
(1837 - 1892)
=
Alice
(1843 - 1878)
d. of Victoria
Q. of Gt. Britain

(1)Caroline
B. of Nidda
(1848 - 1879)
d. of Ludwig Willich
v. Pollnitz
=
HEINRICH
(1838 - 1900)
=
(2)Emily
B. of Dornberg
(1868 - 1961)

ANNA
(1843 - 1865)
=
Fried. Franz II
GD. of Mecklenburg
-Schwerin
(1823 - 1883)

WILHELM
(1845 - 1900)
=
Josephine
(1857 - 1942)
B. of Lichtenberg
d. of Philipp Von Bender

VICTORIA
(1863 - 1950)
=
Louis
Pr. of Battenberg
L. Mountbatten 1917
M. of Milford-Haven
(1854 - 1921)

ELIZABETH
(GD. Yelizaveta
Feodorovna)
(1864 - murd. 1918)
=
Sergei Alexandrovitch
GD. of Russia
Son of Alexander II
(1857 - murd. 1905)

(1)Victoria Melita
(1876 - 1936)
d. of Alfred
D. of Saxe-Coburg
(div 1901) married 1905
GD. Kirill of Russia
(1876 - 1938)
=
ERNST LUDWIG
GD. of Hesse (1892-1918)
(1868 - 1937)
=
(2)Eleonore
(1871 - k. 1937)
d. of Hermann
Pr. of Solms-
Hohensolms-Lich

ELIZABETH
(1895 - 1903)

GEORG DONATUS
(1906 - k. 1937)
=
Cecilie
(1911 - k. 1937)
d. of Pr. Andrew of
Greece

LUDWIG
(1908 - 1968)
=
Margaret
(1913)
d. of Auckland
L. Geddes of Rolvenc

LUDWIG
(1931 - k. 1937)

ALEXANDER
(1933 - k. 1937)

JOHANNA
(1936 - 1939)

| AMALIE (1754 - 1832) | = | Carl Ludwig Her. Pr. of Baden (1755 - 1801) | WILHELMINE (Natalia Alexeyevna) (1755 -1776) | = | Pavel I GD. (later Emp. of Russia) (1754 - murd.1801) | LUISE AUGUSTE (1757 - 1830) | = | Carl August GD. of Saxe-Weimar-Eisenach (1757 - 1828) | FRIEDRICH (1759 - 1802) | CHRISTIAN (1763 - 1830) |

| FRIEDRICH AUGUST (1788 - 1867) | EMIL MAXIMILIAN (1790 - 1856) | GUSTAV FERDINAND (1791 - 1806) |

| ALEXANDER (1823 - 1888) | = | Julie Pr. of Battenberg (1825 - 1895) d. of Johann Moritz C. von Hauke | Alexander II Emp. of Russia (1818 -murd. 1881) | = | MAXIMILIANE (Maria Alexandrovna) born Princess of Hesse (1824 - 1880) | ELIZABETH AMALIA (1821- 1826) |

| LUDWIG (LOUIS) Pr. of Battenberg L. Mountbatten 1917 M. of Milford-Haven (1854 - 1921) | = | Victoria (1863 - 1950) d. of Ludwig IV | ALEXANDER Pr. of Bulgaria 1879 - 1886 C. of Hartenau 1889 (1857 - 1893) | = | Johanna Maria Louise (1865 - 1951) d. of Johann Loisinger | Beatrice (1857 - 1944) d. of Victoria Q. of Gt. Britain | = | HEINRICH (Henry Maurice) Royal Highness (1858-1896) |

| IRENE (1866 - 1953) | = | Heinrich Pr. of Prussia (1862 - 1929) | FRIEDRICH (1870 - 1873) | ALIX (Alexandra Feodorovna) (1872 - ex. 1918) | = | Nikolai II Emp. of Russia (1868 - ex.. 1918) | MARIE (1874-1878) |

| OLGA (1895 - ex. 1918) | TATIANA (1897 - ex. 1918) | MARIA (1899 - ex. 1918) | ANASTASIA (1901 - ex. 1918) | ALEXEI (1904 - ex. 1918) |

"AN UNCLOUDED, HAPPY CHILDHOOD OF PERPETUAL SUNSHINE"

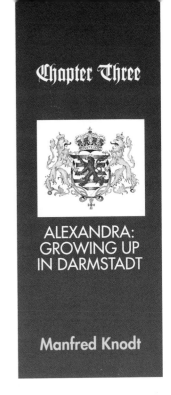

SUNNY

rincess Victoria Alix Helena Louise Beatrix, who was to become the last Tsarina of Imperial Russia, was born in the New Palace in Darmstadt on June 6, 1872, at 3.45 in the morning. She was the sixth child and fourth daughter of Prince Louis of Hesse and Princess Alice, a daughter of Queen Victoria. Her mother wrote to the British Queen: *"Alix we chose for Alice, as they murder my name here . . . they pronounce it 'Alicea'."*

Two years after Alix's birth, in 1874, the last child, Princess Marie Victoria Feodora Leopoldina, was born to complete the family. The New Palace had been built for the couple and was occupied in 1866, four years after their wedding. It looked like a Victorian mansion rather than a German castle. Queen Victoria had made a contribution to the building expenses, which far exceeded what had been expected.

Darmstadt, with a population of 30,000, was the capital of the Grand Duchy of Hesse (originally Hesse-Darmstadt) with three Provinces – Upper-Hesse, Starkenburg and Rhine-Hesse, whose boundaries were set by the Congress of Vienna in 1815. Within the 153 square miles of the Duchy, the population grew from 600,000 in 1815 to 850,000 in 1871, when the German Empire was founded, after the Franco-Prussian war. "Grand Duke" was the title introduced by Napoleon I when he re-organised the German duchies in 1806 in the Rhine-Federation under his leadership. The Grand Dukes of Hesse (from 1817 onwards the full title was of Hesse and by the Rhine, to mark the acquisition of the province on the Rhine) could claim the allegiance of devoted subjects. Many soldiers who had taken part in the victorious war over France in 1870-1871 were proud veterans. The people did not care that the foundation of the new German Empire now meant that their Grand Dukes were taking orders from Berlin and were obliged "at least once a year" to pay

A drawing of Alix by her mother, Princess Alice, with the inscription "Sunny" June 1873.
(Facing page) Young Alix with her elder brother Ernst Ludwig and little sister Mary of Hesse.

The new palace in Darmstadt in its original condition in 1866. Alix's grandmother, Queen Victoria, made a contribution towards the cost of the building which far exceeded expectations. (Facing page) Princess Alice of Hesse with all her children. Standing: (on the left) Elizabeth, who matured into a beautiful young woman and after her marriage to Grand-Duke Sergei, enjoyed the sumptuous lifestyle of the Russian court; Prince Louis Ludwig of Hesse holding Marie. Sitting: Ernst, little Alix by her mother. In front: Irene kneeling, and Victoria on the right.

homage to the Emperor as their "first among equals". The Duchy was agricultural and the experience which Princess Alice brought with her from the highly developed, industrial Great Britain had a beneficial effect on the lives of her new German subjects. With her passion to improve living conditions, especially where the sick and poor were concerned, Princess Alice was the right Grand Duchess in the right place at the right time. The "Alice Women's Society for Nursing" was founded to train nurses while the "Alice Hospital" and the "Alice School for Education of Girls for Employment" of 1867 responded to the actual needs of her subjects. They still exist and do good work, the best possible memorials for a Grand Duchess who will never be forgotten.

The baby Alix was nicknamed "Alicky", "Sunny" and "Princess Sunshine". Alix was a welcome arrival for her three sisters and two brothers, who were all aged between two and nine. The first born was Victoria (1863-1950), who would marry in 1884, Louis Prince of Battenberg (1854-1921), her father's first cousin. As a German boy of 14, he joined the British Navy and became its First Sea Lord in 1912, but had to resign when World War I began. Louis and Victoria of Battenberg had to alter their name to "Mountbatten" when the British Royal Family changed from Saxe-Coburg-Gotha to Windsor. Their famous son was Lord Louis Mountbatten, Earl of Burma, who would have a profound influence on Prince Charles until his murder by the IRA in 1979.

The second child was Elizabeth, born on November 1, 1864. In 1884, she married Grand Duke Sergei of Russia, son of Tsar Alexander II and Maria Alexandrovna, born Princess of Hesse. Again a very close relationship: Sergei's mother and Elizabeth's grandfather, Charles of Hesse, were sister and brother. Elizabeth, known to the family as "Ella", later to be Russian Grand Duchess Yelizaveta Feodorovna, was a decisive influence on her little sister's destiny. Alix went for the first time to Russia for Ella's wedding in 1884 and met, as a girl of 12, the 16 year-old Cesarevitch Nikolai. When Sergei was assassinated in 1905, his wife renounced her worldly life, became a nun and matron of the Sts. Mary and Martha's Cloister which had hospital, orphanage and home for invalid soldiers. After her assassination in 1918 her body was found and brought to Peking by a monk, aided by the retreating White Guards regiments. The coffin was finally transferred to the Russian Orthodox Chapel on the Mount of Olives in Jerusalem. Ella had wanted to be buried there ever since she and Sergei had been present at its consecration in 1888. In 1981, the Russian

Orthodox Church outside Russia canonized Ella, together with all the martyrs of the Russian Revolution including Nikolai II and Alexandra Feodorovna. In April 1992, the Patriarch of Moscow and the Synod accepted the canonization of Yelizaveta Feodorovna and named July 5 as her Saint's Day. The canonization of the other Romanov martyrs has been left open.

Irene Louise Marie Anna (1866-1953) was the first of the Hesse children to be born in the New Palace. Her name, which means peace, was chosen to mark the end of the war for supremacy between Prussia and Austria. Irene married her first cousin Henry, Prince of Prussia (1862-1929), son of Victoria, in 1888 and so she became known as Empress Frederica, because for 99 days her husband was the German Emperor, following his father William I (1797-1888). Henry's eldest brother was the last German Emperor William II (1859-1941, Emperor from 1888 till 1918). Henry was Admiral of the German Fleet and had his home near Kiel in Hemmelmark.

Ernst Ludwig Albert Karl Wilhelm, born on November 25, 1868, was the last reigning Grand Duke, from 1892 till 1918. In his habits and thinking, he was very English. His mother tried to influence and educate him in the same manner in which she had been brought up in England by Queen Victoria. This lasted for ten years until Alice's death, but it was effective, as the ideal of the "English Gentleman" became Ernst's own vision as well. On Alice's death, the grandmother tried to take their mother's place and made the eldest daughter, Victoria, her ally, and through her gave instructions to the other children.

The bond between Ernst Ludwig and his sister Alix was especially strong. Victoria and Ella having left Darmstadt in 1884, Irene in 1888, Ernie and Alix were the only children still there to console their lonely father. Of course, the married sisters came home as often as possible and the Court Circular shows that no event in Darmstadt of any importance took place without the participation of the sisters and their husbands. Official events, after Ernst Ludwig's accession in 1892, were numerous. The consecration of the Russian Chapel, built and paid for by Tsar Nikolai II himself in 1899; the "Nouveau Art" Exhibitions in 1901, 1908 and 1914; and the wedding of Prince Andrew of Greece to Alice of Battenberg (parents of Prince Philip, Duke of Edinburgh) in October 1903.

(Top) Alice of Hesse and her husband Prince Louis. (Above) A pencil drawing by Alice of herself and her son Friedrich Wilhelm August Victor Leopold, who suffered with haemophilia and died at a very young age when he fell from a window. (Facing page) Darmstadt 1870. Portrait of Grand Duchess Alice of Hesse, daughter of Queen Victoria, with two of her daughters Elizabeth (left) and Victoria.

After Ernst Ludwig's birth came Friedrich Wilhelm August Victor Leopold Ludwig. It was through this son that the tragedy of the "Royal Curse" of haemophilia arrived. In February 1873, his mother discovered that "Frittie" (his family nickname) was suffering from haemophilia. Queen Victoria had transmitted the disease, which exclusively affects males, to her daughters, Victoria the Princess Royal, Alice and Beatrice and her youngest son, Leopold. Frittie's life ended tragically. On the morning of May 29, 1873, when Alice was still in bed, her two sons Ernie and Frittie came to say good morning. Afterwards they played a game of who could reach the first window of the room next door. That morning, the window was half open when Frittie reached the frame. It gave way and he fell through, landing on a stone balustrade twenty feet below. By the evening, he was dead.

The shock for Alice, and her only remaining son, Ernie, was traumatic. Alice wrote to her mother: *Ernie is always praying for Frittie and speaks always of him when we walk together. When we went to the Crypt with wreaths the children had made to put*

on Frittie's coffin, Ernie said to all of us 'Whenever I die, you must die too and all the others, why can't we all die together? I will not die alone as Frittie did!'".

The last of Prince Louis and Alice's seven children, Princess Maria Victoria Feodora Leopoldina, was born May 24, 1874. As the sad memories connected with Frittie's death were still on everybody's minds in the Palace, the baptism took place in the Heiligenberg Castle on July 11. To this last daughter, only four years were granted. In November 1878, all the children except Elizabeth were ill with diphtheria and Maria died on the 16th. While the children and their father, who had also been infected, were recovering, Grand Duchess Alice was struck by diphtheria and died on December 14, on the same date her father, Prince Albert, the Prince Consort, had died 17 years earlier.

Alix was baptised in the New Palace on July 1, her parents' wedding day. The mother wrote to the baby's grandmother, Queen Victoria: *"Baby is like Ella, only smaller features and still darker eyes with very black eyelashes and reddish brown hair. She is a sweet, merry little person, always laughing and a dimple in one cheek, just like Ernie"* (August 14, 1872). In later years Alix told her lady-in-waiting, Baroness Sophie Buxhoeveden, to whom she confided some of her secrets, "that her earliest memories were of an unclouded, happy babyhood, of perpetual sunshine ...".

Alix spent her babyhood mainly with her younger sister Maria and two English nurses, Mary Anne Orchard and Margaret Hardcastle Jackson. Strongly interested in education in general and especially that of her children, Grand Duchess Alice explained her principles in her letters to her mother: *"It is a fault of the parents to educate daughters just to be married. It shall be my effort to educate my daughters in such a way not to see marriage as the only purpose of their future; life is also meaningful without being married. Marriage just for the sake of being married is one of the greatest mistakes a woman can make"*. (April 15, 1871).

Before the New Palace was completed in 1866, the young couple lived for some months in the Prince Charles Palace, and later in the Hunting Castle in Kranichstein. Queen Victoria came to inspect her daughter's new life, and stayed one night with numerous family members and staff in the small castle before leaving for Coburg. Victoria's visits were rare and to all the sad events in the family, such as funerals, she would send her sons. The Queen came for the confirmation of Victoria and Ella in 1880, for Ernie's confirmation in 1885, and to Victoria's wedding in 1884. As Hesse became more and more of an annexe to the British Royal Family, the British influence grew. A British Ambassador and an Anglican Chaplain were appointed; English and German customs were sometimes combined – for example, Christmas tree and German Christmas goose with English turkey and plum-pudding.

The mother being so active in social work, her children, from their earliest days, were also involved. So young Alix learned to visit hospitals on her mother's behalf. This gave her an affinity for people in need and the need to help them. Mother Alice's example made all of her children very charitable. The early death of her mother – Alix was only six years old – was a watershed in her life. The elder sisters were fast growing into womanhood and starting lives of their own. The lady-in-waiting of the four sisters, Baroness Wilhelmine Senarclens Grancy, was of the old school, always preaching discipline, restraint and self control; principles which Alix adopted, an added impetus which suited her developing character.

When Alix reached the age of sixteen, Margarete von Fabrice became her special lady-in-waiting. She was in her twenties, very religious with high ideals, and she influenced Alix in a positive way. But she was also, like Alix, shy. When Alix started school education, a special tutor, Anna Textor, joined Miss Jackson. Alix gave all of her energy to her lessons and always had a strong sense of duty. Equipped with a very retentive memory, by 15 she was well grounded in history, literature, geography and all matters relating to England and Germany. She learned French, which she would need later in Russia where it was the language spoken in fashionable salons. English was used every day, she spoke and wrote it to her brother and sisters, later to her husband and children as well. Like her

Osborne, July 23, 1885.
Wedding photograph of Princess Beatrice, Queen Victoria's daughter, and Prince Heinrich of Battenberg. Back row (from left to right): Alexander Prince of Bulgaria, Princess Louise of Wales
Princess Irene of Hesse, Princess Victoria of Wales, Prince Franz Josef of Battenberg.
Middle row: Princess Maud of Wales, Princess Alix of Hesse, Princess Maria Louise and Princess Helena Victoria of Schleswig-Holstein. Front row: Princess Victoria Melita, Princess Marie and Princess Alexandra of Edinburgh, the newly-wed Princess Beatrice and Prince Harry of Battenberg.

Darmstadt, 1888. (Above) Left to right: Alix's brother-in-law Grand-Duke Sergei Alexandrovitch, the 16 year-old Alix, her father Grand-Duke Louis IV, and Sergei's wife, Grand Duchess Yelizaveta (Ella), and brother Ernst Ludwig.

(Right) Alix's 1885 watercolour from one of her notebooks.

(Facing page) Alix prepares for her first ball in 1889. Arranging her hair is her English nurse, Mrs Orchard, while her sister Yelizaveta Feodorovna supervises. "Ella" and her husband Sergei came specially from Russia to be at Alicky's side at this important event. As Sergei had become very fond of his charming young sister-in-law, he persuaded her father to allow Alicky another visit to Russia, to stay with them at their home in Ilyinskoye.

Coburg 1894. Queen Victoria surrounded by the blue blood of Europe, in Germany, for the wedding of Ernst of Hesse and Victoria Melita (Ducky). Standing: (left to right) Heinrich of Prussia; her son-in-law Friedrich III, King of Prussia; her grandson, Kaiser Wilhelm; her son, Prince Albert Edward (later Edward VII King of Britain). Sitting beside Queen Victoria is her daughter Victoria, married to Friedrich III. (Facing page) From around 1877: In front of the hall of Wolfsgarten Castle (left to right) Irene, Elizabeth, Alix and brother Ernie. On the stairs: Victoria and father Louis.

mother, she was musically talented and played the piano well, but was very shy about playing in front of other people. When visiting her grandmother in England, Victoria would help her beloved grand-daughter to overcome this shyness through piano performances for friends and family members. The piano teacher for Alix and her sisters and brother was William de Haan, Director of the Darmstadt Opera. Alix was a good needlewoman and designed attractive trifles which she gave to her friends or to charity bazaars. Her interest in art grew and was developed through her brother Ernie, who made Darmstadt world famous as founder of an "Artists' Colony" with artists like Joseph Maria Olbrich, Peter Behrens, Ludwig Habich and others regarded as leaders of the Art Nouveau movement.

The widowed Grand-Duke Louis spent more and more time in England, in the various homes of his mother-in-law, Queen Victoria, and on these visits he was regularly accompanied by Ernie and Alix. Two events which lightened the series of tragedies the family had experienced came with the marriage of Victoria to Louis of Battenberg in Darmstadt in April, and Ella to Grand Duke Sergei, in June, 1884. Queen Victoria, along with the Prince and Princess of Wales, came to Darmstadt for the Battenberg wedding, but the joy was clouded by the morganatic wedding of the widowed, 47 year-old Louis to the 30 year-old divorced wife of a Russian ambassador, on the same day. Only Louis' daughters knew of their father's marriage and it was kept secret from Queen Victoria. But the minute she learned of it, the Queen forced Louis to have the marriage annulled and Darmstadt's Prime Minister, von Stark, who had officiated at the morganatic ceremony as registrar, was dismissed.

The wedding of sister Ella in Russia gave Alix the first opportunity, in 1884, to travel to Russia with her father and Ernie. As a child, Ella had always been the peacemaker among her brother and sisters, the personification of unselfishness, with a strong sense of humour. She was particularly beautiful, which led her first cousin, the German Kaiser, to love and admire her from his early visits to Darmstadt. As a student in Bonn, he wrote

poems for her – eliciting neither response nor reaction from Ella. She had chosen Sergei, younger brother of Tsar Alexander III. Queen Victoria disliked marriages of family members with Russian Princes and Princesses. But Ella had made her decision without asking permission from "Granny". *"I am glad Ella says she is happy"*, the Queen wrote to her eldest daughter Victoria on February 15, 1887, *"but it is the whole position in such a corrupt country, where you can trust no one and where politics are so antagonistic to one's own views and feelings which is so sad and distressing to us all"*.

In 1889 the first Ball for Alicky was arranged to celebrate her "coming out". Her sister Ella, with her husband Sergei, came especially from Russia to be at Alicky's side at this important event. As Sergei had become very fond of his charming young sister-in-law, he persuaded her father to allow Alicky another visit to Russia to stay with them in their home in Ilyinskoye. This visit, and another in 1890, took place against the wishes of grandmother Queen Victoria. For a long time she had fostered the hope of making Alix Queen of Great Britain by marrying her to Albert Victor, Duke of Clarence and Avondale, the eldest son of the Prince of Wales (1864-1892). "Eddy", as the Prince was known, was willing to follow his grandmother's orders, but Alicky wasn't.

"I regretted Alix going to Russia again", the Queen wrote to her daughter Victoria, on July 15, 1890. *"I heard that Ella was determined to try to get a marriage with another Russian, and this would grievously hurt Uncle Bertie and Aunt Alix as well as me. But it may not be true, and if you take care and tell Ella that no marriage for Alicky in Russia would be allowed, then there will be an end to it . . ."*

A new era started back in Darmstadt as Alix now was more involved in official functions, assisting her father as the new "First Lady" of the Grand Duchy. The Princess was loved by all, high and low, but most of them did not know the suffering every public appearance caused her. Her shyness was a great handicap she would never overcome, painful in a position such as hers. But even worse, many were to mistakenly interpret it as arrogance. During the two years from 1890 until her father's death on March 13, 1892, Alix was mostly at home. She acted as host for the many visitors at Wolfsgarten Castle. At the end of 1891, Queen Victoria became reconciled to the fact that Alicky would never change her mind concerning marriage with Eddy. So Eddy was engaged to Mary of Teck, only to die suddenly on January 14, 1892. The following year Mary married Eddy's younger brother, George, Duke of York, who was to become George V. Both are the grandparents of the present Queen Elizabeth II.

The Grand Duke's death was a great shock to Alix. Ernst Ludwig now became Grand Duke, at the age of 23, when he would have preferred to continue his university studies in Giessen. Queen Victoria, never one to shun the responsibility of choosing even her grandchildren's marriage partners, had decided that Princess Victoria Melita of Edinburgh would be the right wife for Ernie. The consent of the subjects of her marriage policy was soon given – after the Queen had ordered them to agree in her presence. Seven years later, this marriage was to be the first arranged by her to officially fail in divorce. But Victoria did not experience the failure; it happened shortly after her death.

Early in 1894, the Queen had to admit that neither Nicky nor Alicky had given up their hopes of getting married. In spite of the fact that Ella's own conversion to the Orthodox faith had done her no harm, the Queen blamed her for not encouraging them to take the religious difficulty more seriously. So Alix, visiting Coburg for Ernie's wedding with "Ducky" (Victoria Melita) on April 19, 1894, was more or less willing to surrender to this religious necessity.

The Queen had great difficulties in adjusting to the situation she had done her utmost to prevent. In spite of her inevitable acceptance of the decision, on May 25, 1894 she expressed her strong feeling to her daughter Victoria: *"The more I think of sweet Alix's marriage the more unhappy I am! Not as to the personality, for I like him very much, on account of the country, the policy and differences with us and the awful insecurity to which that sweet child will be exposed. To think she is learning Russian and will probably have to talk to a priest, my whole nature rises up against it in spite of my efforts to be satisfied. But I will try and bear it and make the best of it. Still the feeling that I had laboured so hard to prevent it, and that I felt at last there was no longer any danger and all in one night everything was changed. Ella should never have encouraged it originally as she did".* On October 21, 1894, her tone was still very angry: *"My blood runs cold when I think of her so young most likely placed on that very unsafe Throne . . ."*

(Top) Ernst Ludwig with his first wife Victoria Melita and their daughter Elizabeth who died at a young age in 1903. (Above) Victoria and Ernst Ludwig. (Facing page) A portrait of Alix before her engagement.

THE HOUSE OF
SAXE-COBURG-GOTHA
& WINDSOR

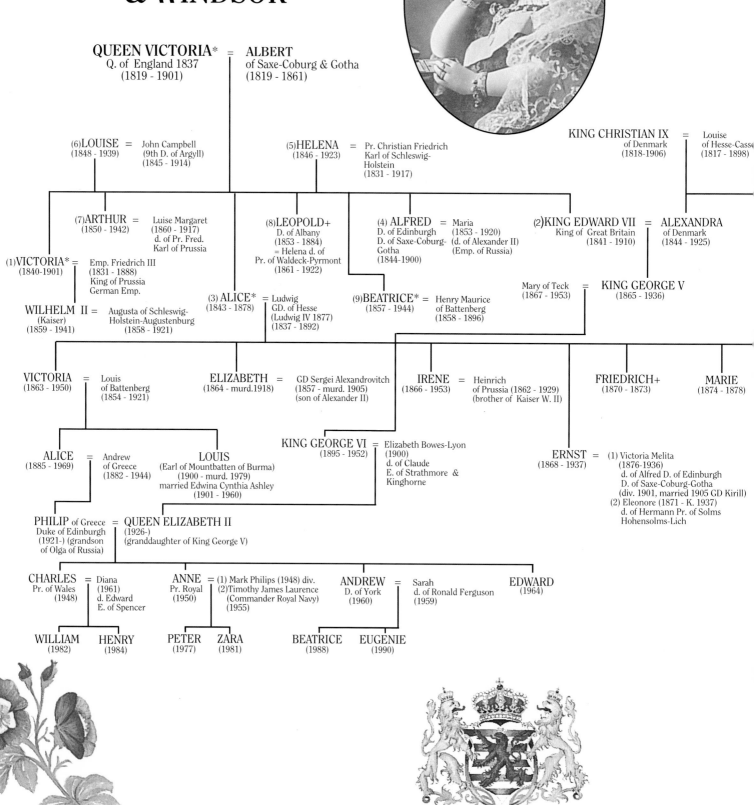

QUEEN VICTORIA* = **ALBERT**
Q. of England 1837   of Saxe-Coburg & Gotha
(1819 - 1901)   (1819 - 1861)

KING CHRISTIAN IX = Louise
of Denmark   of Hesse-Cassel
(1818-1906)   (1817 - 1898)

(6)**LOUISE** = John Campbell
(1848 - 1939)   (9th D. of Argyll)
(1845 - 1914)

(5)**HELENA** = Pr. Christian Friedrich
(1846 - 1923)   Karl of Schleswig-
Holstein
(1831 - 1917)

(7)**ARTHUR** = Luise Margaret
(1850 - 1942)   (1860 - 1917)
d. of Pr. Fred.
Karl of Prussia

(8)**LEOPOLD+**
D. of Albany
(1853 - 1884)
= Helena d. of
Pr. of Waldeck-Pyrmont
(1861 - 1922)

(4) **ALFRED** = Maria
D. of Edinburgh   (1853 - 1920)
D. of Saxe-Coburg-   (d. of Alexander II)
Gotha   (Emp. of Russia)
(1844-1900)

(2)**KING EDWARD VII** = **ALEXANDRA**
King of Great Britain   of Denmark
(1841 - 1910)   (1844 - 1925)

(1)**VICTORIA*** = Emp. Friedrich III
(1840-1901)   (1831 - 1888)
King of Prussia
German Emp.

Mary of Teck = **KING GEORGE V**
(1867 - 1953)   (1865 - 1936)

WILHELM II = Augusta of Schleswig-
(Kaiser)   Holstein-Augustenburg
(1859 - 1941)   (1858 - 1921)

(3) **ALICE*** = Ludwig
(1843 - 1878)   GD. of Hesse
(Ludwig IV 1877)
(1837 - 1892)

(9)**BEATRICE*** = Henry Maurice
(1857 - 1944)   of Battenberg
(1858 - 1896)

VICTORIA = Louis
(1863 - 1950)   of Battenberg
(1854 - 1921)

ELIZABETH = GD Sergei Alexandrovitch
(1864 - murd.1918)   (1857 - murd. 1905)
(son of Alexander II)

IRENE = Heinrich
(1866 - 1953)   of Prussia (1862 - 1929)
(brother of Kaiser W. II)

FRIEDRICH+
(1870 - 1873)

MARIE
(1874 - 1878)

ALICE = Andrew
(1885 - 1969)   of Greece
(1882 - 1944)

LOUIS
(Earl of Mountbatten of Burma)
(1900 - murd. 1979)
married Edwina Cynthia Ashley
(1901 - 1960)

KING GEORGE VI = Elizabeth Bowes-Lyon
(1895 - 1952)   (1900)
d. of Claude
E. of Strathmore &
Kinghorne

ERNST = (1) Victoria Melita
(1868 - 1937)   (1876-1936)
d. of Alfred D. of Edinburgh
D. of Saxe-Coburg-Gotha
(div. 1901, married 1905 GD Kirill)
(2) Eleonore (1871 - K. 1937)
d. of Hermann Pr. of Solms
Hohensolms-Lich

PHILIP of Greece = **QUEEN ELIZABETH II**
Duke of Edinburgh   (1926-)
(1921-) (grandson   (granddaughter of King George V)
of Olga of Russia)

CHARLES = Diana
Pr. of Wales   (1961)
(1948)   d. Edward
E. of Spencer

ANNE = (1) Mark Philips (1948) div.
Pr. Royal   (2)Timothy James Laurence
(1950)   (Commander Royal Navy)
(1955)

ANDREW = Sarah
D. of York   d. of Ronald Ferguson
(1960)   (1959)

EDWARD
(1964)

WILLIAM   **HENRY**
(1982)   (1984)

PETER   **ZARA**
(1977)   (1981)

BEATRICE   **EUGENIE**
(1988)   (1990)

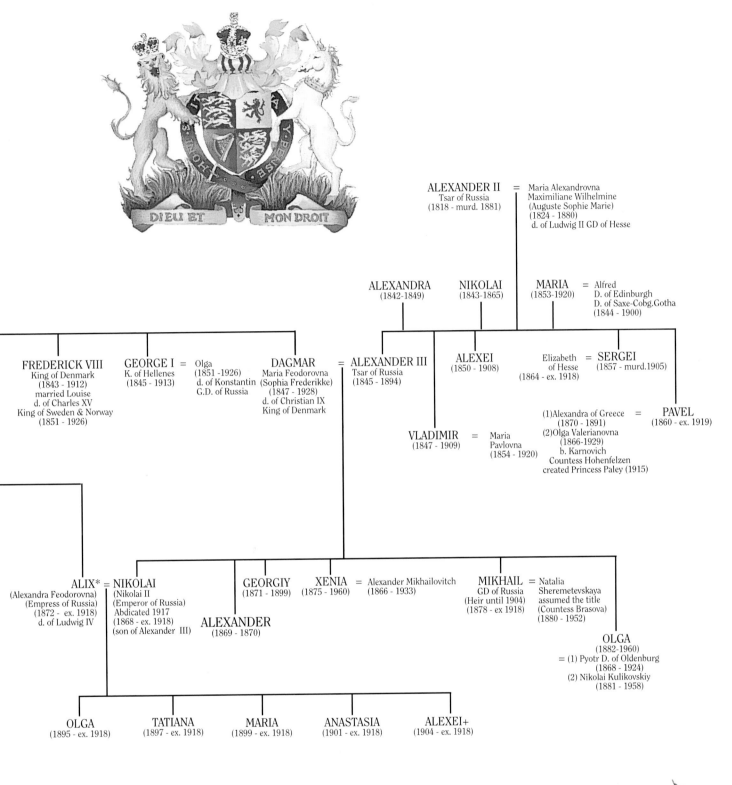

ALEXANDER II
Tsar of Russia
(1818 - murd. 1881)
= Maria Alexandrovna
Maximiliane Wilhelmine
(Auguste Sophie Marie)
(1824 - 1880)
d. of Ludwig II GD of Hesse

ALEXANDRA
(1842-1849)

NIKOLAI
(1843-1865)

MARIA
(1853-1920)
= Alfred
D. of Edinburgh
D. of Saxe-Cobg.Gotha
(1844 - 1900)

FREDERICK VIII
King of Denmark
(1843 - 1912)
married Louise
d. of Charles XV
King of Sweden & Norway
(1851 - 1926)

GEORGE I
K. of Hellenes
(1845 - 1913)
= Olga
(1851 -1926)
d. of Konstantin
G.D. of Russia

DAGMAR
Maria Feodorovna
(Sophia Frederikke)
(1847 - 1928)
d. of Christian IX
King of Denmark
= **ALEXANDER III**
Tsar of Russia
(1845 - 1894)

ALEXEI
(1850 - 1908)

Elizabeth
of Hesse
(1864 - ex. 1918)
= **SERGEI**
(1857 - murd.1905)

VLADIMIR
(1847 - 1909)
= Maria
Pavlovna
(1854 - 1920)

(1)Alexandra of Greece
(1870 - 1891)
(2)Olga Valerianovna
(1866-1929)
b. Karnovich
Countess Hohenfelzen
created Princess Paley (1915)
= **PAVEL**
(1860 - ex. 1919)

ALIX*
(Alexandra Feodorovna)
(Empress of Russia)
(1872 - ex. 1918)
d. of Ludwig IV
= **NIKOLAI**
(Nikolai II
(Emperor of Russia)
Abdicated 1917
(1868 - ex. 1918)
(son of Alexander III)

ALEXANDER
(1869 - 1870)

GEORGIY
(1871 - 1899)

XENIA
(1875 - 1960)
= Alexander Mikhailovitch
(1866 - 1933)

MIKHAIL
GD of Russia
(Heir until 1904)
(1878 - ex 1918)
= Natalia
Sheremetevskaya
assumed the title
(Countess Brasova)
(1880 - 1952)

OLGA
(1882-1960)
= (1) Pyotr D. of Oldenburg
(1868 - 1924)
(2) Nikolai Kulikovskiy
(1881 - 1958)

OLGA
(1895 - ex. 1918)

TATIANA
(1897 - ex. 1918)

MARIA
(1899 - ex. 1918)

ANASTASIA
(1901 - ex. 1918)

ALEXEI+
(1904 - ex. 1918)

"KISS HER HAND . . . THAT IS YOUR TSARINA-TO-BE"

𝕿he very fact that she was born to the Grand Ducal House of Hesse seemed to promise Alexandra a chance to ascend the Russian throne, following in the footsteps of her relations – Tsarina Natalia Alexeyevna, Tsar Pavel I's wife, and Tsarina Maria Alexandrovna, Alexander II's wife (Cesarevitch Nikolai's grandmother) – who were from the Grand Duchy of Hesse-Darmstadt. Besides, St. Petersburg society remembered an episode recounted by Baroness Anna Pilar von Pilhau, Tsarina Maria Alexandrovna's maid-of-honour. During the Russian Tsar and Tsarina's visit to Darmstadt, Grand Duke Ludwig IV of Hesse and his wife Alice had presented their children to them. Pointing to little Alix, the Tsarina instructed her maid-of-honour: "Kiss her hand– that is your Tsarina-to-be". On a mournful rainy October day in 1894 this prophecy was to be fulfilled: Alix adopted the Orthodox Christian name of Alexandra Feodorovna, and later took her place as Tsarina on the right of her sovereign husband, Tsar Nikolai II.

This marriage could have been a rather conventional one contracted according to age-old traditions, or out of political convenience – or just to fulfill Nikolai's grandmother's prediction. But the couple had to endure many difficulties and overcome obstacles to withstand the gravity of traditions which normally make love surrender to the interests of the State. They had first met ten years before. Spring was merging into summer when Alix came to a far-off country to attend the wedding ceremony of her beloved elder sister, Ella, and Grand Duke Sergei Alexandrovitch, Tsar Alexander III's brother. One of the brightest impressions that caught her imagination was the sun. It seemed unusual to Alix.

The young Nikolai and (facing page) the girl who was to become his bride, Princess Alix of Hesse. (Inset) Pages from the young Alix's notebook, while she was in Russia for her older sister Ella's wedding. "The sun rises in Peterhof one hour and seven minutes earlier than in Berlin" the twelve year-old Princess noted. This was the year they first met, July 1884.

59

She put down in her little notebook: *"The sun rises in Peterhof one hour and seven minutes earlier than in Berlin . . ."* Her kind heart, sweet disposition and long golden hair had earned her the nickname "Sunny" among her kin and she often found something in the changing face of the sun that could correspond to her own state of mind: *"At last glorious bright sunshine – what a difference it makes . . ." "At times the sun is marvellous, and then the days are so dark again . . ." "The morning is grey, the weather can't make up its mind whether it will rain, or the sun will peep out through the clouds . . . The sun, the clouds, the snow give way to one another."* It was so much like her life . . . and the lives of those who were dearest to her, her "Sunlight", the beloved Nicky, and their four daughters with gentle, sweet hearts and beautiful faces, and their little "Sunbeam", their son, their pride and hope . . .

The small solar system Alix created for herself would be snuffed out thirty-four years later in the dirty, scantily lit basement in the Ipatyev's House in Yekaterinburg . . . and night would fall, "the long lonely night". But, in 1884, when Alix and Nikolai first met, their tragic fate was still remote and everything was quite different. They seemed to have an eternity in store . . .

Then it was a time of sunshine and beginnings. Alix came to Russia, and the Heir to the Crown, Grand Duke Nikolai Alexandrovitch, a dear boy of sixteen, met her. Recollecting the events of the day, Cesarevitch Nikolai would admit in his diary on May 27, 1884: *"We went to meet Uncle Gega's [Grand Duke Sergei Alexandrovitch] fiancée beautiful Ella, her sisters and brother. The whole family dined at half past seven. I sat next to little twelve-year-old Alix, and I liked her awfully much."*

Nothing out of the ordinary occurred during the next three days. The Cesarevitch and his new friends enjoyed their games in the expansive grounds of the imperial residence Alexandria in Peterhof. Then, suddenly, on May 31, an entry in the Cesarevitch's diary appeared : *"Alix and I were writing our names on the back window of the Italian house (we love each other)".* And the next day he would remark that Alix *"was sure to sit by my side. We played and ran in the garden. Alix and I exchanged flowers."*

The young Cesarevitch may have been a bit self-assured, rather common among young people of his age, as Alix would never have made such confident assertions in her diary. But this confidence quickly vanished when he found himself in an awkward situation. As a token of the sincerity of his emotions, Cesarevitch Nikolai presented a diamond brooch to Alix. She dared not reject it at once, but gave it back the next day at the children's party in the Anichkov Palace. Ten years later the brooch would return to Alix, and it would be one of her most treasured presents. Soon she returned home, leaving Nikolai with sweet memories of her visit. *"I keep thinking of dear Alix",* he would admit in his diary.

It is not known whether Alix also thought of Nikolai once she left Russia. Did she ever think of him now that thousands of miles separated them? She filled the pages of her tiny notebooks with quotations from the Bible, Sophocles, Byron, Goethe, Pliny, Shakespeare, and many others, her interest in these writers revealing a spiritual maturity that belied her years. Yet, she never mentioned the Russian Prince. But among the charming pictures that filled her diaries and notebooks, there appeared coded notes. Alix devel-

(Top) Empresses Natalia Alexeyevna, Tsar Pavel I's wife, and (above) Maria Alexandrovna, Alexander II's wife and Nikolai's grandmother, were from the Grand Duchy of Hesse-Darmstadt. The girlish sketch and watercolour are from Alix's notebook in 1885.

МАЙ.

31. Четв. Ап. Ерма.
12 Iюня.

A formal portrait of Nikolai in uniform from 1888. (Inset) His diary entry recording that first encounter in 1884 : (May 28) "... we played with Ernst and Alix ..." (May 30) "... we went for a ride with Ernst and Alix ..." May 31) "... Alix and I were writing our names on the back window of the Italian House (we love each other). .."

oped this secret code herself, and she would often use it later on. Who did she think about, when she coded her entries, so commonly interspersed with hearts – the "mysterious" symbol that holds no ambiguity for lovers? She also started to draw some charming pictures featuring brides in wedding dress.

Children's souls are pure and naive. However skillfully children try to hide their little secrets, their "buried treasure", they never succeed for they do so with an amazing openness and sincerity, which in many adults, withers and shrinks with every passing day. And although Alix tried her best to hide her secret, she still failed. Having developed an interest in the Russian language and attempting to learn it, she further revealed the seriousness of her intentions. She must have thought about Nikolai, hoping for a sequel to the romance which began in the spring of 1884.

Thirty-two years later, in her letter to her husband, then Tsar Nikolai II, she would avow: *"Oh to have wings and fly over every evening to cheer you up with my love. Long to hold you in my arms, to cover you with kisses and feel that you are my very Own, whoever else dares call you 'my own', - you nevertheless are mine, my own Treasure, my Life, my Sun, my Heart! – 32 years ago my child's heart already went out to you in deep love."* The date was January 2, 1916, a day of "nice bright sunshine and 20 degrees of frost" – but by then the sun had already begun to set on their lives .

Five years were to pass before Alix and Nikolai met again. Nikolai remembered the girl from the far-off country. In his thoughts he recalled the bright days of their first meeting and her arrival revived the memories. Alix plunged into the life of the Russian Court – taking part in official receptions, balls and parades. Many were inclined to regard Alix as the Cesarevitch's fiancée. The private visit to her sister, Grand Duchess Yelizaveta Feodorovna, promised to acquire an official character, which would result in her engagement to the Heir. It was not just the public that wished for a wedding – it was what Nikolai himself wished, and he had even told his parents about his desire.

Like many beautiful girls, the Princess from Darmstadt displayed rather independent and reserved manners, but it was not the cold restraint of a 'belle de salon'. Anyone with an unbiased observant eye could detect that she was of a subtle and delicate disposition. But, at the same time, she was resolute, with an innate impulsiveness. Her conduct revealed the strict upbringing of her grandmother, Queen Victoria.

This remarkable woman had tried to inculcate in her grand-daughter all the qualities she herself possessed. Who knows, probably while walking in the grounds of Windsor Castle she told Alix about her romantic meeting with the young Russian Heir Alexander Nikolayevitch (later Tsar Alexander II) who in 1838-39 visited several West European countries. He arrived in Great Britain in April 1839, and was received by Queen Victoria, then unmarried. The following extracts from Queen Victoria's diary, May 29-30, 1839, suggest that she felt some affection for the young Grand-Duke: *"I never enjoyed myself more. We were all so merry, . . . I got to bed by 1/4 to 3 but could not sleep till 5. . . I*

Unlike Nikolai, Alix did not write about her feelings, but some of her sketches indicate that she was far from indifferent to the Russian heir after their meeting. Sketches more and more began to feature a young girl in a wedding dress and the diary entry mentions *"There is one, and he is a love, and so are you, you little dove."*
(Facing page) The young Alix with older sister, Irene. Her family's photographs were treasured by Alix and kept in her albums when she became Tsarina.

really am quite in love with the Grand Duke; he is a dear, delightful young man"; "I felt so sad to take leave of this dear, amiable young man whom I really think I was a little in love with". Victoria's brief flirtation with Alexander came to nothing however, and for a while it looked as though Alix was about to repeat her grandmother's experience.

The private life of sovereigns cannot belong to them completely; they have to sacrifice their emotions for the benefit of their country. And this applied to the Russian Heir as well. Alix's second visit was not a successful one, and it could have turned out to have been her last one. Sharp tongues gossiped that Nikolai's mother, the Tsarina, disliked "cold arrogant" Alix. In fact, things were not as plain as that. Banking on an alliance between Russia and France, Alexander III expected his son to play the main part in these political intrigues. Cesarevitch Nikolai was supposed to marry the Princess of the Orléans House, Hélène, daughter of the Count de Paris. To his parents' great surprise, Nikolai, ever so gentle and obedient, rejected the proposal. Yet, for the time being, he did not insist on his marriage to Alix. But it was only for the time being . . .

In August 1890, Alix came to Russia again. But this time the loving couple were separated by a great distance. The despair of lovesick Nikolai seemed to be infinite. He wrote: *"God, how I wish to go to Ilyinskoye [the estate of Grand Duke Sergei Alexandrovitch and Yelizaveta Feodorovna, Alix's sister, in the suburbs of Moscow] . . . Alix and Victoria are staying there; if I don't see her now, I shall have to wait for another whole year, and it's so hard!!!"* (Diary entry; August 20, 1890). But the distance between St. Petersburg and Moscow was insurmountable then, and the exclamation marks at the end of Nikolai's record are easily understood.

Alix was well aware of the intricate situation in which they were both embroiled. The undisguisedly cold reception on the part of Nikolai's parents added to Alix's personal, no less complicated, feelings concerning her religious convictions. The prospect of becoming Nikolai's fiancée and then wife meant obligatory conversion to the Orthodox religion. "The marriage of the Heir to the Throne or the eldest male in His generation to a person of different faith shall not be contracted otherwise but after her conversion to the Orthodox faith", read Article 40 of the Fundamental Laws of State, which was beyond all debate. Matters seemed to have reached a deadlock. Life went on as usual, but it didn't bring about any desirable changes.

"A year and a half have passed away since I spoke about it with Papa in Peterhof, and nothing has changed", Nikolai wrote in his diary in December 1890. *"My dream is to marry Alix H. [of Hesse] some day. It's ages I have loved her, but still deeper and stronger since 1889 when she spent 6 weeks in Petersburg. For a long time I resisted my feeling trying to deceive myself that my fondest dream was unfeasible . . . The only obstacle and gulf between her and me is the question of religion. There is no other impedi-*

Alix's introduction to Russia came when her older sister Ella (facing page) married the Grand Duke Sergei Alexandrovitch, Nikolai's uncle. Ella had to embrace the Orthodox religion as did Alix later on.
(Above) Grand Duke Sergei Alexandrovitch who was Governor General of Moscow.

(Right) Queen Victoria with family members and friends at Osborne House in August 1887. (From left to right) standing: Princess Marie and Princess Victoria Melita of Edinburgh; far right Mohamed Bukhsh. Seated: the Duke of Connaught, Queen Victoria; (to her left:) Alix of Hesse, Princess Alexandra of Edinburgh, Princess Irene of Hesse and Beatrice, Princess Henry of Battenberg (back view). (Above right) Ella in the sitting room on her estate at Ilyinskoye. Alix's older sister, Ella, then in Russia having married Grand Duke Sergei Alexandrovitch, wrote to Nikolai on May 31, 1891, expressing her anxiety over the "nasty accident in Tokyo", during his visit to Japan. She refers to "Pelly" – a secret code-name for Alix – and comments on her father being upset about her changing religion, this, she points out, will be the biggest obstacle between Nicky and Alix: "Dear Nicky, Thank God that you are now quite well & on your way home. . . Poor Pelly was in an anguish. I telegraphed several times to her father as it was impossible to send her the details giving you another name . . . You will have to fight a battle my dear, not for love but to give her courage and persuasion as my changing religion although all my family were very kind, got upset Papa very much and in the country made a bad impression. Luckily grandmama and all the English relations looked at it from quite another view and found it natural wife & husband should try to be of one belief – Grandmama wrote to me once asking if I was not perhaps encouraging a certain marriage and that what she found against it was that two sisters should not be in the same country. How us being here will make a difference . . ." (Facing page) Ella and Alix in a beautiful portrait taken during Alix's visit to her sister. Ella played an important role in Alix's life. The relationship between the two sisters suffered when Ella defended Dmitriy Pavlovitch, who was brought up by her like a son, when he took part in the killing of Rasputin.

66

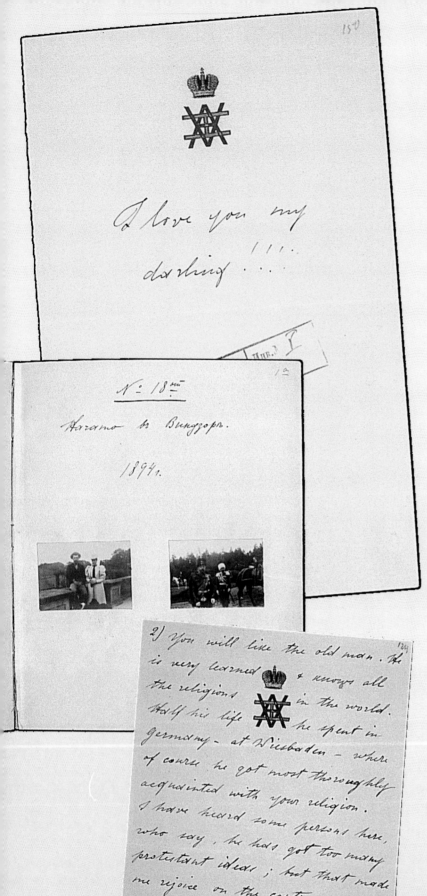

Nikolai's simple *"I love you my darling"* note to Alix in contrast (above) to Alix's poems addressed to Nicky in October 1894: *"For my own beloved darling, Nicky dear, from y. deeply loving, truly devoted Alix." "May love and peace/ and Blessing without end / Wreath all your path with flowers/ Oh my friend! / And if a thorn should touch /you where they grow/ Believe, indeed I would not / have it so."*

(Left) The opening pages of one of Nikolai's diaries with two photographs and the note in his handwriting *"No.8, begun in Windsor".*

(Bottom left) Nicky's letter to Alix on the arrival of an Orthodox priest to instruct her for conversion to the Orthodox religion. *"... You will like the old man. He is very learned and knows all the religions in the world ... I have heard some persons here, who say, he has got too many protestant ideas; but that made me rejoice on the contrary, because I think bigots only can say such things! .. He is not going to hurt y.' feelings, sweety, of that I am sure ! .. "*

Facing page: (top left) Alix commiserates with Nikolai on the death of his Aunt Hattie, and tells of the arrival of Fräulein Schneider, who was to teach her Russian: *"...My precious Darling, Fondest thanks for your dear letter ... Fräulein Schneider has arrived — mad little woman insists on only talking Russian with me, I stand grinning at her, without being able to understand anything, my memory is too bad ... "* (May 14, 1894).

(Top & bottom right) Nikolai apologises for being a "stern teacher" in this letter correcting Alix's Russian: *" ... only don't think me too severe a judge. Well! now the lesson begins. You wrote a sweet thing ... the second word ought to be ... — means — of mine. Excuse me, darling, only I don't know — it is so difficult to explain it in writing! Then there follows two phrases, perfectly well written, especially as you were composing alone! ... (loves) instead of be loved ...The last sentence is beautifully put in — so many thanks, you sweet little girly, for taking that trouble of writing me in Russian. My officers want me now, so I must leave you, dearest Alix, because they have decided to drink to your health & so I must go ...Now you shall see whether I am fit to continue a letter after; the task may be a difficult one, but I will have to do it, knowing that tomorrow is my own darling's dear birthday ... I have just seen the telegram the officers have despatched off to you. Poor little dear — the last bit of your incognito shall vanish, but I think I shall go on writing to my beloved Baroness S. I leave directly for Gatchina, as I have not seen Papa for two days. — I hope Madelaine has not forgotten my commission and gave you the little birthday present. Now I must end this scribble ! Oh! my love, how I long for you, today still more than ever — could I only clasp you & press you to my heart. I pray to God — that the year you have come into, should be one of utter happiness & eternal sunshine for you! Good-bye, my primrosy. With thousand blessings, kisses, wishes and tenderest love, my own sweet one, love & ever your deeply loving, true & devoted Nicky."*

(Bottom left) Nikolai, still writing about the "incognito" *"... It makes me laugh out loud having to put that incognito address of your's. Fancy me writing to a baroness when I am engaged to a darling little Princess of Hesse! Our post at home will be simply shocked when they are going to see so many of my letters sent to a baroness!! — When we are once married and start on a voyage, to Italy for instance (Venice, Florence) we shall travel under the name of Count & Countess Reventlov — won't we Sweety? Of course we must try and not to meet with the real R's else we might get into no end of muddles! and qui pro quos? Hmm ..."*

No. 14.
Windsor Castle.
May 14th 1894

My precious Darling,

Fondest thanks for your
dear letter, I received this morning.
How terribly sad poor old Aunt
Katty's death. Was it not very
sudden? I am glad Hélène
was there; how unhappy she
must be, but it is lucky she
is married. What sorrows
this life does bring! — Fräulein
Schneider has arrived — dear
little woman insists on
only talking Russian with
me, & I stand grinning at
her, without being able to understand anything, my memory
is so bad — she tries to teach

2) It makes me laugh out loud
having to put that incognito
address of yours! Fancy me writing to a baroness when I
am engaged to a darling little
Princess of Hesse! Our post at
home will be simply shocked
when they are going to see so many
of my letters sent to a baroness!!
— When we are once married &
start on a voyage, to Italy for
instance (Venice, Florence) we shall
travel under the name of Count &
Countess Reventlow — won't we sweety?
Of course we must try and not
meet with the real R's, else we
might get into no end of muddles!
& qui pro quos? Hum! — Now I
shall be good & tell you how we came here.

few faults you have made — only don't think
me too severe a judge. Well! now the lesson
begins. You wrote a — sweet thing: men never
notice my — the second word ought to be — moi-
because moi — means — of mine. Excuse me darling, only I don't know — it is so difficult to explain
in writing. Then there follow two phrases perfectly
well written, especially as you were composing alone!
Amuse, think men madame know (by me). Had
you wrote madame (loves) instead of be loved — madame.
The last long sentence is beautifully put in
so many thanks, you sweet little girly, for taking
that trouble of writing me in russian. — My officers
want me now, so I must leave you, dearest Alix
because they have decided to drink to your health
& so I must go. Now you shall see —
bit to —

a chorus — wh. touched me greatly. I have
just seen the telegram the officers have
despatched off to you. Poor little dear — the
last bits of your incognito shall vanish, but
I think I shall go on writing to my beloved
Baroness S. — I leave directly for Gatchina,
as I have not seen Papa for two days. —
I hope Madelein has not forgotten my commi-
sion & gave you the little birthday-present.
Now I must end this scribble! — Oh! my
love, how I long for you, today still more
than ever — could I only clasp you & press you
to my heart. I pray to God — that the year
you have come into, should be one of utter
happiness & eternal sunshine for you!
Good-bye, my primrose. With thousand blessing
kisses, wishes & tenderest love, my own sweet one,
ever & ever your deeply loving, true & devoted Nicky

(Above) A young Queen Victoria and Alexander II spent a few elated days together in the spring of 1839 in England and she wrote in her diary: *"...I never enjoyed myself more. We were all so merry..."*
(Right) Alix's brother, Ernst, with his first wife Victoria Melita on their wedding day in 1894. (Facing page) Queen Victoria visited Coburg for Ernst's marriage which was to coincide with the engagement of Nikolai and Alix. While there, she posed for this picture with family and relatives. From left to right: (In front): Princess Beatrice of Coburg and Princess Feodora of Saxe-Meinengen. (First row) Kaiser Wilhelm of Germany; Victoria and her daughter Victoria; (Second row) Prince Alfred of Saxe-Coburg-Gotha; Nikolai and Alix, her sisters Princesses Victoria of Battenberg and Irene of Prussia; G.D. Maria Pavlovna (wife of G.D. Vladimir Alexandrovitch); Duchess Marie of Saxe-Coburg-Gotha daughter of Alexander II). (Third row) Edward, Prince of Wales, later Edward VII; Princess Beatrice of Battenberg; Princess Philipp of Coburg; Duchess Alexandra of Hohenlohe (daughter of Duke Alfred of Saxe-Coburg); Princess Charlotte daughter of Friedrich III (married to Bernhard III Duke of Saxe-Meinengen; Duchess Marie of Connaught. (Fourth row) Prince Heinrich of Battenberg; G.D. Sergei Alexandrovitch; Prince Ferdinand of Rumania; G.D. Vladimir; Duke Arthur of Connaught. (Fifth row) Prince Ludwig of Battenberg; G. D. Pavel Alexandrovitch; Prince Philipp of Coburg; Count Mensdorf; Princess Maria of Rumania; G.D. Yelizaveta Feodorovna; Alfred of Saxe-Coburg-Gotha.

ment, I'm nearly certain that our feelings are reciprocal. God's will be done. Trusting in His mercy, quiet and obedient, I face the future". That last sentence in the entry is highly significant – the very essence of Nikolai's philosophy is distilled there.

Then came 1894, the year in which Nikolai assumed power from his father's hands and later shared it with his darling Alix. In January 1894, Tsar Alexander III had fallen dangerously ill with pneumonia, which caused complications with his renal disease, and the Family Council decided to hasten the Heir's marriage. The eldest member of the Romanov House, Grand Duke Mikhail Nikolayevitch, was entrusted to discuss the delicate

question with Nikolai, who asserted that he loved Alix of Hesse, and wouldn't marry any other. The parents had to give in – and so their permission for the marriage was obtained.

An opportunity to put the plan into action soon presented itself. Early in April, the Russian delegation – with the Heir to the Throne at its head – left for Coburg to attend the wedding of Alix's brother, Grand Duke Ernst-Ludwig von Hesse, and Princess Victoria Melita of Saxe-Coburg-Gotha. But besides the official purpose of the mission there was, apparently, another purpose, even more significant for Nikolai and all of Russia – to arrange the Cesarevitch's engagement to Princess Alix. Proof of this was the presence of Archpriest Ioann Yanyshev and Catherine Schneider. The former had introduced Nikolai's mother, then Princess Dagmar of Denmark, afterwards Tsarina Maria Feodorovna, to the fundamentals of the Orthodox religion in 1864-1865. The latter taught Russian to Alix's eldest sister, Ella, before her marriage to Grand Duke Sergei Alexandrovitch in 1884. The parallels were obvious.

On April 4, 1894, Nikolai Alexandrovitch, accompanied by his uncles Grand Dukes Vladimir Alexandrovitch, Sergei Alexandrovitch and Pavel Alexandrovitch, arrived in Coburg. The day he had looked forward to was nearing. Behind were ten years of longing and waiting which now seemed as short as one day. Ahead were the excruciatingly long hours of expectation. They met on April 5 /17. *"God! What a day! After coffee, at about 10 o'clock, I went to Aunt Ella's residence to see Alix. She has become remarkably pretty, but looked quite sad. The two of us were left alone, and then began between us the conversation, which I had long strongly wished for and at the same time had very much feared. We talked till twelve, but with no result, she still objects to changing her religion. Poor girl, she cried a lot. . ."*

(Above) Nikolai's record of his engagement to Alix in his diary— he has drawn three lines under the date (Friday, April 8) for emphasis! *"A wonderful, unforgettable day in my life, the day of my engagement to dear beloved Alix . . . all the day through I was in a sort of trance, not quite aware of what had really happened to me . . ."* (Right) Another reminder of the great day on that day's Palace menu – Nikolai scrawled *"on the day of our engagement"*. (Facing page) A pretty but sad Alix gazes pensively at the camera for this portrait. Nikolai gave Alix many gifts which included a pink pearl ring, a chain bracelet with a large emerald and a sapphire and diamond brooch. Grandest of all was a sautoir of pearl, which was a gift from Alexander III. Created by Fabergé, it was worth 250,000 roubles.

Vendredi, le 3/20. Avril 1894.

Déjeûner dinatoire.

Potage Pohlebka.

Oeufs de vanneaux.

Poulets à la paprica.

Côtelettes de mouton sautées.

Salade.

Pointes d'asperges en légume.

Gaufres à la crême.

Was it a failure? No, Nikolai would be patiently waiting, entrusting all to God's will. Alix's diary entries were disappointingly plain and digressive – matter-of-fact statements of the events, no more. Yet, on April 7/19, Alix ciphered some notes in her diary and underlined the date in a special way, which was so unlike her. What was it that had excited the Princess so much that it made her use the mysterious code? It was the wedding day of Ernst Ludwig and Victoria Melita. During the ceremony Nikolai and Alix were sitting side by side, and she couldn't but feel his eyes on her. *"The pastor delivered an excellent sermon, and its contents so wonderfully corresponded with the very essence of the problem we are facing now. I eagerly wished I could peep into Alix's heart at that moment!"*

That evening, April 7, the Princess must have felt restless, in suspense for the day to come. She had to make her choice: say "No" again, or pronounce the eagerly anticipated "Yes". April 8. Friday. *"A wonderful unforgettable day in my life – the day of my engagement to dear beloved Alix. After 10 she came to Aunt Miechen [Grand Duchess Maria Pavlovna], and after a talk with her we explained ourselves. God, what a mountain has lifted from my shoulders, what gratifying pleasure it will be for dear Papa and Mama. The whole day I've been walking in a sort of trance, not quite aware of what had really happened to me . . ."* Nikolai drew three lines under the happy date for emphasis, and every word written by him exuded joy.

Recounting the events in a letter to his mother, Tsarina Maria Feodorovna, the Cesarevitch wrote: *"Oh God, what happened to me then. I cried like a child, and she did too, but her expression had changed at once: her face was lit with a tranquil content. No! Dear Mama, I cannot explain to you how happy I am! And I am sad that I am not with you and I cannot embrace you and dear Papa at this moment. The whole world turned for me, everything: nature, people, places, all seem to be nice, dear and lovable. I could not write at all, my hands were trembling. And besides, really, I had not a single moment free. I had to answer hundreds of telegrams and I wished terrifically to sit in a corner alone, with my sweet bride. She has quite changed: she is cheerful and amusing, and talkative and tender. I do not know how to thank God for such a boon of His . . . "*

That April of 1894 would stand out in their memories till their last day. Their walks in private amid the fragrant spring countryside, the cheerful sounds of the military band playing in their honour, the celebratory fireworks flushing high in the sky, and the flowers, lots of them – these memories would return in their thoughts, supporting them in the moments of trial and tribulation.

Those twelve days which Nikolai and Alix spent together after their engagement were coming to an end. And their separation was nearing. Not long before they parted, they exchanged verses, and now each of them had words written by their lovers' hand to give them strength to live through all hardships. *"For my own beloved darling Alix from her deeply devoted and loving Nicky. In remembrance of a lovely stay in Coburg. April 1894."*

On his return to Russia after their engagement, Nikolai wrote to Alix from Gatchina enclosing a dried bluebell bloom in his letter, which – apart from a few words in Russian – is written in their common language, English. "April.30/May 12. My loving soul Alix. Hello, I am not so polite as you my sweet one, because I omit the two letters at the end of the 'me' word. Your dear letter No. 7 did me so much good, for which I thank you my darling little girl and kiss her fondly many times. At last you got my first letter from home, it is such a pleasure reading the answers to one's letters and after this one many others shall follow ." (Facing page) Nikolai gave this handsome portrait of himself to Alix with the dedication: "again & again the same old face Nicky. Coburg 1894"

*" Peace be around thee where'er thou rovest
And all that thou wishest and all that thou lovest.
Come smiling around thy sunny way.
If sorrow o'er this calm should break
May even thy tears pass off so lightly,
That like spring showers they'll only make
The smiles that follow, shine more brightly . . ."*

And these are the words of Alix's "spell":

*"I want a heart not heeding
What others think or say,
I want a humble spirit
To listen and obey,
To serve Thee without ceasing,
Tis but a little while,
My strength, the Master's promise,
My joy, the Master's smile."*

Alix left for Darmstadt, and later she sailed off to England to her grandmother Queen Victoria, while Nikolai stayed in Coburg before he returned to Russia. It was then that the daily correspondence between them began. Those tender messages most wonderfully united the hearts and souls of the lovers while distance and time separated them. On

again & again the same old face Nicky

Coburg 1894.

the same day, Nikolai and Alix began writing this great novel in letters. There has never been anything like it to be found among their equals in blood and status. Every letter was numbered, and each number marked a day apart, a day of anxiety, sorrow and expectation. There were 653 of them in all. Tsarina Alexandra Feodorovna would write her last letter to her husband on March 4, 1917, several hours after Nikolai II had abdicated the throne; and as ever, hope was the keynote. "*. . . Only I feel and foresee glorious sunshine ahead.*"

The first page of the novel was begun on Wednesday, May 2, 1894, in Coburg and Darmstadt, simultaneously. "*PALAIS EDIN-BURGH COBURG No. 1. This sad Wednesday, April 20/May 2, 1894. My sweet darling beloved Alix! Oh! it was too awful saying goodbye like that with a lot of people looking on from all sides! I shall never forget the sweet sad and yet smiling expression of your angelic face looking out of the window as the train was beginning to move!*"

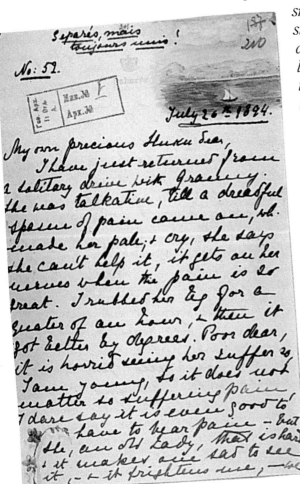

"*Darmstadt. May 2nd 1894. Wednesday evening, 11.5 No. 1. My own precious Darling, I'm lying in bed, but cannot go to sleep before I have written to you, as speak, alas, we cannot. Oh, how I miss you, it is not to be described and how I long for the two hours all alone with you – no goodnight kiss and blessing, it is hard. But our thoughts will meet, won't they? . . .*" On May 4, already in Windsor, Alix wrote to her "own precious Nicky dear": "*I shall never forget those first days and what a beast I was to you, forgive me, my love. Oh, if you only knew how I adore you and the years have made my affection for you grow stronger and deeper, and I wish only I were worthier of your love and tenderness. You are much too good for me!*"

The separation was too hard upon them and they were so eager to be together again. An "eternity" had passed before they met again – on June 8, 1894, the Imperial Russian yacht *Pole Star* with Nikolai on board sailed up the river Thames, and the lovers could hold one another in their arms at last. Alix was "even more beautiful and sweeter than before", as Nikolai wrote to his mother.

They spent several days in Walton, and then they went to Windsor to meet Queen Victoria – "old dear Granny". Prepared for a strict and austere regime while visiting the old Queen, Nikolai was surprised at the freedom Alix and he were given. They were so happy and contented then. And Nikolai's diary was the most trustworthy witness to that.

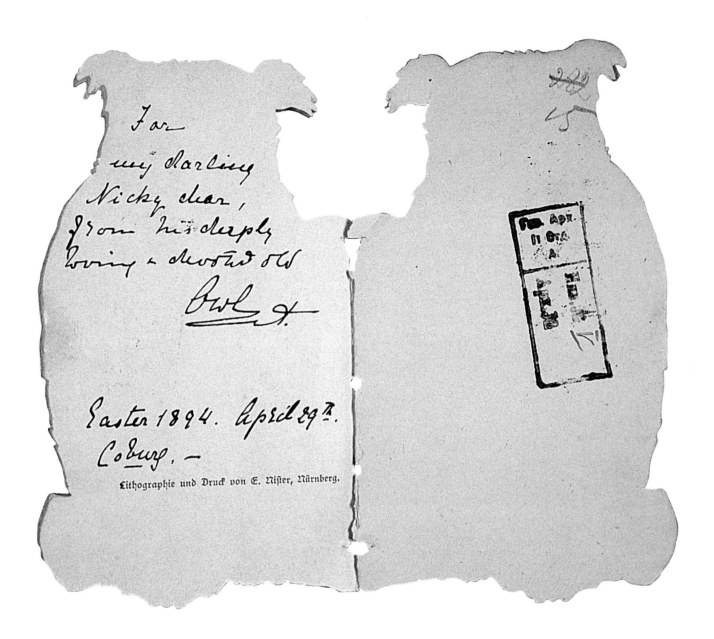

For
my darling
Nicky dear,
from his deeply
loving & devoted old

[signature]

Easter 1894. April 29ᵗʰ.
Coburg, —

Lithographie und Druck von E. Nister, Nürnberg.

Its pages were now open for Alix's entries as well. Some of the poems entered in the diaries could have been written by them, especially those by Nikolai. Most of the verses are well written, although some look like hackneyed rhymes and others are amateurish. With her extensive reading and love for quotations Alix must have copied most of them, while some of Nikolai's verses look original. Alix would playfully draw a heart and write down her "oath" in it: "toi toi toi toi", or just put down a few phrases. And there's a poem dedicated to him:

> "The clock is striking in the belfry tower,
> And warns us of the ever fleeting hour,
> But neither needs time, which outward glides,
> For time may pass away, but love abides.
> I feel his kisses on my fever'd brow;
> If we must part, why should it be now?
> Is this a dream? Then waking would be pain,
> Oh, do not wake me, let me dream again."

From this moment on, her entries would often appear in his diary and her reticence in expressing her feeling towards Nikolai, so typical of her before, would be melted by their great love. *"I'm yours, you are mine, of that do be certain. You are locked in my*

heart, lost is the little key. You must now stay inside forever". That was her farewell to Nikolai when he was leaving England . . . and over and over again there was intolerable separation, hopes and memories.

"To love and to care not when amarants fade
On earth be bathed in sunshine or shade!
To love and to be loved again,
Whatever the joy, whatever the pain.
To love and to tell it on soft summer eves
Amid the rustling of green summer leaves,
To feel sweet moments vanish away
And to know there is still so much to say.
To love as we love in the bye and bye,
Together to live, together to die.
One hope, one faith, both loyal and brave
Through life heart to heart, side by side in the grave."

(Top) the newly-engaged couple enjoy an outing.
(Above) Alix's exercise-books from the period 1891-94 with notes on various subjects, and including exercises in the Russian language.
(Facing page) a formal pose to mark their engagement.
(Inset) Nikolai's letter to Alix (written in pencil) on a sheet bearing the stamp "Osborne". The letter however, was written on board the yacht *Pole Star* when Nikolai was departing from England. "Good-bye! My sweet angel, my beloved little Alix! God bless you for all your kindness and goodness to me. Once more be quite sure in your N's love, who is too happy for any word to possess such a treasure as you are. Ever your own for life, Nicky."

Chapter Five

THE WEDDING OF NIKOLAI AND ALEXANDRA

Vladimir Oustimenko

'GOD GRANTED ME THE HAPPINESS I COULD NEVER DREAM OF – HAVING GIVEN ME ALIX . . .'

"May time who sheds his blight o'er all
And daily dooms some joy to death,
O'er thee let years so gently fall
They shall not crush one flower beneath".

(Above) A picture postcard which Alexandra gave to her husband in 1895. Whenever they were apart they were united by the written word.
Facing page: A beautiful portrait of Empress Alexandra Feodorovna taken in 1895 in St. Petersburg by Pasetti.
(Inset) Part of the music score played at Nikolai and Alexandra's wedding. "The Wedding March" dedicated to "Their Imperial Majesties" by composer Boris Shell, "The humble faithful subject".

These lines written by Nikolai at the joyous time of his engagement to Alix, sound like a prayer. The Russian Tsar-to-be, whose sincere and deep faith was mixed with a presentiment that his life would be full of grief and suffering, must have had a foreboding that these sorrows were imminent, and he seemed to want to shield his beloved from sorrow and distress in his invocation to Heaven: "*. . . May that side the sun's upon, Be all that e'er shall meet thy glances*". Fate was to decree otherwise. It threw joy and sorrow into the scales in equal parts for Nikolai and Alix.

Early in autumn, the Heir came to Darmstadt. Suddenly he was called back to Russia to the sick-bed of his dying father. Alix soon followed Nikolai – the wedding had to be arranged with speed. They were about to cross over the line that divided their most

80

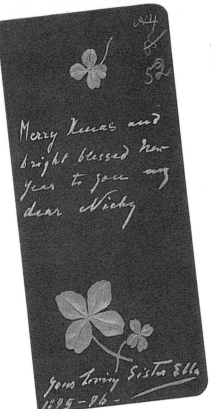

untroubled and brightest days, not yet burdened with a heavy load of responsibility for the destinies of the vast country. A new life began beyond that line.

In the Crimea, not far from Yalta, amid the lovely countryside with its warm, mild air, so like some wonderful liqueur secreted from a mixture of the sea and mountain winds, the first act of the tragedy was being staged. On October 10, Alix arrived in the Crimea. The day before she had sent a telegram to Livadia, the summer residence of the Imperial family. She informed the Cesarevitch that she wished to adopt the Orthodox faith. The Heir met his bride in Alushta, halfway between Simferopol and Yalta. *"My Lord"*, Nikolai entered in his diary on October 10, 1894, *"what a joy to meet her in my homeland and have her near – as if half my anxieties and grief fell off my shoulders."*

The environment in which the Princess of Darmstadt found herself was rather uncomfortable. It could be partly accounted for by the fact that Tsar Alexander III was mortally ill, but the main reason was the traditional cold indifference of the Imperial court. Her heart disapproved of those crowded dinners, the bustle and vanity of a court life which wouldn't give up its habits, even in those grim days when, in the room next door, the father of her beloved Nicky was dying.

On October 20, 1894, Tsar Alexander III passed away. *"My God, my God, what a day! The Lord has called to him our adored, dear, fondly loved Papa. My head turns, I wouldn't wish to believe – so much seems impossible, the horrible reality . . ."* This diary entry reveals both the fear and agitation which crept over Nikolai on the day of his father's death. The Imperial Crown he inherited at the age of twenty-six seemed too heavy for him. The young Tsar was not prepared for it as he could never have thought that his father, such a robust and strong man, would be so suddenly stricken down.

On October 21, the day after the death of Alexander III, Alix was consecrated and given the Orthodox name of Alexandra Feodorovna in commemoration of the Blessed Martyr, Tsarina Alexandra. *"And even in our deep grief, God grants us a gentle and bright joy. At ten o'clock my dear sweet Alix was consecrated, and then she, dear Mama, Ella and I took Holy Communion together . . . Amazingly well and distinctly, Alix recited her responses and prayer,"* Nikolai described the event in his diary. On adopting the Orthodox faith, the title of the Russian Grand Duchess was conferred on Alexandra Feodorovna. Now the date of the wedding ceremony was to be decided. The new Tsar, his mother and bride assumed that the wedding would take place in Livadia – modestly and quietly, without pomp. But the numerous members of the Imperial Family insisted that the wedding take place in St. Petersburg, after the funeral, so that the nuptial ceremonies could be observed as becomes the Russian Tsar. They won the majority at the Family Council.

On October 27, the funeral procession started for Yalta, and then moved onto St. Petersburg. On November 1, the funeral train arrived in the capital. Within a short period Russia was to witness events which, albeit in close succession, were essentially so remote from one another – the funeral of the father and the wedding of the son. Nikolai and Alexandra were on the verge of despair. Things were even more exasperating because they saw so little of each other in those days. The Tsar was absorbed in the endless concerns of state which, to some extent, provided a distraction from dismal thoughts. As is the wont of those of a spiritual nature, Alexandra sought refuge and comfort in her love for Nikolai. Every day, he found in his diary tender words of love and eternal faithfulness. *"Love, however low it may speak, speaks yet distinctly to the heart, love's accent is a voice from the light of heaven, love is earnest and joyous, forbearing and vigorous. Death cannot*

(Above top) Christmas and New Year best wishes from Ella to Nikolai: *"Your loving sister Ella 1895/96".*
(Above) Another card from Ella to Nikolai and Alexandra sent in the years 1894/95: *"For both dears! The Sun! The flowers! Love without end and blessings for New Year".*
(Facing page) Tsarskoye Selo 1898. A charming portrait of Ella and Alexandra who chose to dress identically. All these photographs were put in their albums with much love and care and were deeply treasured. For the next seven decades the Bolsheviks were careful to preserve every one of these mementoes.

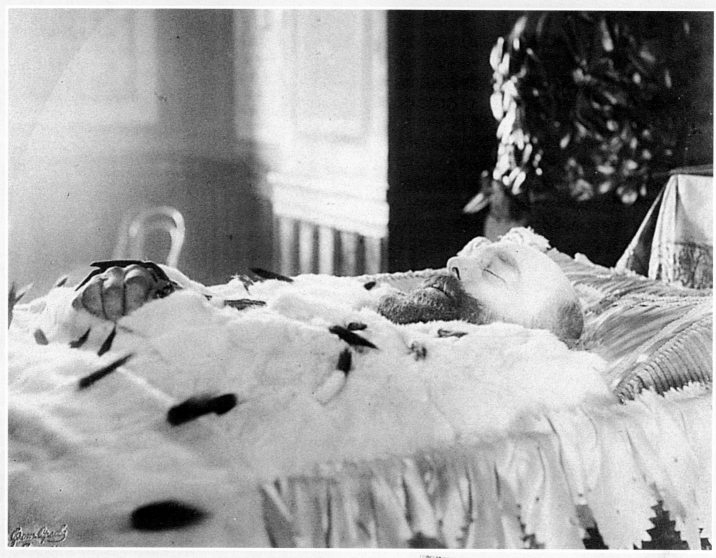

(Above) Alexander III lying in State on November 11, 1894.

When Alexander III was still alive, on October 15, Alix wrote in Nikolai's diary: "*Darling boysy, me loves you, oh so very tenderly and deep. Be firm and make Drs. Leyden and the other G. come alone to you and tell you how they found him, and exactly, what they wish him to do, so that you are the first always to know. You can help persuading him then too, to do what is right. And if the Dr. has any wishes or needs anything, make him come directly to you. Don't let any others be put first and you left out. You are Father's dear son and must be told all and be asked about everything. Show your own mind and don't let others forget who you are. Forgive me lovy.*"

Alix felt it was her responsibility in times of crisis to offer advice to Nikolai and urge him to be stronger and assert his power.

(Right) Copy of the letter Nikolai wrote to Queen Victoria expressing his great sorrow: "*My darling Grandmama, I must write you a few lines as the messenger leaves tomorrow. I cannot tell you what awful and trying days we are living through now! Your dear kind telegrams touched us all more than words can say! Ten days have already passed since that terrible event happened – it seems to me a nightmare – I cannot yet believe that my deeply passionately adored & beloved Father has been taken away from us! Though I knew how seriously ill he was . . . – poor dear Mama . . . She bears her grief and sorrow wonderfully! Sweet dear Alicky's presence is such a comfort to me – I don't know how else I would have stood it – Dear aunt Alix & uncle Bertie being here – help also Mama in her pain . . . I am deeply grieved, that it is impossible for Alicky to come and say good-bye, before our wedding to you – but as probably Mama is going south soon & Lent before Xmas begins on the 14/26 Nov. the marriage has to be hastened! . . .*"

Facing page: (top) The funeral procession of Alexander III. A sad Nikolai stands alone, just behind the funeral carriage. On November 7, on the day Alexander III was buried, Alexandra wrote in Nikolai's diary: "*I cannot express in words what I feel for you, but Darling you know my tender sympathy . . . your duties are many, and hard ones too, may God give you strength . . . let her, who will, God grant, be soon your little wife share all with you, joy and sorrow*".

(Far left) The condolences sent to Nikolai from the British Residents in St. Petersburg.

(Left) The letter of respect the Anglo-Russian Literary Society sent from London on November 1894:

"To His Imperial Majesty,
The Emperor Nicholas II.
Sire,
May it please your Majesty, we the undersigned . . . crave permission to lay before His Majesty, the expression of our profound emotion at the loss sustained by the Russian nation through the sad demise of His Imperial Majesty ALEXANDER III, and our sympathy with the sorrowing hearts of His bereaved people . . .
We humbly pray Almighty God to be the stay and support of Your Imperial Majesty in this hour of trial . . . We have the honour to be,
Your Imperial Majesty's
Most dutiful and obedient servants,
President: Ed. A Cazalet.
Members of Committee:
John Davis,
Will. F. Machin,
E. Demar Morgan,
J. Wolfe Murray,
John Pollen,
Alex Kinloch, Hon. Sec."

shatter love. Love's silence is beautiful and sweeter often than words, what love unites, no fate can separate, love will one day unite all the loving ones." (Alexandra's entry in Nikolai II's diary No 18, p.132. November 5, 1894.)

On November 7, Tsar Alexander III was buried in Sts. Peter and Paul's Cathedral, the resting place since the 18th century of the Imperial family of the Romanovs. Twelve months' mourning was decreed for the whole country. And, again, in those tragic days, Alix's words are addressed to her beloved one: *". . . I cannot express in words what I feel for you, but Darling you know my tender sympathy, having only so shortly gone through the same sorrow and without a Mother"* [Alix alludes to her father's death], *"but we have not lost our dear Ones, they have only gone before, and are waiting for us. It is a comfort to try and live and act as they would have wished and try and follow in their footsteps. They are near us I am sure and love us deeply. – Your duties are many, and hard ones too, may God give you strength to bear and fulfil them – let her, who will, God grant, be soon your little wife share all with you, joy and sorrow."* (Alexandra's entry in Nikolai II's diary No 18, p.136. November 8, 1894.)

Death, though, had to give way to Life. The interval between them was so short that it seemed that in the same room where the orange-blossom was prepared for the wedding dress of the bride, the floor was still strewn with petals from the funeral bier. To Alexandra, it did seem *"a mere continuation of the masses for the dead with this difference that now I wore a white dress instead of a black."*

On November 14, at 8 a.m., a 21-gun salute from the Fortress of Sts. Peter and Paul rang out to herald the beginning of the celebrations for the wedding of His Imperial Majesty Nikolai II to Her Highness Most Sacred Grand Duchess Alexandra Feodorovna. *"My Wedding Day"*, Nikolai would write in his diary, *"We all had coffee together, and then we went to dress: I put on my Hussar uniform, and at half past eleven Misha* [Mikhail Alexandrovitch, Nikolai II's youngest brother] *and I went to the Winter* [Palace]. *All along Nevskiy* [Prospect] *there stood the Guards of Honour to salute Mama and Alix as they drove by. While her toilet was being made in the Malachite* [Room] *we all were waiting in the Arab Room . . . "*

"Now the door of the Malachite Room opens wide and the bride appears, beautiful and resplendent in a white silver dress with a diamond necklace and a diamond crown. Over her dress she wears a robe of golden brocade with an ermine lining and a long train, carefully borne by five attendants." *"At 10 min.* [utes] *past twelve the procession moved to the Bolshaya* [Grand] *Church,"* Nikolai continued. Their proceeding from the inner chambers is accompanied by a salute of 51 salvoes. The wedding procession is a magnificently spectacular sight: the blue blood of Europe – princes, dukes, counts, earls and barons, are followed by gallant guards, officers and eminent dignitaries, hof-couriers and chamber-couriers, gentlemen of the imperial bed-chamber and chamberlains, hof-meisters and hof-meistresses, ladies-in-waiting, chamber maids-of-honour and other ladies of the court.

"At the entrance to the Cathedral the nuptial train is met by the Most Reverend and Right Honourable Metropolitan of St. Petersburg and Ladoga, members of the Holy Synod and the court clergy. Now the Emperor ascends the dais in the centre of the Cathedral. His mother, the Dowager Empress, brings the High Betrothed Bride to him and retreats. The solemn rite begins. From the altar the court archpriests carry out the gold wedding rings on gold dishes. Pronouncing the established prayer Their Imperial Majesties' confessor, Father Ioann Yanyshev, takes the rings and places them on the fingers of Nikolai and Alexandra. The wedding crowns are raised over their heads. And then the wedding commences as a continuation of which, after the recital of the Holy Gospel . . . declared will be 'Of the Most Sacred and the Most Autocratic Our Great Sovereign His Imperial Majesty

(Above) Nikolai's diary record of his wedding day, he put three lines under the date. "November 14, Monday. My Wedding Day. We all had coffee together, and then we went to dress: I put on my Hussar uniform, and at half past eleven Misha [Mikhail Alexandrovitch, Nikolai II's youngest brother] and I went to the Winter [Palace]. All along Nevskiy [Prospect] there stood the Guards of Honour to salute Mama and Alix as they drove by. While her toilet was being made in the Malachite [Room] we all were waiting in the Arab Room . . . At ten minutes past twelve the procession moved to Bolshaya [Grand] Church, and I came out of it a married man . . . (Facing page) An autographed portrait of Alix to Nicky: "From a very loving Alix. 1894."

(Above) A "lubok" print of Nikolai and Alexandra portraying the journey to their honeymoon, five days in Tsarskoye Selo. These few days together were a memento that they treasured all their lives.
(Facing page) A stunning portrait of Nikolai and a radiant Alexandra taken in Coburg in 1894.

Nikolai Alexandrovitch of All Russia and His Consort the Most Sacred Her Imperial Majesty Alexandra Feodorovna'.

"The newlyweds express thanks to Her Imperial Majesty Maria Feodorovna and then they receive congratulations from those present. Then comes the thanksgiving service with genuflection. And the choir breaks into the song: 'We praise Thee, O God!' In the Fortress of Sts. Peter and Paul, a 301-gun salute marks the conclusion of the wedding ceremony. Now they are to make their way back through the same galleries of the Winter Palace, this time in the reverse order: the Memorial Room of Peter the Great, the Armorial Hall, the Field-Marshals' Hall, the Small Antechamber, the Memorial Room of Nikolai I, the Concert Hall and finally, the Malachite Room." (Excerpt from "The Wedding Ceremonial" approved by His Imperial Majesty).

In the days that followed came an endless chain of receptions, boring and cheerless. Their hearts and souls strove for peace and seclusion. They were granted five days honeymoon in Tsarskoye Selo. They went there on November 22. *Words cannot describe what bliss it is for us both to live in such a lovely place as Tsarskoye,"* Nikolai admitted in his diary (November 25).

Alexandra's entry in her husband's diary on November 26 reveals the extent of her love for him: *"Ever more and more, stronger and deeper my love and devotion grows and my longing for you. Never can I thank God enough for the treasure He has given me for my very own, – and to be called yours, sweety, what happiness can be greater. Never shall I forget this place, already dear to me on account of the remembrance of 1889, and now – our first quiet time together. God bless you, my beloved little husband, I cover your sweet face with kisses."*

Nikolai wrote on the same day: *". . . My bliss is boundless – it's such a pity we have to leave Tsarskoye which has become so dear a place for both of us: it is the first time after our wedding that we've spent some days in private and lived in perfect concord."*

"Never did I believe there could be such utter happiness in this world, such a feeling of unity between two mortal beings. I love you – those three words have my life in them ." (Alexandra's entry in Nikolai's diary, November 26).

At the honeymoon's end Nikolai would dedicate a poem to his "darling, little Wify":

"Why did we marry?
Why did we marry – you and I?
Ah! me, why did we in our youth
I vowed I loved; and your reply,
Heart-sung, yet silent, seemed the truth.
Beside our love's now swelling tone
How faint was that first throb, dear heart!
It was a babe that since has grown
Big as the world of which we're part.
Aye, bigger yet, like paradise;
For when you fold me to your breast,
Or I drink deep from your dear eyes,
The world's forgot', with all the rest.
Give more, dear nobler half! I thirst
For all the love you once kept hid.
What if we did not love at first?
Thank God, sweet wife, we thought we did."

As the year of 1894 – tragic, full of anxieties and grief, yet such a happy one for Nikolai and Alexandra – drew to its close, they came to Tsarskoye Selo to see out the Old Year. *"The last day of the old year – what happiness to spend it together. Sweetest Angel, if little wify ever did anything that displeased you or unwillingly grieved and hurt you in the*

(Above) Manifesto of Nikolai II on the occasion of the adoption of the Orthodox Faith by his fiancée Princess Alix von Hessen. October 1894. (Facing page) Portrait of Nikolai II in uniform.

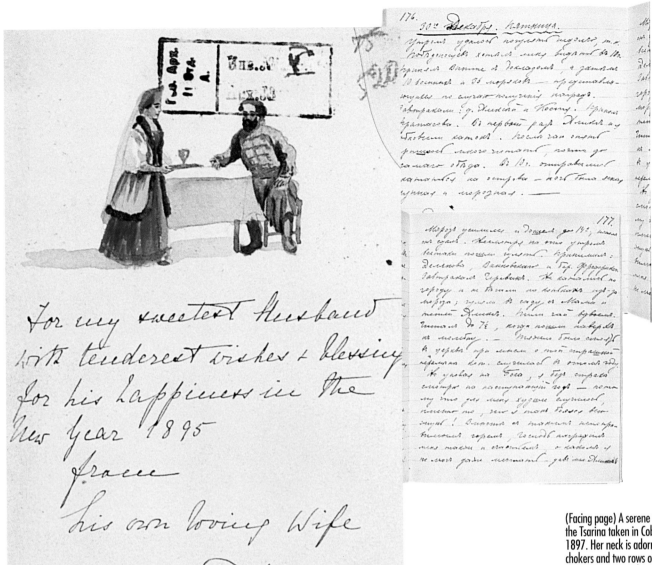

past year – forgive her darling. So deep and pure and strong my Love has grown – it knows no bounds. God bless and keep you." (Alexandra's entry in her husband's diary No 18, p.176. December 31, 1894).

And Nikolai wrote: *". . . It was so hard to stand at church with the thought of the dreadful change that has happened this year. Yet, confiding in God I look forward to the coming year without fear, – because the worst thing for me has happened, and that was what I had feared all my life. But along with this inconsolable grief God granted me the happiness I could never dream of – having given me Alix."*

(Facing page) A serene portrait of the Tsarina taken in Coburg in 1897. Her neck is adorned with two chokers and two rows of pearls and she is wearing pearl earings. She had a real love of pearls and her collection was remarkable. (Left) A card Alexandra gave to Nicky for the New Year: *"For my sweetest husband with tenderest wishes and blessing for his happiness in the new year 1895, from his own loving wife, Alix. St Petersburg."* (Above) Two pages from Nikolai's diary December 31, 1894. Alix wrote first: *"The last day of the old year – what happiness to spend it together. Sweetest Angel, if little wife ever did, if anything, that displeased you or unwillingly grieved & hurt in the past year – forgive her darling! So deep & pure & strong my love has grown – it knows no bounds. God bless & keep you."* (continued by Nikolai) *"It was so hard to stand at the church with the thought of the dreadful change that happened this year [he refers to his father's death]. Yet confiding in God I look forward to the coming year without fear because the worst thing for me has happened, and that what I feared all my life. But along with this incontrollable grief God has granted me the happiness I could never dream of giving me Alix . . ."* Again, grief and happiness seem to be interwoven in Nikolai's heart.

93

'THANK GOD, EVERYTHING HAS BEEN GOING QUITE SMOOTHLY . . . BUT TODAY A GRAVE SIN HAS BEFALLEN'

A commemorative Coronation mug. (Facing page) A painting of the crowned Tsar. These portraits, known as "lubok paintings" were very simple and unpretentious. They appeared in Russia early in the 16th century. Originally, they were prints made of an engraving carved on a bast (lubok), and it is from this Russian term that the pictures derived their name. The pictures portrayed renowned war heroes, prancing on horseback. They featured various scenes from the lives of saints, illustrated proverbs, or folk songs. The technique of printing later changed, but the name – lubok – survived, denoting cheap popular prints. Their image being pellucid, their cost very cheap, the luboks found their way into every peasant and petty merchant house, sometimes whole collections adorned their walls. An indispensable part of traditional old Russian art, "luboks" have become collectors' items.

ourning for Tsar Alexander III was over by the autumn of 1895 and was replaced by the preparations for the coronation of the new Tsar. The ceremony of the Sacred Coronation was scheduled for May 1896. In accordance with the time-honoured tradition it was to take place in Moscow, the former capital, yet still pre-eminent city of Russia. The specially appointed Coronation Commission was assiduously preparing for grandiose festivities. Considerable sums were allotted for repairing and decorating palaces, imperial theatres and places for outdoor fêtes and spectacles in Moscow. Banners and standards, the purples and the regalia, as well as liveries for top officials and vestments for dignitaries, garments for heralds and other vestments were to be specially made for the occasion.

The coronation gown of Tsarina Alexandra Feodorovna cost 4,920 roubles, with the other items prepared for her for the ceremonies amounting to 12,000 roubles. It is noteworthy, however, that the sums were only a tenth of the expenditure for her predecessor, Tsarina Maria Feodorovna, in 1883. The total sum allotted for the Coronation celebra-

(Above) Photograph from the coronation album 1896. The stunning splendour of the Imperial procession, the pageantry and the regalia was a spectacle crowned by Kings and Queens of Europe. On the morning of May 9, not only the pavement, but the ledges and the roofs of the houses were swarming with people, every pair of eyes fixed on the Triumphal Gates – and then His Majesty the Tsar appeared. As befitted the occasion, he rode escorted by his lavishly brilliant suite. The Tsar was mounted on the half-bred English horse Norma. Princess Victoria was invited to the Coronation and to Queen Victoria, who was eager to hear about it, she gave an account of the ceremony: "The coronation is over ... it was a most beautiful and impressive sight. Aunt Minnie [Maria Feodorovna] in her crown and robes headed our procession into the church. She looked marvellous, but I have never seen sadder eyes than hers ... It was indeed a sad and sorrowing sight to see her standing all alone before her throne, waiting for the new Emperor and Empress to come. I think her youthful looks made it all the more pathetic. We waited about an hour in the church before Nicky and Alicky appeared, he looked very grave and serious and she remarkably handsome, with hair unadorned and a small string of pearls around her neck..." (Facing page) A "lubok" portrait of the Tsarina in her coronation robe.

tions in 1896 amounted to 965,925 roubles, while the expenditure for the Coronation celebrations in 1883, when Tsar Alexander III was crowned, totalled 2,715,704 roubles.

The most prominent artists and decorators were engaged in embellishing the palaces and streets of Moscow. Special coins and medals were minted to commemorate the Sacred Coronation. The Russian celebrities Vasiliy Vasnetsov and Alexander Benoit designed the watercolours for the menus of the festive meals. The composer Alexander Glazunov dedicated a cantata.

In early May 1896, hordes set out for Moscow searching eagerly for "bread and circuses". Everybody was looking forward to the arrival of the Imperial Couple. On Monday May 6, 1896, Tsar Nikolai II and his consort, Tsarina Alexandra Feodorovna, arrived at the Petrovsky Palace, several miles outside Moscow. The next two days were devoted to the preparations for the Ceremonial Entry in the Kremlin. On the morning of May 9, cavalry and foot soldiers moved to music all over the city, lining the route for the Imperial procession. His Imperial Majesty's Own Escort, the Horse-Guards, the Life-Guards Uhlan, Dragoon, Cuirassier, Hussar and Cossack squadrons and regiments, the grenadiers as well as riflemen, sappers and military schools' cadets, made up an impressive, picturesque throng, with horses, guns and all sorts of arms, all of them subject to strict regulations and discipline. Gathered under their regimental standards, these crack troops represented the pride and glory of the Russian Army.

The miles-long passage formed by the troops led to the centuries-old walls of the Kremlin. Deployed inside were the battalions of the Life Guards Semyonovsky and Preobrazhenskiy regiments, the first regiments of the regular Russian army created by Peter the Great. Commanding the troops was Grand Duke Vladimir Alexandrovitch, Nikolai II's uncle. Nine volleys from the guns of the Tainitskaya Tower rang out, and the bells of the Assumption Cathedral peeled. Not only the pavements, but the ledges and the roofs of the houses were swarming with people, every pair of eyes fixed on the Triumphal Gates.

Two hours of expectation, waiting for the Imperial procession to appear, crawled by, the suspense creeping over the crowd. At last the gun salute rang out from the Kremlin to herald the departure of the Tsar and the Tsarina from the Petrovsky Palace. Hardly had the sound of the guns receded than the bells of all the churches of Moscow joined in the joyous cacophony. The people, as one, uncovered their heads and devoutly crossed themselves. Tears sparkled in the eyes of many. From all the churches that the

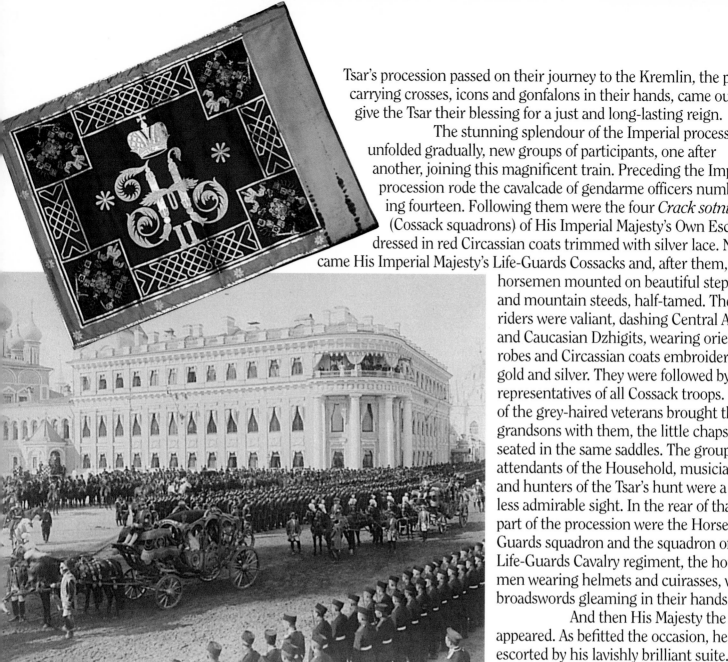

Tsar's procession passed on their journey to the Kremlin, the priests carrying crosses, icons and gonfalons in their hands, came out to give the Tsar their blessing for a just and long-lasting reign.

The stunning splendour of the Imperial procession unfolded gradually, new groups of participants, one after another, joining this magnificent train. Preceding the Imperial procession rode the cavalcade of gendarme officers numbering fourteen. Following them were the four *Crack sotnias* (Cossack squadrons) of His Imperial Majesty's Own Escort, dressed in red Circassian coats trimmed with silver lace. Next came His Imperial Majesty's Life-Guards Cossacks and, after them, horsemen mounted on beautiful steppe and mountain steeds, half-tamed. The riders were valiant, dashing Central Asiatic and Caucasian Dzhigits, wearing oriental robes and Circassian coats embroidered in gold and silver. They were followed by the representatives of all Cossack troops. Some of the grey-haired veterans brought their grandsons with them, the little chaps seated in the same saddles. The group of attendants of the Household, musicians and hunters of the Tsar's hunt were a no less admirable sight. In the rear of that part of the procession were the Horse-Guards squadron and the squadron of the Life-Guards Cavalry regiment, the horsemen wearing helmets and cuirasses, with broadswords gleaming in their hands.

And then His Majesty the Tsar appeared. As befitted the occasion, he rode escorted by his lavishly brilliant suite. The Tsar was mounted on the half-bred English horse Norma, a thirteen-year-old light-grey dapple mare. The most splendid part of the procession were the fourteen coaches and phaetons covered with gold leaf and velvet, the train drawn by six horses harnessed in tandem. Some of the coaches, in the style of Louis XV, dated back to the reign of Tsarina Catherine II and Tsar Pavel I. The coaches were adorned with paintings by the famous artists Boucher, Watteau and Gravelot. The other carriages, austere and massive, yet even more luxurious, came from the XVII century. Each of the crack horses, beautiful and graceful, with golden trappings, was led by an equerry.

The Dowager Tsarina, Maria Feodorovna, travelled in the golden carriage, the top of which was adorned with the Imperial Crown encrusted with precious stones. In the next carriage, a golden coach decorated with paintings, came the young Tsarina. The procession reached the Kremlin. Here, at the Chapel of Our Lady of Iver, the Tsar dismounted and helped his mother, and then Alexandra Feodorovna, out of their carriages. It was a tradition with all the Russian Tsars that their every entry to the Kremlin territory be marked by worship to the icon of the Blessed Virgin of Iver, one of the most revered icons in Moscow. The icon was a replica of the icon kept in the Iver Monastery at Mount Athos, Greece, and it was brought to Russia in 1648. The Tsar, the Dowager Tsarina and the Tsarina attended the Assumption, the Archangel and the Annunciation Cathedrals, after which they proceeded to the Kremlin Palace. There they were to remain while the final preparations for the Sacred Coronation were being made, the ceremony fixed for May 14.

May 10 and 11 were days of ceremonial receptions for the ambassadors and envoys extraordinaire. On May 12, Trinity Sunday, the Banner of State was consecrated. On

(Top) One of the banners displayed during the Coronation. (Above) View of the Kremlin and the procession. The Dowager Tsarina, Maria Feodorovna, travelled in the golden carriage, whose top was adorned with the Imperial Crown. In the next carriage, a golden coach decorated with paintings, came the young Tsarina. (Facing page) In glorious sunshine, Nikolai II under the canopy, carrying the Sceptre and the Orb.

(Right and facing page top) Photographs of the tragic events that took place in the Khodynskoye Pole (meadow) during the Coronation on May 18, 1896. During the celebrations the people were given a "kerchief" (larger than a handkerchief; such souvenir kerchiefs were made in Russia on various national occasions, with a special printed pattern commemorating the event) with a mug and some sweets bundled inside. The giving out of the ration and presents was traditional; at Alexander III's coronation there was perfect order, which amazed all foreign spectators. The Times correspondent wrote that it would be impossible to keep order if such an event were to be held in Britain. Events took a tragic turn at Nikolai II's Coronation, and many people were killed. On the arrival of the Police and the Cossacks, the meadow resembled a battlefield. On the evening of May 18, a horrifying entry would pierce his diary's pages: *"Till this day, thank God, everything has been going quite smoothly, but to-day a grave sin has befallen and it's dreadful . . . about 1300 people were trampled down! . ."*

The same evening, the Tsar and the Tsarina had to attend the ball given by the French Ambassador, the Marquis Louis-Gustave de Montebello, in their honour. Nikolai's uncles put pressure on him not to disappoint the French. Once more the Family Council had their way, the show had to go on. The Imperial couple, shocked and dismayed, had to dance the night away.

Facing page: (bottom left) The Coronation March music and cover. The composer was V.I. Glavatch and the text read: *"Glory to the Dawn of Joy! Glory to the Orthodox holiday and the autocratic Throne of the Tsar of all Russia! Glory, Glory, Glory to the Russian Tsar! Glory, Glory, Glory to the Reigning Couple! . ."*

(Bottom centre) Coronation souvenir mug with the Russian Crown and the initials N & A for Nikolai and Alexandra.

(Bottom right) Souvenir edition of the Newspaper "Syn Otechestva" (The Son of the Fatherland), the political, scientific and literary newspaper. It carried two poems dedicated to the Coronation by K. Medvedskiy and D. Togolskiy and carried an article explaining the significance of the event and gave a short historical survey.

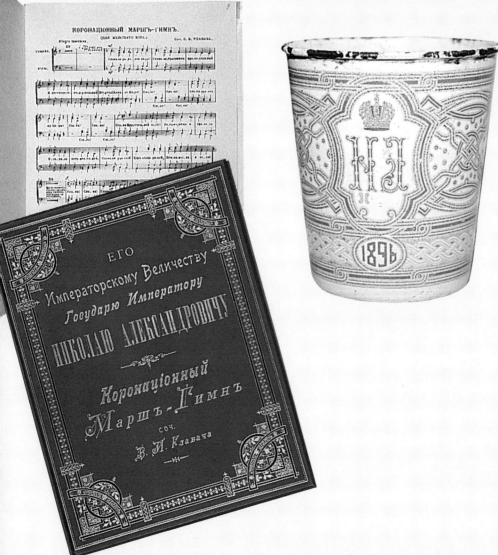

(Above) Two of the tickets given out to view the crowning of the new Russian Tsar. The top one was issued to view the Coronation from the Kremlin's ground. The other for permission to enter the Church of the Assumption Cathedral. (Above right) Supper menu during the coronation festivities dated May 23, 1896, designed by Lippart.

(Right) The poem and its cover written and given to the Tsar by the Czechs people as testimony of the Coronation.

(Far right) Coronation greetings from the French Artists and Industrialists who took part in the French Exhibition in 1891 in Moscow, and their thanks to the Tsar for the warm welcome they received at the time.

Facing page: (top) The crowd creating a corridor for the Coronation procession. Never before had the Russian people witnessed so many national events so close together. The funeral of Alexander III, the wedding of the Royal couple, culminating with the splendid and glittering Coronation. (Bottom left and right) Dinner menus to commemorate the Coronation, dated May 15 and May 19, 1896, illustrated by Lippart. The menus, just like the illustrated greetings sent from all over Europe, were works of art themselves.

102

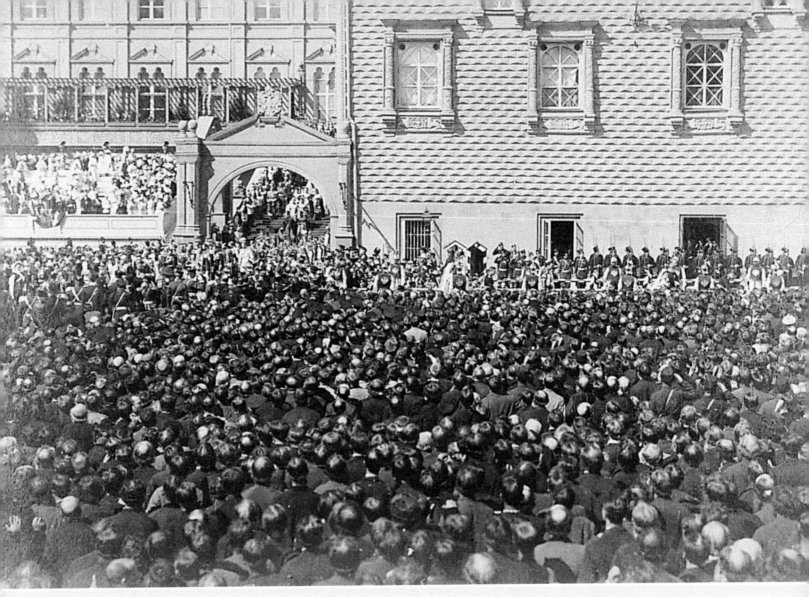

May 13, Whit Monday, the Imperial Regalia were delivered from the Armoury to the Throne Hall of the Kremlin Palace. The preparations were over.

The morning of May 14, 1896, dawned with a glorious sunrise over Moscow, glistening on the golden cupolas and crosses of Moscow cathedrals. On all belfries of the city the bell-ringers held their bell-pulls awaiting the pre-arranged signal. Noiselessly, officials and their assistants carried the Imperial Regalia, the Chain of the Order of St. Andrew for Her Majesty the Tsarina, the Sword of State, the Banner of State, the State Seal, the Purple for His Majesty the Tsar, the Orb, the Sceptre, the Small Imperial Crown, the Great Imperial Crown – all arranged in a strict order of succession – towards the Assumption Cathedral. Silent and obeying barely audible commands, the aides-de-camp to the Tsar, the generals of the Suite and the Horse-Guards troop lined up along the route, on both sides of the Imperial Regalia up to the Red Porch. The Hof-Marshal, the Hof-Marshal-In-Chief and the Supreme Marshal, each with a mace in his hand, silently took their places. The canopy was carried up to the lower steps of the Red Porch. The tassels and the poles of the canopy were held by thirty-two adjutant-generals, with their juniors at the poles.

"Escorted by the Minister of the War Office, the Minister of the Imperial Court, the Commander of the Imperial Residence, the Adjutant-General-of-the-Day, the orderly Major-General of the Suite and the Commander of the Horse-Guards regiment, the Tsar appears on the Porch. Following him, Tsarina Alexandra Feodorovna comes out accompanied by four ladies-in-waiting, maids-of-honour of the day. The Tsar and the Tsarina take their places under the canopy . . ."

"*. . . The procession set out only at half past ten. Luckily, the weather was marvellous, and the Red Porch was a brilliant sight,*" Nikolai II would reflect in his diary. "The silence is abruptly shattered by church bells heralding that the procession has started. The dignitaries come out to the parvis of the Assumption Cathedral to welcome the monarchs. Palladius, the Metropolitan of St. Petersburg, offers Their Majesties the Holy Cross for kissing, and Ioannakius, the Metropolitan of Kiev, sprinkles them with holy water. Having entered the Cathedral, the Tsar and the Tsarina perform the thrice-repeated worship and kissing of the holy icons, and then they ascend the steps of the dais in the centre of the Cathedral. On the top of the dais there are the thrones of the Tsars Mikhail Feodorovitch [the first tsar of the Romanov dynasty, who ascended the throne in 1613] and Ivan III [the Grand Duke of Moscow since 1462, who created the title of 'Tsar of All Russia' in the 15th century]. The Imperial Regalia are placed at their side. The Metropolitan of St. Petersburg suggests Nikolai II make his public confession, after which the Tsar is offered the Holy Book to read his prayer. The last word of the prayer uttered, the Metropolitan solemnly enunciates: 'The blessing of the Holy Spirit be with Thee. Amen'.

"The Tsar takes off the chain of the Order of St. Andrew, and the Metropolitans of St. Petersburg and Kiev dress the Tsar with the Purple, with the diamond Chain of the Order of St. Andrew. His Majesty bows his head. The Metropolitan Palladius makes the sign of the cross over him, and laying his hands on the Tsar's head pronounces two prayers. Nikolai II orders the Imperial Crown be given to him. From the hands of the Metropolitan the Tsar accepts the Crown and places it on his own head. Then he orders the other insignia be handed over to him. With the Sceptre in his right hand and the Orb in his left, the Tsar sits down on the throne of Tsar Mikhail Feodorovitch.

"A few moments later he rises to his feet, hands over the regalia to his attendants and summons the Tsarina. She kneels before the Tsar on a crimson cushion bordered with golden lace. He takes off his Crown and touches the Tsarina's head with it. Then the Small Crown, the Purple and the Chain of the Order of St. Andrew are handed over to the Tsar and one after the other he places the regalia on Alexandra Feodorovna.

"The Sceptre and the Orb are in the Tsar's hands again. The Cathedral choir break into song ,wishing the Tsar and the Tsarina many years of life and reign, and the singing is accompanied with the toll and a salute of 101 salvoes . The Tsar gives the Sceptre to his attendants, genuflects and recites the established prayer. Then he rises to his feet,

while the Metropolitan of St. Petersburg and all present at the ceremony, kneel down to supplicate their prayer on behalf of all the Russian people, and the choir sing: 'We praise Thee, O God.'

"Then begins the Divine Liturgy – the Holy Unction of the Russian Monarchs. The Tsar, followed by the Tsarina, descends the dais. Pacing on the floor covered with crimson velvet bordered with golden lace, the Tsar, and after him the Tsarina, step for a moment on the golden brocade to be anointed with the holy myrrh, Metropolitan Palladius pronouncing: 'The Seal of the Gift of the Holy Spirit'. And the bells and a salute of 101 salvoes herald the perfection of the Unction. The Eucharist concludes the rite which originated in the historical depths of Orthodox Russia.

"The Tsar's train proceeds to the Archangel and the Annunciation Cathedrals. Having performed the appropriate rites there, the procession makes for the Red Porch. At the first step the Tsar and the Tsarina leave the canopy and enter the Palace." (Traditionally, for every coronation a set of new procedural instructions was drawn up. The Ministry of the Court described these procedures in "The Ceremony of the Holy Coronation" from which these extracts are taken).

The Imperial couple needed some rest before the ceremonial meal in the Hall of Facets . . . That evening, tired yet utterly gratified, the Tsar would write in his diary: "... *All that happened in the Assumption Cathedral, though it seems but a dream, is not to be forgotten for life!!!*"

If only his diary would always contain such joyous entries . . . but on the evening of May 18, a horrifying diary entry would pierce the pages: *"Till this day, thank God, everything has been going quite smoothly, but today a grave sin has befallen. The crowd who spent the night in the Khodynskoye Pole* [meadow] *pending the giving out of a dinner and a mug, pressed upon the wooden constructions, and there was a terrible jam, and it's dreadful to add, about 1300 people were trampled down! . ."*

"A grave sin" – Nikolai would take the blame upon his soul. So often somebody's death or suffering had cut short the serene sequence of bright and placid days. Nikolai took it as a confirmation of his hard lot, his destiny from the very day of his birth – May 6, 1868, the martyr St. Job's Day. In 1896, that very date was to be the first day of the Sacred Coronation celebrations. Astounded by the fabulous glitter of the Coronation, Russia soon shuddered at the dreadful bloodshed that belied the splendour.

Chapter Seven

THE FAMILY
LIFE OF NIKOLAI
& ALEXANDRA

**Vladimir Oustimenko
Lyubov Tyutyunnik**

"IT WAS THE HOLIEST AND THE PUREST FAMILY . . ."

"If you wish to become more loving, look for loving hearts, if you wish to become purer daily, then seek earnestly for purer ones".
Alexandra's entry in Nikolai's diary, November 3, 1894.

(Above) Postcard to Emperor Nikolai II from his wife Empress Alexandra Feodorovna. It reads: *"A Happy New Year, 1914, to you my Darling, fr. Wify".*
(Facing Page) A formal portrait, taken in 1899, of the Tsar and Tsarina with their three daughters – baby Maria in her mother's arms, Tatiana standing and eldest daughter Olga sitting in front.

Alexandra dedicated those words to her beloved Nikolai a few days before his father's funeral. Those were the days when Nikolai had just accepted the crown, and he desperately needed the comfort and encouragement his darling Alix so willingly rendered. Both Nikolai and Alexandra could readily admit that this maxim laid down one of their guiding principles. The course of their life would always swing abruptly between the extremes – from "Light", "Bright Sunshine" to "Pitch Black", "Night" – as the Tsarina so aptly labelled those periods in her correspondence – and then Sunshine again . . . Love ruled the world of this Sunshine, and the Tsarina would assert: "There is only one hope in our despairing night: that hope is Love".

The tendency to represent the last Russian Tsar and Tsarina as exalted persons obsessed with mysticism and renouncing the joys of physical existence, appears not only primitive but utterly erroneous. Like all those of human bondage, they trod the Earth, between the Sunshine and the Dark, the Joy and the Sorrow, the Triumph and the Subversion. The material world imbued with human passions, sensuality and enjoyment, could not but affect them, but it failed to absorb them completely. Their souls would invariably strive for the Cosmos.

The earthly love of Nikolai and Alexandra, their relations as man and woman, father and mother, and – last but not least – Tsar and Tsarina, stemmed from the spiritual values of Christianity which recognises love as the essence embracing the Heaven and Earth, the Divine and the Human. They were destined for each other, and their love was the load with which God had chosen to burden and to crown them, as the greatest trial and

the greatest gift for their hearts and souls. Faith was the philosophy of their life, an indispensable condition of their existence on earth comprising the physical and the spiritual. Brought up as a true believer, Nikolai II was sustained in all his daily life by his religious convictions, which his wife soon learned to share. Having overcome so many hesitations, the young emotional lady fell under the spell of the meditative, mystical spirit of her new religion; enthralled with the splendour of the orthodox liturgy served in old white churches with the blue smoke of incense spreading its sweet, permeating scent, the blinking of hundreds of candles reflected upon the holy faces in ancient icons; the austere chanting of the choir which captivated the listener. Reading orthodox books, learning about Russian history, visiting orthodox monasteries and worshipping to their numerous sacred relics, the neophyte immersed herself in the depths of orthodoxy.

There was another circumstance which could not but leave its mark upon Alexandra's character, and to some extent it accounted for the "deepest, fervent, unending" love she felt for her husband. Having lost her mother early in her childhood, Alix had suffered acutely from the lack of a mother's caresses and affection, and due to this awareness she knew better than anybody the true value of these emotions. Now she tried to repay her beloved Nikolai, whom she worshipped and adored, for his love. Her gratitude was infinite, and it made her love even more intense.

Neither sham exaltation nor hypocritical timidity ever marred the sweet sincerity of their relations. They spoke of their love with an amazing candour, and their devotion and confidence grew with every new day of their togetherness. Years failed to blight the youthful vigour of their love, and their attachment, matured and ingrained, proved unaffected by all storms and stresses that befell them. Nobody could explain their emotions better than Nikolai and Alexandra did themselves. The Tsarina's letters, carefully stitched in volumes, read like novels – indeed, they are more eloquent than novels, for even the most sophisticated fiction can never surpass reality.

"... *Twenty years tomorrow that you reign and that I became orthodox. How the years have flown, how much we have lived through together ... My prayers and thoughts and very, very tenderest love will follow you all the way. Sweetest of loves, God bless and protect you and the holy Virgin guard you from all harm. My tenderest blessing. Without end I kiss you and press* [you] *to my heart with boundless love and fondness ..."* (Alexandra to Nikolai; No 239; 20.10.1914)

"... *Beloved One, I kiss you, oh so tenderly and wish I could share your loneliness. You have not a soul to talk to, to feel near you, who understands you and with whom you can talk about anything which comes into your head ..."* (Alexandra to Nikolai; No 462; 15.03.1916)

"... *God bless and protect you and give you success in all undertakings, guide and guard you from all harm. Passionately I press you to my heart, kiss you with infinite tenderness, eyes, lips, forehead, chest, hands, every tenderly loved place which belongs to me ..."* (Alexandra to Nikolai; No 465; 26.03.1916).

More reserved in expressing his emotions in letters, Nikolai wrote to his "own beloved One": "... *Tenderest thanks ... for all your love and caresses during those six days we were together – if you only knew how that keeps me up and how it recompenses me for my work, responsibility, anxiety, etc. Really I do not know how I could have stood it all if God had not wished to give you* [to] *me as wife and friend! I mean it earnestly. Sometimes*

(Top) Watercolour by Grand Duchess Maria autographed, and titled *"To the Dawn. Tsarskoye Selo. May 25, 1909"*. (Above) Another watercolour by Maria and younger sister Anastasia, autographed and titled by Maria, *"The Curious. Krylov's fable. Tsarskoye Selo, December 25, 1910."* (Facing page) Tsarskoye Selo, 1900. A charming photograph of Maria, aged two, wrapped in a coat shawl and matching hat.

it is difficult to say such a truth and I find it easier to put it on paper – out of stupid shyness . . ." (Nikolai to Alexandra; 31.12.1915).

"My own precious beloved One, Again you leave us two [Nikolai and Cesarevitch Alexei] *to return to your work and tiresome worries! I thank you lovingly and deeply for having come here and for all your love and caresses. How I will miss them!! . . . I shall miss you especially in the evenings, which were ours. God bless your journey and your coming home. Do take care of yourself and don't overtire yourself. I kiss your sweet face lovingly and tenderly, my own Sunny, my Wify, my little girly of bygone days. Clasping you once more in my loving arms – ever my precious Darling, your very own hubby Nicky".* (Nikolai to Alexandra; 12.10.1916).

Contributing to the harmony of their alliance was the fact that Alix unreservedly shared her husband's views on their august predestination and his firm belief that autocracy was the only possible form of policy in Russia. Filling in the questionnaire of the All-Russian census of Population in 1897, in compliance with his political creed, Nikolai indicated his occupation: "Master of the Russian Land", and referring to his wife he wrote down: "Mistress of the Russian Land".

Born into a small German grand duchy, but also, granddaughter of the Queen of the mighty British Empire, Alix had been brought up in quite different traditions, but her astute mind and keen insight meant she very soon understood that western models could not apply in her new Motherland. Wholeheartedly Alexandra assimilated the idea of autocracy without which, she believed, *"Russia could not exist"* (Alexandra to Nikolai; No 330; 22.08.1915), and she encouraged her husband: *"Be more autocratic, My very own sweetheart, show your mind".* (Alexandra to Nikolai, No 318; 15.06.1915)

(Facing page) Formal portrait of Nikolai II, Alexandra Feodorovna and baby Olga, St. Petersburg, May 3rd 1896, taken by the photographer Levitskiy. That day Nikolai wrote in his diary: *"At 2.15 went to Levitskiy Jnr. to be photographed because the old one is ill. The photographs were taken in a variety of shots – the two of us, with our daughter, and each of us alone. Hope that one and a half hour's suffering will give some results."*
(Above) Nikolai's diary for November 3/4 1895, recording the birth of Olga. The Tsar drew three lines under the name of his first child.

As a true autocrat, Nikolai II believed that he bore the supreme responsibility for the destiny of Russia, and he had no intention of shifting it off either upon the ministers or the "people's elected representatives". Refuting the assessments by some contemporaries, Aide-de-Camp to the Tsar, Colonel Mordvinov pointed out that Nikolai II's most outstanding feature was allegiance to his principles. All throughout his reign the Tsar had to withstand incessant pressure from those who demanded a "constitution" and a "responsible ministry", and criticism from those who alleged he was "weak", "constantly hesitating" and "acting at somebody else's bidding". For many years Nikolai II's critics failed to embarrass him, which Mordvinov inferred, revealed that the Tsar's political convictions were well thought-out and deeply held.

All of Nikolai II's close acquaintances pointed out that the Tsar's most distinguishing traits of character were kindness, cordiality, tact and ingenuousness. Whenever he had to reprimand, he would always try to mollify the rebuke with some token of courtesy. Evil and bloodshed went counter to his nature. Confirming the latter assertion is Nikolai II's diary entry of January 9, 1905, the ill-famed "bloody Sunday". That day the Tsar being away from the capital, Fullon, the Governor-General of St. Petersburg, ordered troops to shoot at the workers' peaceful demonstration which was moving to the Winter Palace to submit their petition to the Tsar. In the evening of the tragic day the Tsar wrote in his diary: *"Oh Lord, how painful and hard! . . .",* and General Fullon was dismissed *"for direct non-fulfilment of his duty."*

Like his father, Nikolai II was fond of physical work, and he took special pleasure in long walks, cutting firewood or clearing snow in the park. His personal needs were very modest, his clothes very plain, and he liked common Russian food: *borsch* (vegetable soup with beetroot), *schi* (cabbage soup), *kasha* (dish of cooked grain or grits). At dinner he enjoyed a glass or two of his favourite port or madeira.

Like most of the Romanovs, Nikolai dedicated himself to military service. He valued the spirit of officers' honour and the fellowship fostered in the Russian army. Grand Duke Alexander Mikhailovitch recalled that the Cesarevitch's modesty won him popularity among the officers in the regiment. When his father, Tsar Alexander III, died, Nikolai held the rank of a colonel. He was a battalion commander in the Life Guards Preobrazhenskiy regiment – having become the Tsar, he deemed it inappropriate to create himself general.

The Tsar felt perfectly at ease in the warm, friendly atmosphere of the officers' mess and he liked to dine with the regiment. Usually in a large dining-room, about a hundred places were laid. Old regimental silver glistened in the bright lights of the hall, adding to the glamour of the feast. Voyeikov, the palace superintendent, remembered that the Life Hussars, in accordance with Russian tradition, treated the Tsar to a "silver cup served on a gold dish", as the old Russian drinking-song has it. The dinners never descended into carouses, and thanks to Nikolai II's tact and courtesy, the atmosphere at the parties was informal and friendly.

Military manoeuvres, reviews and parades were very popular in Russia at this time. These took place in St. Petersburg, Tsarskoye Selo or Krasnoye Selo. The ladies of the Imperial Family graced the events with their presence. Traditionally, the Tsarina and the Grand Duchesses were appointed patrons of regiments. Alexandra Feodorovna was patron of the Uhlan Life Guards regiment, Olga Nikolayevna was patron of the 3rd Hussar Yelizavetgradsky regiment, Tatiana Nikolayevna had the patronage of the 8th Uhlan Voznesensky regiment, and Maria Nikolayevna was patron of the 9th Dragoon Kazansky regiment. The Romanov ladies took a sincere interest in the life of their regiments, acted as protectors and attended regimental feasts and parades, at which they would wear the dress uniforms of their regiments.

Absorbed in domestic concerns and the care of the children's upbringing and education, the Tsarina rarely involved herself in the intricacies of affairs of State, till the beginning of World War I. However, she was aware of her responsibilities in serving her new Motherland. She devoted herself to charity activities, seeing in them an opportunity to help her husband and to get to know her country and people better. In 1896 Alexandra Feodorovna became patron and chairwoman of the Women's Patriotic Society which undertook to sponsor the guardianship of orphans, to promote the education of girls from poor families, and to organise aid for the victims of wars and natural calamities.

A good mother to her own children, Alexandra Feodorovna was a caring mother for the people of her new country, and she wholly deserved the respectful name which since ancient times the people of Russia had used to honour their Tsarina – *Matushka* (Dearest Mummy). Her most cherished aspiration was a better, more decent life for the Russian people. On one of the Society's reports she appended the resolution urging "to bear it in mind that caring for the poorest is the duty of our society", and the proposal to exclude gymnastics from the school curriculum was adamantly rejected: "I find thera-

Maman.

J'aime maman, qui promet et
qui donne
Tant de baisers à son enfant,
Et si doucement lui pardonne
Toutes les fois qu'il est méchant.
Tatiana.

Tzarskoë Selo.
14 avril, 1905.

66

T. H.

(Top) Watercolour by Grand Duchess Tatiana with a dedication to her mother written in French "I love mama . . . Tsarskoe Selo, 17 April 1905". (Above) Coloured pencil drawing by Tatiana, autographed "T.N. 19 December 1908. T. S". (Facing page) Tsarskoye Selo. Formal portrait from 1897, of Alexandra Feodorovna holding baby Tatiana with little Olga .

peutic gymnastics indispensable in our climate".

A major pursuit in Alexandra's charity activities was raising funds for and establishing a network of Houses of Diligence, meant "to improve the working class and to arrange broad aid for the population during the years of natural calamities". In 1904, at the Tsarina's personal expense and in accordance with her plan, a Nurses' School with an orphanage was founded in Tsarskoye Selo. As the Tsarina intended, Russian nurses were to replace foreign governesses so that foreign influence could be excluded from the upbringing of the Russian child. The Tsarina also presided over the Guardians Board for Maternity and Child Protection, whose objective was the promotion of measures to reduce infant mortality in the country.

(Below) Three watercolours with Olga's initials, "O.N.", and on the reverse "Olga January 1911". (Bottom) A poem dedicated to her mother from Olga, July 17, 1903. Underneath a commentary by tutor Petrov, "This poem was handwritten . . . It wasn't finished because letter 'B' was spoiled . . . replaced by another sheet . . ." (Facing page) Peterhof, 1899. Olga with sister Tatiana sitting in a toy carriage, taken at the Imperial Palace on the Baltic shore.

An admirer of Russian traditional crafts, Alexandra Feodorovna contributed a lot to furthering their development, and her special interests were those domestic industries, the so-called *promysels*, peasants' non-agrarian pursuits, especially those which involved the work of peasant women, such as highly artistic embroidery and lacemaking. She instituted a special committee for these arts, and in a letter to her husband the Tsarina wrote: *"We shall interest the governors and spread it all over the country and for the wounded* [too] *and then have art and taste in it like in my school of folk art. Oh Sweety, what a lot one can do, and we women can help so much. At last all have woken up and are ready to help and work. This way we shall get to know the country, peasants, governments . . . better and be real union with all. May God help me in that way to be of some use to you, Sweetheart".* (Alexandra to Nikolai, No 529, 24.06.1916)

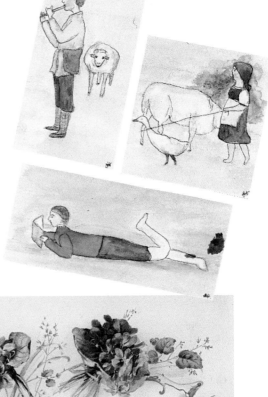

Fully aware of the heavy responsibility that lay on her husband's shoulders, Alexandra Feodorovna willingly tried to ease the load. *"Whenever I can be of smallest use, tell me what to do – use me – at such a time God will give me the strength to help you – because our souls are fighting for the right against the evil".* (Alexandra to Nikolai, No 330, 22.08.1915)

Everybody close to Her Majesty noticed her infinite kindness and magnificence. Her magnificence was positively unlike the arrogance which appears so common in people spiritually insignificant and superficial – which was ascribed to the Tsarina by the court scandal-mongers. Quite the contrary, hers was the sublimity of all her aspirations, incentives, sentiments and actions.

Neither Nikolai nor Alexandra liked the bustle of crowded official receptions and balls which used to be held in the Winter Palace, St. Petersburg. The social season in the Winter Palace, in the winter of 1903, was closed with two costume balls. The seventeenth century held special fascination at that time, and all the guests were arrayed in traditional Russian *boyar* costumes lavishly adorned with furs, encrusted with diamonds and precious stones and beaded with pearls. It seemed as if all family jewels of their eminent ancestors had been taken out of the bottoms of old chests for display. Some of the costumes, though, were exact copies made with unequalled craftsmanship. Nikolai wore a copy of the original full dress of Tsar Alexei Mikhailovitch – a *caftan* of golden brocade and a cap trimmed with sable. The Tsarina was garbed in a copy of the outfit of Tsarina Maria Ilyinishna, the first wife of Tsar Alexei Mikhailovitch. It was a traditional Russian dress of brocade with silver ornamentations and an *ubrus* (traditional

Russian headdress) studded in diamonds and pearls.

The ball opened with the polonaise from Glinka's opera "*A Life for the Tsar*", performed by the court orchestra, the musicians in XVIIth century dress. The Imperial couple were standing at the entrance of the Arab Room and the guests came dancing past them. The Tsarina cut a glamourous figure, "a perfection of beauty and majesty", one of the witnesses remarked.

Despite its splendour, the Tsarina found court etiquette "annoying for their private life". She would even demand that the number of the guards be reduced. It especially irritated her – and the children found the regulation ridiculous – that, according to the established order, each time the imperial family passed the guards post as they strolled along the alleys in the Livadian park, the guard immediately reported on the telephone to the palace superintendent. The Tsarina insisted that the absurd order be abolished. She also thought that the entourage that accompanied Their Imperial Majesties on various functions was excessive. In a private talk with the palace superintendent she grumbled that their every journey involved a whole train of automobiles which hampered regular traffic and unreasonably drew everybody's attention. Later, the Tsarina's decision to cut the number of the entourage, as well as other restrictions on the social life of the court, aroused the displeasure of the *beau monde* . . . which would gradually turn into hatred.

The most valued treasure for the Tsar and the Tsarina was their family, a secluded world inaccessible to outsiders. All the members of the family were united with sincere feelings of love, mutual respect and friendship. The relations between the parents and their children were cordial and simple, without a shade of estrangement and formality

A glimpse of the Imperial nursery in 1898 with Olga and younger sister Tatiana surrounded by their toys. (Facing page) The Tsarina with baby Maria and Olga in 1899.

Alix. 1901.

which had been the norm in the families of Nikolai's ancestors when the children had been fully in the charge of numerous nurses, governesses and tutors. Alexandra Feodorovna took her duties as a mother most seriously and she dedicated herself to caring for her children. Absorbed with the many duties of State and Court life, the Tsar could not spend as much time with his children, but in hours of leisure, "unwatched by immodestly peeping eyes he would willingly join the youthful amusements". In the evenings, the children loved it when "Papa" read for them, or they arranged some small entertainments – staging amateur plays, watching cinematography, or looking at the pictures in their father's numerous photo-albums. Nikolai II was very fond of photography; he was quite an expert and had excellent taste. With his good-natured humour and a keen eye, he caught funny little scenes and characteristic features of people. The children would later start keeping photo-albums of their own in which they would assiduously paste pictures and write captions. "The Little Girls" – Maria and Anastasia – even coloured in the photographs.

Five children were born to the Tsar and the Tsarina. On November 3, 1895, their first-born arrived, and the happy father would record in his diary: *"At exactly 9 p.m.* [we] *heard the baby squeak and we all breathed freely. The daughter sent to us by God was named Olga ... When all the worries were gone and all the horrors over, there began quite a blissful state of awareness of what had happened".* Indeed, it was the beginning of a special state, the opening to an immense world, the infinite plenitude of which is expressed in one single word: FAMILY.

Within the next six years three more daughters joined them: Tatiana, on May 29, 1897; Maria on June 14, 1899; Anastasia on June 5, 1901. On July 30, 1904, the long-expected Heir, Cesarevitch Alexei, was born, and his arrival seemed to settle the problem of direct succession to the Throne, which had been a matter of serious concern for the Imperial couple.

The children were divided into "The Big Ones" (Olga and Tatiana) and "The Little Ones". Each of the Grand Duchesses had a Russian nurse, and as the girls grew older, the nurses became their maids. The girls were brought up "in the English manner": they slept on hard camp beds, with few pillows; they took a cold bath every morning and a warm one every evening; their clothes were simple, very often outgrown dresses and shoes handed down from the elder to the younger; the daughters spoke English with their mother and Russian with their father; Alexei spoke only Russian.

When the time came, teachers from St. Petersburg university and gymnasiums were brought in. The Russian artist Dmitriy Kardovskiy, professor of the Academy of Arts, famous for his historical paintings, became their drawing master. Of all the tutors the favourites were Pyotr Vasilyevitch Petrov, who taught Russian language and literature; their tutor of French, the Swiss Pierre Gilliard whom, according to the Russian tradition, the children called Pyotr Andreyevitch, or sometimes playfully "Zhilik"; and the Englishman Sydney Gibbs, or Sydney Ivanovitch, or even "Sig", a pet-name formed of the first letters of his full Russian name which punningly formed the name of a freshwater fish of the salmon species. Their religious instructor was Father Alexander Vasilyev.

All these people remained faithful to the Tsar's Family till their last day. Petrov, who died in Peterhof in 1918, preserved the last letters from the Tsar's daughters from Tobolsk and Yekaterinburg. Pierre Gilliard wrote several books of reminiscences noted for their profound approach and keen observations. Having returned to Great Britain, Sydney Gibbs adopted the Orthodox faith and took monastic vows under the name of Father Nikolai. He was the founder of the Orthodox Church in Oxford.

Watercolour by Grand Duchess Anastasia sent to her father on March 9, 1915.
In an accompanying letter she wrote: *"My Golden Papa Darling! Terribly terribly, thank you for your photos . . . Loving you, your daughter Nastasulya. Shvybzik.*
A.N.R.P.K.Z.S.G."
Anastasia's letter vividly illustrates her exuberant sense of fun.
(Facing page) A 1901 portrait of Alexandra with baby Anastasia, signed "Alix."

The children's life and classes were strictly scheduled, the time table having been approved by the Tsarina. Indispensable in their time table was outdoor physical exercise. As Anna Vyrubova recollected, the Tsarina never allowed the children to be idle. Like their mother, the Grand Duchesses were good at embroidery and knitting. Alexei could knit a little too. In a letter to his father, he informed that he had begun *"knitting a scarf of wool of different colours"*. (December 16, 1915).

The tutors submitted regular reports to the Tsarina which recorded their pupils' progress and peculiar features. The Cesarevitch was "very inquisitive and very quick on the uptake", he liked to have stories read to him, had a good memory and easily memorised poems. Grand Duchess Olga Nikolayevna displayed the greatest aptitude for learning. By the age of eight she developed "an interest in reading, diligence, and a sound tenacious memory"; she was "resourceful and witty". The infant Tatiana always tried to follow Olga's example. She had a good memory and was fond of reading, but she was physically less strong and tired easily. She was rather slow at mathematics. As Sobolev, the master of mathematics, pointed out, one of the major difficulties the girls came across was that they knew "little about everyday relations which recur in arithmetic problems". Both sisters, Olga and Tatiana, were quite good at playing the piano and had excellent voices.

In winter, the family lived at Tsarskoye Selo, in the Alexander Palace. On fine days the children played in the park; they went sledging or skating, made snowmen, or even built fortifications of snow. When the weather was nasty the youngest came down from the upper rooms into the Tsarina's room – the renowned "mauve boudoir" adorned with a mass of flowers, lilacs or roses. A big basket with toys was there for the children, and they would sit playing on a vast carpet that covered the floor, while their mother relaxed on

An official portrait of Nikolai II and Alexandra Feodorovna and family: (left to right) Olga, Maria, Anastasia, Alexei and Tatiana. Postcard copies of this photograph were sold to raise money for charities. (Facing page) Portrait of Nikolai and Alexandra taken in 1895 in the early years of their marriage. Photographer L. Pasetti.

Russia

her couch, doing some needlework and raising her eyes now and then to watch the children. They spent summers in Peterhof, on the coast of the Gulf of Finland, staying in the Alexandria residence, or sailing to the Finnish fiords on the imperial yacht *Standard,* which had been built for Tsar Alexander III in Denmark. The yacht was unique for its impeccable exterior and magnificent, luxurious interior decoration. They delighted in boating and picnicking on the isles, gathering mushrooms and berries, romping around, or playing lawn-tennis. In the lines of Robert Louis Stevenson,

"Happy hearts and happy faces,
Happy play in grassy places –
This was how in ancient ages
Children grew to kings and sages".

In spring and in autumn the family went to the Crimea. Here, specially for Nikolai II's family, the architect Krasnov had erected a fascinating, Italianate palace. It was faced with the local white Akkerman stone, its interior was exquisite and the plate-glass windows gave plenty of light. Everybody in the family believed that it was the loveliest place in the world.

There were not too many official visits abroad. Usually they visited their relations in Germany, Denmark and England. The Tsar's diaries and albums of photographs featured these delightful events. In May 1908, Nikolai II met Britain's King Edward VII and Queen Alexandra – Nikolai's aunt – in Reval. That day Nikolai was wearing the uniform of the British Horse Guards. He described the event in his diary: *"May 28, Wednesday . . . At 1 o'clock on board the 'Standard' there was a great luncheon. Uncle Bertie* [Edward VII] *created me admiral of the British Fleet. I visited their cruiser 'Minotaur' and took a general look at it. Then* [I] *moved to the turbine yacht 'Alexandra' where all the relations were staying. Having made a round* [of the yacht], *we went to the 'Polar Star'* [the imperial yacht on which travelled Dowager Empress Maria Feodorovna] *and Mama treated us to tea. About 6 o'clock returned on board the 'Standard'. Played with the children and read. At 8 1/2 the two of us* [Nikolai II and Alexandra Feodorovna] *went to* [the yacht] *'Victoria and Albert' for ceremonial dinner.* [I] *created uncle Bertie Admiral of our fleet".*

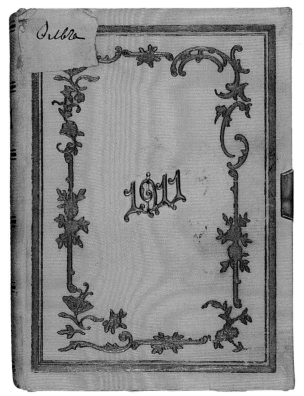

As the children grew up, their features and inclinations became more distinct. The eldest, Grand Duchess Olga Nikolayevna was a slender, graceful blonde, her blue eyes blazing with playful slyness, her nose slightly turned up. She inherited her father's eyes and his temperament – his kindness, sincerity, honour and dignity, though she lacked his renowned self-restraint. According to Pierre Gilliard, Olga was the most gifted and well-educated of all the sisters. She was of a romantic nature with an artistic leaning and a passion for reading. She even tried her hand at writing poetry. Affable and good-humoured, she would readily forgive others' weak points and tricks. On July 11, 1911, Olga's name day, officers of the *Standard* gave Olga a frivolous present. Storming with indignation, Olga's younger sister Tatiana, then fourteen, described the prank in a letter to Auntie Olga Alexandrovna: *" . . . Olga received a mass of presents and a lot of flowers. I am so sorry you are not with us now. In the morning officers gave me an envelope for Olga, and I gave it to her. What do you think it was? There was a cardboard frame with a portrait of* [Michelangelo's] *David cut out from a newspaper. Olga laughed at it long and hard. And not one of the officers wishes to confess that he had done it. Such swine, aren't they?"*

In November the same year Olga turned sixteen – coming of age for a grand

The cover of Grand Duchess Olga's 1911 diary, lavishly decorated.
(Facing page) Autographed 1914 portrait of Grand Duchess Olga Nikolayevna.

duchess. Her birthday presents from her parents were two necklaces – one of thirty-two pearls and the other of thirty-two diamonds. That evening the Livadian palace was host to a most resplendent full-dress ball. The huge glass doors of the grand dining-room were open wide, and the palace was filled with the lovely fragrance of the southern night and the thundering of the surf. Among the guests were grand dukes and their wives, officers of the local garrison, their friends, and, of course, officers of the favourite yacht *Standard* . . .

Olga was closer to her father than to her mother. From the age of eight she would often accompany Nikolai II to church, or to regimental reviews, to the theatre or for a walk in the park. There was a very special, confidential relationship between father and daughter, and years later the Tsar would often share his news and thoughts with her. Olga's relations with her mother were not so smooth. Once, on the spur of the moment, the Tsarina complained to Nikolai: *"You cannot understand how terribly I miss you – such utter loneliness. The children with all their love still have quite other ideas and rarely understand my way of looking at things, the smallest even – they are always right and when I say how I was brought up and how one must be, they can't understand, find it dull. Only when [I] quietly speak with Tatiana she grasps it. Olga is always most unamiable about every proposition, though may end by doing what I wish. And when I am severe – sulks me. Am so weary and yearn for you . . ."* (Alexandra to Nikolai; No 460; March 13, 1916).

A signed watercolour by Tatiana, *"Christ Has Resurrected!"* Poem by A. Korinthskiy. Tsarskoye Selo. April 18, 1910.
(Facing page) A 1910 portrait of Grand Duchess Tatiana Nikolayevna.

As the girls grew up, the Tsar's family had to face the problem of arranging suitable marriages for their daughters. The proposals arriving from the Greek, Rumanian and Serbian houses found no enthusiastic response in the hearts of the Grand Duchesses. They did not feel like living abroad. In a letter to her husband Alexandra Feodorovna shared her concern: *"I send you my very very tenderest loving, thoughts and wishes and endless thanks for the intense happiness and love you have given me these 21 years. Oh, Darling, it is difficult to be happier than we have been, and it has given me strength to bear much sorrow. May our children be as richly blessed – with anguish I think of their future – so unknown! Well, all must be placed into God's hands with trust and faith. Life is a riddle, the future hidden behind a curtain, and when I look at our big Olga, my heart fills with emotion and wondering as to what is in store for her – what will her lot be!"* (Alexandra to Nikolai; No 338; 12.11.1915)

Rejecting a proposal from a foreign prince, Olga declared: "I am Russian, and I wish to remain Russian". But the Russian Grand Dukes Boris Vladimirovitch and Dmitriy Pavlovitch also met with rejection. Not that Olga was cold-hearted. Delicate and sweet, her heart was open for love and happiness. There must have been someone who had won the heart of the young Tsarevna. Some entries in her diary seem to divulge the secret. In her diaries of 1915-1916 she often mentions "darling", "little" Mitya (the pet-name for Dmitriy). She must have known him before, but she would first mention him on August 12, 1915: *"One thing is the most important – [I] talked with Mitya again"*. For several months afterwards she would mention every meeting with him – only a line or two – practically every day: *"Talked with Mitya – he feels a bit depressed, little one"* (August 30); *"Mitya also helped me"* (September 3); *"Sat long with Mitya"* (October 7); *"Talked with golden Mitya over the telephone . . . – nice, sweet he is"* (October 20); *"Sat with Mitya, golden one"* (December 20); *"Awfully nice it was with Mitya, little golden one"* (December 23); *"It was nice to be sitting with him. Then Mitya's mother came, such nice, looking so much like her little one . . . Then I talked with Mitya. He's leaving for the city* [St. Petersburg] *today"* (January 3).

Sometimes he left Tsarskoye Selo for several days, and returned, and she would miss him when he was away: *"It is miserable without Mitya"* (January 7); *"It's very dull without the little one"* (January 23); *"At 12 Mitya golden one arrived. Stood together in the*

Мария

1910

corridor. How glad [I was] *to see him"* (January 25). One day he would leave for the front, and they would never meet again. He never wrote to her directly; at least the Grand Duchess never mentioned any correspondence between them; sometimes they spoke on the telephone, and wrote to "Anya" and "Bibi": *"Mitya wrote to Anya.* [He] *will stay in the city till tomorrow on regimental matters. It's dull without him"* (February 4); *"Mitya sent Bibi a postcard"* (February 10); *"Bibi wrote to Little one"* (September 20). Olga would see his mother sometimes, and she would be *"awfully glad, a bit of him she is"* (September 28).

It is not known who this 'Mitya' was. Was he a wounded officer treated in the infirmary, or maybe he served in the regiment located in Tsarskoye Selo? What happened to him later? He may have perished at the front, or in the dreadful civil war, or he may have escaped abroad to spend many sleepless nights thinking about the beautiful Grand Duchess, or he may have shared the lot of millions of his compatriots, who died in the Cheka massacres . . . No-one knows, and there is scarcely any sense to investigate. Let it remain the secret of the two.

The second daughter, Grand Duchess Tatiana Nikolayenva, "a dark blonde" with deep grey eyes, was an attractive and elegant girl, good-looking, but not as charming as the eldest sister. Contemporaries pointed out that she was the most aristocratic of all the sisters, and they could always feel that she was the Tsar's daughter. She took after her mother, having inherited her strong willpower and imperiousness, prudence and a sense of duty. She was as reticent and concentrated as Alexandra Feodorovna, and, perhaps for this reason, there was a close spiritual connection between them. Tatiana's talent was housekeeping and handicrafts. Like her mother, she was very religious, and seriously believed in Grigoriy Rasputin's miraculous and prophetic gifts. Two of Tatiana's notebooks have been preserved in which she copied his letters and telegrams and recorded his maxims. She took to reading theology and began, at an early age, to ponder over the eternal problems of Good and Evil, Sorrow and Forgiveness, about Man's Destiny on earth, and she would infer: "One has to struggle much because the return for good is evil, and evil reigns".

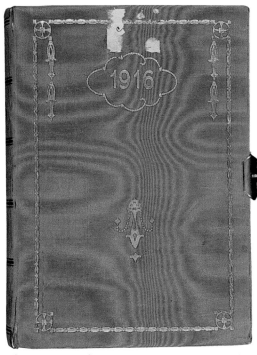

Maria's diary, bearing the date 1916.
(Facing page) Autographed 1910 portrait of Grand Duchess Maria Nikolayevna.

Tatiana's seriousness seemed to belie her age, and yet she was sometimes naive and spontaneous. She wrote to Olga Alexandrovna, July 14, 1911: *"Perhaps you know that Ioanchik* [a peculiar pet-name of Grand Duke Ioann Konstantinovitch] *is engaged to Helene of Serbia, it is so touching. How funny if they might have children, can they be kissing him? What foul, fie!"*

Many observers were inclined to regard Grand Duchess Maria Nikolayevna as the prettiest of the sisters. She was a typical Russian beauty, good-natured, cheerful and friendly. Big-boned, tall, physically very strong, she bore the greatest resemblance to her grandfather, Tsar Alexander III. Her hair was a lighter shade than Tatiana's, but darker than Olga's, and her light-grey eyes were stunning. Her kind-hearted, but rather clumsy complaisance earned her two nicknames in the family: *"Le Bon Gros Toutou"* and just *"Mashka"* (a playful derivation of Maria), which appeared rather apt. In the family she was the most simple, tender and affable. She had a vocation for motherhood. Her sphere was little children. She once wrote to her father: *"Yesterday afternoon Anastasia and I were at the nurses' school, the children drank tea and I fed them with gruel and I thought about you when the gruel ran down their chins and we cleaned their chins with spoons."*

Visiting her father at the Headquarters during the war, and later in the exile in Siberia, she would enjoy talking to officers and common soldiers, asking about their homes, plots of land and children. She would go into every detail of their life, and her unfeigned interest and warm, friendly attitude made her easy and frank. Her parents never discouraged her light and playful manners; she was even skittish sometimes, and they took her innocent flirtations rather humorously. In a letter to her father Maria would describe a

funny incident when she was once cutting ice together with the officers: *"It was such fun. Krylov lost the biggest and the best scrap-iron in the middle of the pond, having fallen on the prow . . . Then Khadov went to help him get the scrap-iron out, and they both nearly dipped. Finally I went to hold them by the uniforms. All this was happening on a piece of ice already drifting, so the sisters held it with hooks . . . In command today was not Fedotov, but the other one, you remember, he came to the tower, the one with such chubby cheeks? So we call him "cheeks". He made a terrific fuss and shouted orders from the bank. Mama was sitting there on the bank, in her armchair, and we all laughed, long and hard"*.

One of Maria's admirers, Nikolai Dmitriyevitch Demenkov, or "Kolya", was an officer of the day in the Tsar's Headquarters in Mogilyov. Having returned to Tsarskoye Selo, Maria would often ask her father to remember her kindly to officer Demenkov, and send him her best regards, and sometimes she would playfully sign her letters to dear Papa: *"Yours Mrs. Demenkov"*.

The baby Anastasia, the youngest of the sisters, promised to become a beauty, but she did not live up to this promise. Her short, stout figure earned her the nickname of "Dumpling". She was notorious for her mischief, a tomboy, "Chieftain of all firemen", *Shvybzik,* and she took pride in all her titles. Undoubtedly, Anastasia was endowed with an extraordinary theatrical gift, which she realised in all sorts of pranks. She was witty, noticing people's weak points and peculiar features and her mimicry was funny and apt. Her winsome candour and inexhaustible buoyancy won everyone's sympathies. She loved dancing and would describe

one of the parties in Livadia, in November 1913, to her grandmother, Dowager Empress Maria Feodorovna: *"I danced a great lot, and at first I felt giddy, but then I was better . . . There were a lot of people, about 40 couples. We threw small garlands of flowers, and the men caught them, and we had to dance waltzes with them . . . It was such fun"*.

Anastasia's letters to her father deserve special attention. Abundant in all sorts of mots and peculiar, low-style words, the epistles could hardly go with prim manners more becoming a princess. Each phrase seemed to explode with fireworks of extravagance:

"My Darling Sweet and Dear Papa!! I want to see you very much. I have just finished my arithmetic lesson and it seems to be not bad. We are going to the nurses' school. I am very glad. Today it is raining and is very wet. I am in Tatiana's room. Tatiana and Olga are here. Tell Bob when you see him that I shall be punching him yet, I am itching to. I try my best to get rid of worms, and Olga says I am stinking, but that is untrue. When you come I shall be washing in your bath. I hope you have not forgotten the 'anegdote', which I told you during our walk. I sat digging my nose with my left hand. Olga wanted to give me a slap but I escaped from her swinish hand. I hope you have got a good picture of Alexei, and you show it to everybody. Tatiana is as stupid as ever. I kiss you a HUNDRED times, my dear darling Papa. Olga is adjusting her trousers. When you arrive I shall be meeting you at the station. Be cheerful and healthy. Squeezing fondly your hand and face. Thinking of you. Loving you ever and everywhere and writing daughter Anastasia".

"My Brilliant Daddy! . . 1000000 times kiss your feet and hands and bow to you. Loving you. Your faithful daughter 13-year-old lass, first name Nastasya (Shvybzik),

(Top) Autographed collage and water colour by Anastasia, Tsarskoye Selo, April 23, 1910. (Above) Another watercolour by Anastasia *"Easter 1911, 10 April Tsarskoe Selo".* (Facing page) Portrait of Grand Duchess Anastasia Nikolayevna, dated 11 May 1914.

last name *A.N.R.P.K.Z.S.G.* [Anastasia Nikolayevna Romanova . . ?] *Patron of the Popskiy* [a Russian adjective, probably derived from the noun "bum"] *Atamanskiy* [Chieftains] *Regiment.*

> *Artichokes, 'artechokes' and 'elmond'-trees and 'elmond'-trees. Never grow on the nose*
> *never grow on the nose I wish they did*
> *I wish they did (thrice and more).*
> *Sleep sweetly and see me in your dreams and I will see you so we are quits".*

Her last letter from Tobolsk to a friend would be so very different: *"It is awfully sad and empty, cannot make out what it is . . ."*

The family was happy in their unity; they felt "cosy", as they used to say, only when they were together, in their own small secluded world. Having gone through great trials together, they preserved the integrity and clarity of their souls, deep faith and dignity, infinite love and devotion, kindness and sincerity. On October 22, 1918, in the town where the inhuman massacre of the Tsar and his family had taken place, Nikolai's former valet, Volkov, choking with tears, would say to Sokolov, the White Russian investigator: *"I cannot explain the characters of the Tsar's Family because I am not a learned man, but I will tell you as I can. I will tell you about them simply: it was the holiest and the purest family . . ."*

An old, yellowed photograph remains. For a moment Time has stopped its progress to the fatal verge . . .

Nikolai II and Alexandra Feodorovna dressed for a costume ball in 1903, held in the Winter Palace, St. Petersburg. His Majesty wore a copy of the original full dress of Tsar Alexei Mikhailovitch – a *caftan* of gold brocade and a cap trimmed with sable. The Tsarina was dressed in a copy of the outfit of Tsarina Maria Ilyinishna, the first wife of Tsar Alexei Mikhailovitch – a traditional Russian dress of brocade with silver ornamentation and an ubrus (a traditional Russian head-dress) studded with diamonds and pearls. On the crown precious stones were placed and Fabergé created a necklace in the old style, using one of the largest sapphires in the world.
(Right) A faded photograph of Alexandra Feodorovna. The brightly flowered hat the Tsarina is holding provides a stark contrast to the plain white dress she is wearing.

> *"Enamelled cross in the tab*
> *Against the jacket's grey.*
> *What radiantly beautiful faces,*
> *They all have long passed away.*
>
> *What resigned and sorrowful faces,*
> *So despairingly pale –*
> *The Heir, the Empress,*
> *The four Grand Duchesses*
> *Doomed to irretrievable bale."*
> Georgiy Ivanov

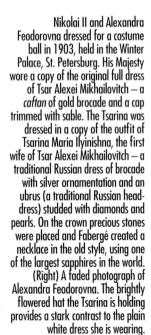

the Romanov
family albums

(Above left) The Orthodox Chapel of St. Maria Magdelena in Darmstadt, the Tsarina's birthplace. Built to allow the Tsar and his family to practise their faith when visiting Darmstadt, Nikolai had soil brought from Russia for the Chapel's foundations to rest upon.
(Insets above) Postcard letter from Alexandra to Nikolai. *"For my own beloved Darling, with very tenderest prayers . . . love you as only can y. own old Sunny."* December 31, 1907.
(Left) Celebrations in Darmstadt for the official visit of Nikolai II and Alexandra Feodorovna (October 1896).
(Facing page) Tsarskoye Selo, 1898. Portrait of Nikolai II and Alexandra Feodorovna by the photographer Gorodetskiy.

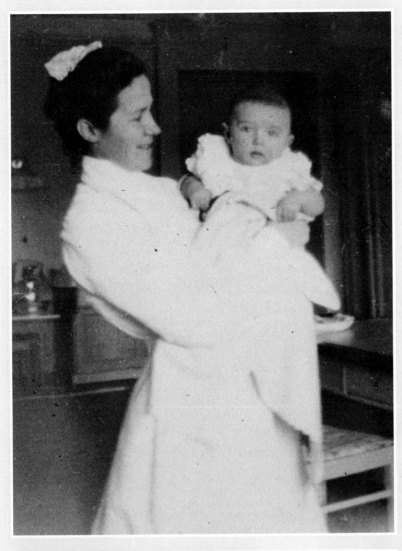

(Above left) Peterhof, 1904. The infant Alexei with his nurse Maria Vishnyakova.

(Above right) Alexandra holding her baby son in a picture taken in Peterhof in1905.

(Above) Tatiana holding Alexei on a white shawl, Alexei has obviously been upset by something and is crying.

(Left) In the grounds of the park in Peterhof (1905) Nikolai holding son Alexei.

Facing page: (top) Olga posing solo and with sister Tatiana at Tsarskoye Selo in 1902.

(Bottom left) Tsarskoye Selo, 1902. Tatiana, Maria and Olga playing with doll and pram.

(Bottom right) "The small pair" Anastasia and Maria in the gardens on a sunny day at Krasnoye Selo,1906.

A set of pictures taken in 1903 in Germany. (Above) The four sisters: (left to right) seated Irene, Alexandra and Victoria; standing behind them is Ella (Right) Nikolai and Grand Duke Sergei Alexandrovitch, husband of Yelizaveta Feodorovna (Ella). Although the pictures look informal they were very much posed.
(Facing page) An 1898 portrait of Nikolai and Alexandra. Nikolai in military uniform and a serene looking Alexandra, in a richly embroidered dress, wearing her favourite necklace.

(Above) 1900, Livadia, Crimea. Nikolai resting in one of his hunting pavilions, lying on a sofa, surrounded by family portraits. The floral pattern of the sofa and carpet was fashionable at the time. (Right) Autumn 1900, Livadia. Nikolai was nursed by his wife while he was recovering from typhoid. *"Nicky was really an angel"* Alexandra wrote to her sister Ella, *"I refuse to have a nurse and we have managed perfectly ourselves . . . I read to him almost all day long."* Shortly after Nikolai's recovery Queen Victoria died and the pregnant Tsarina was unable to attend her beloved grandmother's funeral. (Facing page) 1901. Nikolai strolling with his dog.

In remembrance of our rides together. 1903

Nicky

(Left) 1898. Nikolai and Alexandra crossing a border (probably leaving Germany) to change train carriages. The Tsarina casually dressed and very fashionable in a short cape and hat. For once, the camera has caught a cheeky, happy expression on Alexandra's face.

(Below) Tsarskoye Selo, 1903. The Imperial couple riding together. Alexandra was an excellent horsewoman.

Facing page: (bottom) Nikolai on horseback with the inscription "*In remembrance of our rides together. Nicky 1903.*" (Inset) A coloured pencil drawing with a note by the tutor Petrov: "*Drawing by Empress Alexandra Feodorovna for Grand Duchess Olga Nikolayevna, August 1904. Alexandra*". (Top) Alexandra with her five children: (left to right) Anastasia, Alexei, Olga, Tatiana and Maria by the lake in the park in 1906.

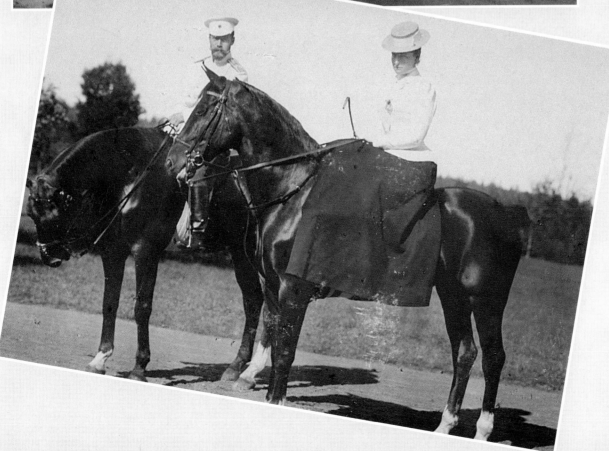

(Above left) Olga and Tatiana trying to lift younger sister Maria on the terrace of the farm in Alexander Park. The grounds of the Alexander Palace were reserved for the Imperial family. (Above) 1902, a nursery picture of Princess Elizabeth, the daughter of Ernst Ludwig of Hesse, who died at the tender age of eight, with her cousins Olga and Tatiana. (Left) Three sulky and barefoot Grand Duchesses — Anastasia, Olga and Maria — pose for the camera at Peterhof, 1905.
(Facing page) A 1906 portrait of Alexandra Feodorovna and Cesarevitch Alexei.

(Above) The four Grand Duchesses, Peterhof, 1905, in striped bathing costumes pose playfully for the camera. The girls enjoyed bathing and having fun in the water. Their bathing season began as early as June when the waters in the Finnish bay were still very cold. A sailor from the *Standard* was entrusted with teaching the Grand Duchesses to swim, but years later Olga would confess in a letter to a friend that she never did learn!
(Left) Peterhof 1905. (Left to right) Maria, Olga and Tatiana about to leave for a bike ride.
(Facing page) On board the Imperial yacht, the *Pole Star*. Tatiana and Olga standing above and Maria below, among the officers and sailors, in 1905.

(Above) A very pensive Alexandra in her sitting room, resting near the window.
(Above right) Alexandra with Maria and Anastasia.
(Right) The five children together, Olga holding Alexei, Tatiana, Maria and Anastasia.
(Facing page) More pictures from Tsarskoye Selo taken in 1906. (Top) Little Anastasia wearing a large straw hat and Tatiana looking confidently straight at the camera. (Bottom left) Olga posing, very much the blossoming young lady, surrounded by plants and a large arrangement of flowers.
(Bottom right) On the balcony the four Duchesses: (left to right) Maria, Tatiana, Olga and Anastasia in front.

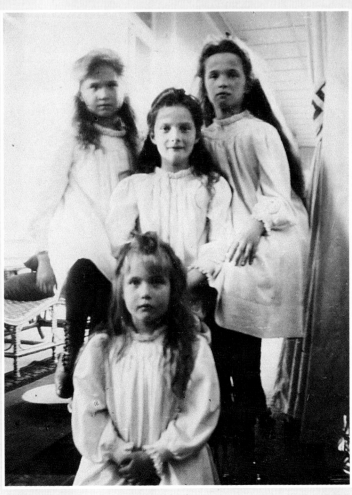

148

(Above left) Tsarskoye Selo, 1906. Alexandra strolling in the park on a sunny day.

(Above) Alexandra enjoying a picnic lunch in the woods (Byelorussia 1900). (Left) Peterhof 1900, Grand Duchess Yelizaveta Feodorovna, elegant as always in a perfect outfit, feeding the birds.

Facing page: (top) Peterhof 1906. A simple and charming picture of husband and wife, resting on a hay stack. These simple family pictures were very dear to Alexandra in later years. These were the times in which Alexandra was happy and relaxed, away from court life and able to have "her Nicky" all to herself.

(Bottom) Peterhof, 1900. Ella (Yelizaveta Feodorovna) and Nikolai on the porch of the palace enjoying a drink and (inset) three pages of a letter Ella sent, in 1905, to her brother-in-law "Nicky" about the death of her husband Grand Duke Sergei, who had been assasinated by terrorists. She expresses her hopes that she will be able to cope, as well as her late husband, in bringing up Maria and Dmitriy, the children of Grand Duke Pavel Alexandrovitch.

On holiday in Finland in 1907. (Top left) Little Alexei, equipped with hat and parasol for a day on the beach, looking so adorable one can imagine how his parents and his older sisters could make so much fuss of him.
(Top right) Maria, Alexei and Nikolai.
(Left) Nikolai carrying a tired Alexei in his arms, followed by Olga and Tatiana, and (above) the sailor-nurse Derevenko keeping a watchful eye on Alexei playing in the water.
(Facing page) The *Standard* 1909. Alexei was Derevenko's personal responsibility and here he conscientiously keeps a grip on Alexei's canine friend.
Derevenko did not share the tragic fate of the faithful Nagorny, who stayed with the family till the very end.

(Above and left) 1908.
On board one of the Baltic
Navy cruisers, little Alexei
enjoys the attention of the
crew.
(Facing page) Pictures from
the *Pole Star* 1900: (top and
bottom left) Prince Nicholas of
Greece teases the cameraman.
(Top right) Grand Duke
Mikhail Alexandrovitch joins in
the fun and (bottom) Nikolai
relaxing at the ship's rail.

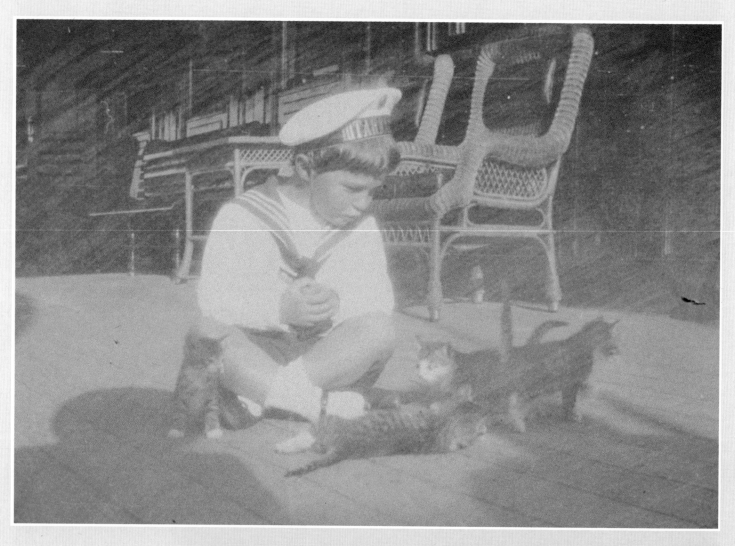

The *Standard*,1908.
(Above) Young Alexei playing with kittens.
(Right) Joining in the fun, Maria and Tatiana.
Facing page: (top) Alexei was a very lively child. In spite of his illness he was full of life and it was very hard to keep him still. Here he is caught at a rather contemplative moment, filling up his little kettle and emptying it in the sea.
(Bottom) 1906. Nikolai II and Alexandra Feodorovna with their children dressed in sailors' uniforms with matching hats posing on the Imperial yacht *Standard*. From left to right: Olga, Anastasia, Tatiana and in front, Alexei and Maria .

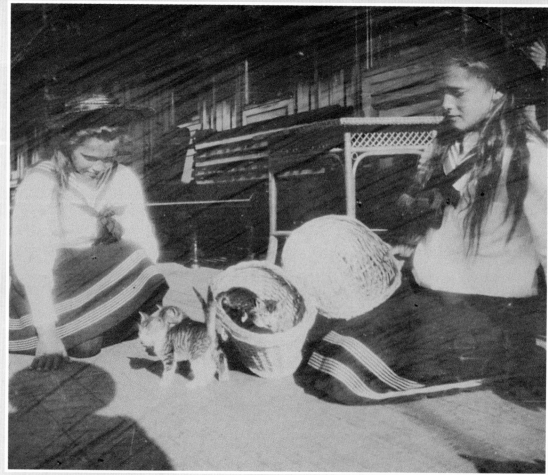

159

with best wishes for a prosperous new year '06 *Willy*

(Above) Nikolai and Kaiser Wilhelm aboard the German cruiser *Berlin*. Nikolai's diary entry, July 11, 1905: ". . . At ten Wilhelm came for coffee. Talked till twelve and the two of us together with Misha [G.D. Mikhail Alexandrovitch] went to the German cruiser 'Berlin'. Took a round of it. We were shown artillery exercises".

(Right) 1907. Nikolai and Alexandra relaxing on the deck of the *Standard*.

Facing page: (top) Reval, May 27, 1908. Edward VII, Nikolai in Highland regiment uniform, and Alexei. Nikolai's diary entry: "Before 10 am I saw the British detachment approaching from the sea, escorted by the Essen's Admiral division of torpedo boats. Having made the round of our vessels from the ports, the yachts 'Victoria and Albert', 'Alexandra' and cruisers 'Minotaur' and 'Achilles' stood on anchor between our lines. In the Scots Grey uniform I went to pay a visit to uncle Bertie and auntie Alix [Edward VII and wife Alexandra]".

(Bottom) May 27-28, 1908. Aboard the yacht Standard (left to right) Princess Victoria, Queen Alexandra and the Tsarina.

(Above) Barton Manor, August 4, 1909. The Imperial Russian family visiting their British relatives. (Left to right) standing: Prince Edward (later Edward VIII), Queen Alexandra, Princess Mary, Princess Victoria, Grand Duchesses Olga and Tatiana. Sitting: Victoria Mary, Princess of Wales, Nikolai II, King Edward VII, Alexandra Feodorovna, George Prince of Wales, Grand Duchess Maria.
Sitting on the ground: Cesarevitch Alexei and Grand Duchess Anastasia.
(Right) Peterhof, 1909. The Tsar's children posing for the camera with their aunties and uncle. Left to right: Alexei, Grand Duchess Olga Alexandrovna, Anastasia, Grand Duke Mikhail Alexandrovitch, Maria and sitting in front Grand Duchess Xenia Alexandrovna.
Facing page: (top) Tsarskoye Selo, 1909. Yekaterininskiy Palace. Maria, Olga, Anastasia, Alexei, Tyutcheva, the governess, and Tatiana.
(Bottom) Tsarskoye Selo, 1907. Yekaterininskiy Palace. Maria, Anastasia, Tatiana Alexei, the Tsarina, Grand Duke Vladimir Alexandrovitch and Olga.

Aboard the *Standard*, 1908. Young Alexei practising his drill with the officers of the Imperial yacht. (Facing page) A proud Nikolai holding Alexei in his arms. From an early age Alexei was introduced to military life, accompanying his father to military parades and army HQ.

(Above) The Tsar's children, formally and beautifully dressed, aboard the *Victoria and Albert*. The children were brought up in a free and relaxed atmosphere but, at the same time, they were very well trained, particularly in foreign languages, which were needed on foreign trips. (Left) Alexandra gives Alexei a piggyback. (Facing page) Happy and relaxed, Alexei and his parents aboard the *Standard* in 1908.

(Above) Reval. July 14,1908. Nikolai II and President Fallières on board the French iron-clad *Verité*. (Left) Alexandra Feodorovna on the *Standard* on the visit to Riga in 1910. The Russian Kingdom was very vast at that time and Latvia, like the other Baltic States, belonged to the Tsar's empire. The ladies of the Court, immaculately dressed, were enjoying the occasion.

Facing page: (top) The *Standard,* 1908. Formal dinner setting for the foreign dignitaries.

(Bottom) Nikolai II welcomes President Armand Fallières, eighth President, until 1913, of the Third French Republic. Nikolai's diary entry, July 14, 1908. *"After eight I began to prepare to meet the French. At 2 their ships appeared on the sea, surrounded by Essen's [Russian Admiral] division of torpedo-boats. At 3 they stood on anchor between our lines. Then arrived Fallières with a big suite. After mutual presentations he reviewed the Guard of Honour and part of the crew and then left. . . At eight we had a big dinner party and we had a drink in his honour."*

The
Three Kittens.

Tsarskoe Selo,
April 23ʳᵈ 1910.

(Left) Tsarskoye Selo,1909. Alexander Palace. Alexandra showing a picture to her daughter Tatiana.
(Inset) Watercolour by Tatiana with a poem by Lermontov: *"When the ripening cornfield is ruffling . . . Tsarskoe Selo, 25, May 1909".*
(Below) Alexandra Feodorovna in the Alexander Palace. The room reflects the style of the time, as we can see the sophisticated pattern of the furniture matches the wall paper and the curtains.
(Facing page) Pictures from Tsarskoye Selo, 1909: (top) Alexandra, who suffered from poor health, a weak heart and recurring headaches, resting on the chaise-longue in her mauve boudoir.
(Bottom) Alexandra with Tatiana, Maria and — on the chaise-lounge — Anastasia.
(Insets) Two watercolours autographed with inscriptions: One by Anastasia, *" The Three Kittens. Tsarskoye Selo, April 23, 1910."* and a story written by Maria:
"1909, Peterhof, 25, August . Once upon a time there lived a father and mother . . ."

168

(Left) Livadia, 1909.
Tatiana and Olga
climbing a ladder resting
against the "Wendy House"
in the grounds of the
estate.
(Inset) Anastasia in the
study room painting.
Facing page: (top left)
Tsarskoye Selo,1909. Olga
playing big sister and
giving her little brother a
piggyback through the
snow.
(Top right) Winter1909.
Olga, Anna Vyrubova and
Anastasia taking a walk in
the snow.
(Bottom) Tatiana and Olga
resting on the signpost
which says "Cape of dear
Sasha".

A set of photographs taken in 1910.
(Above) The Skerries. Anastasia standing underneath a rock, probably playing a trick on the photographer. Anastasia was a great joker who liked to play pranks on relatives and friends.
(Right) Picnicking in the Skerries. Nikolai is caught inside the merry circle. The grown-ups seemed to derive great pleasure from partaking in the children's games. The Tsar of Russia could in these moments forget his worries and the burdens of governing.
(Facing page) Finnish skerries. A very excited Cesarevitch Alexei playing by the sea.

(Right) Kivi-Saari, 1908. Voyage on board the *Standard* to the Skerries. Alexei having fun standing on a stone. (Below left) Finland.1910. Olga shielding herself from the sun with a parasol, and Anastasia. This yellowed photograph evokes the bygone time. (Below right) 1908. Young Alexei proudly helping Derevenko to carry wood. Facing page: (top) The Baltic coast, 1910. Grand Duchess Maria with a toddler, a son of one of the officers. This picture was taken on a walk along the sea coast with her sisters, mother and Anna Vyrubova. All the ladies wore beautiful white dresses with matching hats, but here Maria has removed her hat. Considered the most beautiful of the Tsar's daughters, a "Russian beauty" made of big bones Maria was an easy going, charming girl and had a special affinity for young children. (Bottom) Tsarskoye Selo, 1907. Anastasia with Alexei and Tatiana and Derevenko, behind them, amid officers.

172

Саша Марина Паша Миша

Для П. В.
отъ
Ольга
30го іюня 1906.

Наталіи
отъ
Татьяны.

53

1906.
30 ноября

Марія Анастасія. Оля Татьяна.
1908.

(Left) Krasnoye Selo,1907. A photograph of a slender and graceful Olga.

Facing page: (top left) June 30, 1906. Pencil drawing by Olga, four figures, *"Sasha, Marina, Pavel and Misha. For V.P. from Olga"*, given to tutor Vasilyevitch Petrov as a present.

(Below) Collage with autograph: *"In memory of Tatiana. 1906"*. On the reverse Petrov's note: *"Presented before the lesson on November 30. Kissed her finger"*. These dedications illustrate the close relationship between tutors and pupils, which was encouraged by the Tsar and Tsarina.

(Top right) Finland, August 1908. A pensive Maria.

(Bottom) The Skerries, 1908. The children posing together. They seem naturally to group themselves into "The Big Ones" and "The Small Ones". Alexei seems enchanted with having his photograph taken. He belonged to the set of "The Small Ones". The children loved this time spent with their parents and they especially enjoyed the long walks in the pine forests with their father.The five children autographed the picture, young Alexei having just signed his name with a big "A".

(Above) 1911. Aboard the *Standard*. Nikolai and children, Anastasia and Alexei beside their father and left to right, Maria, Olga and Tatiana.

(Left) Livadia, 1911. Anastasia and Alexei. When they were very young they used to play a lot together. Alexei, restricted by his illness and constant supervision, enjoyed the company of the free spirited Anastasia.

(Far left) 1910, the *Standard*. Father and son by the yacht's lifeboat.

Facing page: (top left) Peterhof, 1910. Anastasia in one of her cheeky moods peeking from behind some paintings.

(Top right) Livadia,1910. Alexandra and Alexei in a quiet moment.

(Bottom) The Skerries, September 1911. Maria and Anastasia collecting flowers.

Germany, Wolfsgarten. October 1910,
(Left) From left to right: Olga, a court lady, Tatiana and Maria out for a walk. As usual, beautifully and uniformly dressed, here in smart coats. (Facing page) 1910. A view of Fredensborg Palace, Denmark, showing the immaculately kept gardens. (Inset) Another view in the courtyard, the children next to a carriage (left to right) Maria, Anastasia, Olga, Tatiana and Alexei in the carriage with two small children. The Tsarina resting on the banister, keeps an eye on the children.

(Above) 1910. The Hunting Lodge. The Tsar's family visiting Darmstadt. From left to right from bottom steps: Cesarevitch Alexei, Grand Duke George Donatus, Prince Ludwig, Grand Duchess Tatiana. Second row: Princess Irene of Prussia, Grand Duchess Maria, Grand Duchess Olga. Third row: Grand Duchess Eleonore, Grand Duchess Anastasia, Prince Heinrich of Prussia, Tsar Nikolai II, Tsarina Alexandra Feodorovna, Baroness von Grancy. Fourth row: Chief Equerry Riedesel Baron Eisenbach, Lady-in-waiting Miss von Butzow, Duke Ernst Ludwig, Captain Baron von Massenbach, Baroness von Rotsmann, Lady-in-waiting Miss Tyutcheva, Lady-in-waiting Miss von Oertzen. Fifth row: Doctor Botkin, Captain Lieutenant von dem Knesebech, Captain Drenteln, Baron Ungern-Sternberg, Chamberlain Baron von Leonhardi.

179

A Merry
Christmas

Tsarskoe Selo
Dec 25ᵈ 1910.

(Left) Germany, 1910. Anastasia at her most charming, wearing an oversized coat and a stunning hat. (Insets) A watercolour with the inscription *"A Merry Christmas. Tsarskoe Selo. Dec. 25, 1910"*, from Maria. Watercolour by Anastasia signed *"A.N. 1912"*.

Facing page: (top) The *Standard*. 1906. Nikolai had this occasion filmed. The four girls and little Alexei running around on the deck, the Tsarina in the background, the crew looking on. Watching this film and seeing the little boy falling over again and again one is amazed, that in spite of his illness, he was allowed to play so robustly. (Bottom left) Livadia,1909. Anastasia and Alexei by the park gates. (Bottom right) March 1909. Three ladies having a chat, Anna Vyrubova, Empress Alexandra and Julia Dehn.

181

(Left)1905, Peterhof. Grand Duchess Tatiana about to go for a bike ride.
(Below left) 1907, the *Standard*. Olga giving Maria a protective hug, 1910.
The four Duchesses were very different in temperament but they were very close and loyal to each other.
(Below right) The three Duchesses and Anna Vyrubova aboard the *Standard*, from left to right ,Olga, Tatiana and Maria. Vyrubova sitting, is familiarly putting her harm around Olga's waist. The Standard was a magnificent yacht. Its drawing rooms, lounges and dining rooms were panelled in mahogany and lit by crystal chandeliers. Built specially for the Tsar in Denmark the yacht was so spacious it could even house the members of the Yacht's brass band and balalaika orchestra.
(Facing page) 1907. Anastasia seated on a piano stool in her mother's boudoir practising her knitting.

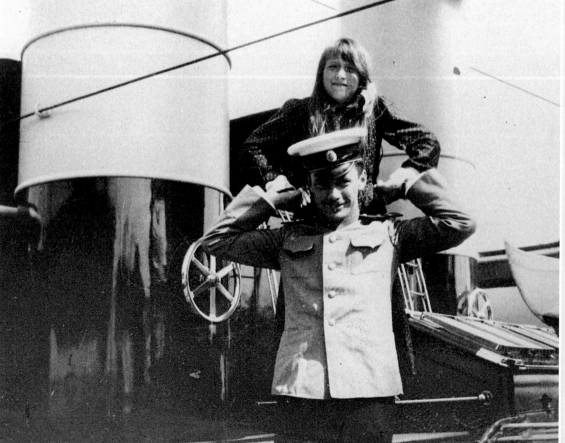

(Above) Sevastopol. September 1911. Flirtatious fun: Olga in front, Maria and one of the Court ladies with the officers of the *Standard*. The officers playing pranks with the two Duchesses. Aboard the Imperial yacht everything was run to perfection but at the same time, the atmosphere was relaxed and the cheerfulness of the children was contagious. (Left) Tomboy Anastasia in a playful mood.

(Left) 1910. An officer of the *Standard* with Olga to his right and Tatiana to his left and Maria in front of them. To the four Duchesses the relationship with the officers of the *Standard* had no feeling of uneasiness and whenever their duty allowed them, the officers joined in the fun. (Below) Sevastopol, December 1913. The *Standard*. Tatiana and a sleeping Maria with Commander Grabbe. (Inset) Tatiana's letter to Auntie Olga Alexandrovna recounting the "swinish" joke the officers of the *Standard* played on Olga's nameday. Tatiana wrote: *". . . Olga received a mass of presents and a lot of flowers. In the morning the officers gave me an envelope for Olga . . . What do you think it was? . . . A portrait of David [Michelangelo] . . . Such Swine, aren't they?"*

Настенька Гендрикова, Мирна Хамаева,
Дэнюс и Агель Гендрикон.

(Above) 1912. On the roadstead near the Finnish coast Tatiana resting after a game of tennis. The Grand Duchess has developed into a striking young woman.

(Left) Prince Ioann Konstantinovitch and his wife Yelena Petrovna (née Princess Helene of Serbia), married in 1911. At the time of their courtship Ioann was the butt of one of Tatiana's jokes.

Facing page: (top) Peterhof, 1912. A day by the sea. Left to right, in front Nastia Gendrikova, Grand Duchess Anastasia, Cesarevitch Alexei, Alix Gendrikova; behind them Grand Duchess Maria, Grand Duchess Tatiana, Inna Balashova and Grand Duchess Olga.

(Bottom) Livadia, 1913. On the tennis court, Tatiana, Lieutenant Rodionov, Maria and Olga.

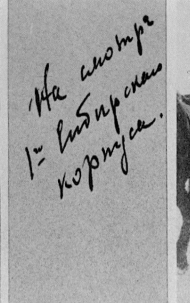

На смотрѣ
1-й Сибирскаго
корпуса.

188

(Left) Oreanda, Crimea, 1914. After a walk Alexandra and her daughter Olga stop for a short rest. (Below) Crimea. May, 14. Nikolai resting amongst the flowers. Various members of the aristocracy had their estates in the Crimea, the place was magnificent with its coniferous forests.

Facing page: (top) Photograph with Nikolai's autograph, *"The parade of the 1st Siberian corps. 1916"*. (Bottom left). An unusual photograph. The officers behind the Tsar have a ghost like quality, almost certainly an accidental, but interesting effect.

(Bottom right) Peterhof, 1913. Nikolai II and Dowager Empress Maria Feodorovna. The Dowager Empress maintained a close relationship with her son, and discussed and gave advice to Nikolai on affairs of state. Nikolai expressed his anger and frustration in a letter sent to his mother, when a British delegation was on its way to meet members of the Duma: *". . . Uncle Bertie was sorry that he was unable to prevent their coming, their famous 'liberty' of course. How enraged they would be if we sent a deputation to the Irish to wish them success in their struggle against their government . . ."*

(Above) Crimea, 1914. The Imperial family on a visit to the Yusupov's estate, "Eagle's Airie" (Orliny Zalyot). Left to right are Anastasia, Olga, Maria, Tatiana and the Tsar. A sunny day but the ground still covered with snow, not uncommon in the Russian climate.

(Left) Tsarskoye Selo, 1916. Olga, Nikolai and Maria breaking the ice in the palace grounds.

Facing page: (Oval) 1916. Grand Duchess Olga Alexandrovna with husband Koulikovskiy Nikolai Alexandrovitch.

(Top Right) Olga Alexandrovna and first husband Prince Peter Alexandrovitch of Oldenburg.

(Bottom left) Tsarskoye Selo, 1913. Maria, Olga, Olga Alexandrovna and Anastasia pretending to be very tired and leaning against her auntie, on the terrace of the Alexander palace,

(Bottom right) 1910-1911. Aboard the Standard Anastasia and Auntie Olga, much younger than brother Nikolai — she was almost a sister to the four Grand Duchesses.

(Above) March 25, 1909. Emperor Nikolai II and Cesarevitch Alexei inspecting the forces at Tsarskoye Selo. The little boy feeling rather fed up, had decided to walk away while the officers were saluting the Tsar.

(Left) Yalta, April 20,1912. Alexandra and Alexei collecting donations for the tubercular patients and giving presents at the Festival of the White Flower.

Facing page: (top) Livadia,1912. Nikolai II and Grand Duke Nikolai Nikolayevitch, in the background Anastasia talking to Uncle Ernst Ludwig von Hessen.

(Bottom left) Crimea, 1913. On the terrace of the Livadian palace a tutor's meeting, (left to right) Gilliard, Vasilyev the religious instructor and Petrov.

(Bottom right) The *Standard,* 1912. Two demure Grand Duchesses, Olga and Tatiana.

193

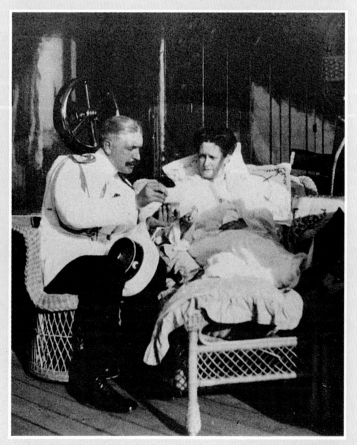

(Above left) Spala, 1913. Empress Alexandra Feodorovna dressed in casual warm clothes but still looking very regal. (Inset) Card from Olga to her mother on her birthday, May 25 1911. *"To Mother, Your daughter's congratulations to You*
On Your birthday wishing you Joy and happiness
So that God may shield Your life of griefs and sorrows forever Olga . . ."
(Left) 1914. Departure from Sevastopol on board the *Standard*, Nikolai, Tatiana, Maria, Olga and Anastasia.
Facing page: (Top left) Stockholm. June 13, 1909. Alexandra during her visit to Sweden.
(Top right) 1914. Alexandra relaxing with a lady of the Court.
(Bottom right) 1913. The *Standard*. Alexandra and Aide-de-camp, officer in chief of the yacht Nikolai Pavlovitch Sablin.
(Bottom left) A domestic scene; Nikolai reading and Alexandra doing needlework.

195

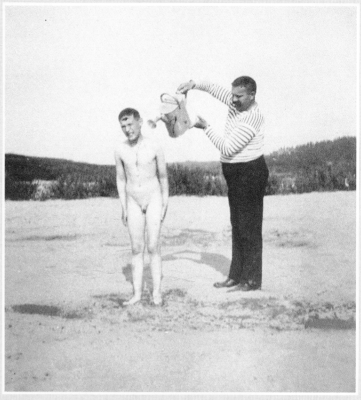

(Left) June 1912. Maria on the deck of the *Standard* during the voyage to the Skerries. (Above) Tatiana at work on one of her drawings. The most aristocratic of the sisters, she was talented at handicrafts and had inherited her mother's strong willpower and sense of duty. Of all the children, she had the closest affinity to Alexandra. (Below left) Olga, Tatiana, Maria, Nikolai, Anastasia and Alexei on their return from a vigorous row in the lake. (Below) Tsarskoye Selo, 1916. Anastasia and Maria pulling faces at the camera. Facing page: (top left) 1916. By the the Dnieper river, near Mogilyov, Nikolai with Olga, Tatiana, Alexei and Anastasia. (Top right) Derevenko washing Alexei after a swim. The Imperial family seemed to have a very natural attitude to life, all the men of the family, even the Tsar went bathing in the nude. (Bottom) September 1913. Father and daughters: Anastasia, Tatiana and Olga visiting the archæological excavations at Khersones, Crimea.

(Above) Meeting of Nikolai II with the President of France Poincaré on July 1914 aboard the yacht *Standard*. Several days later the whole of Europe was in turmoil when Austria declared war on Serbia and Nikolai II ordered partial mobilization.

(Right) Crimea 1914. That day the Imperial family had gone for a walk in a meadow full of long grass and wild flowers. The Tsar, smoking, is resting for a moment.

(Facing page) August 5, 1913. The two Grand Duchesses in uniforms. On the right is Olga wearing the uniform of the 3rd Hussar Yelizavetgradsky H.I.H. Grand Duchess Olga Nikolayevna's Regiment. On the left Tatiana is wearing the uniform of 8th Uhlan Voznesensky H.I.H. Grand Duchess Tatiana Nikolayevna's Regiment.

3^й Гусарскій Елисаветградскій Е. И. В.
Великой княгини Ольги Николаевны полкъ.
5 Августа 1913 г.

472

8^й Уланскій Вознесенскій Е. И. И. Великой
Княгини Татьяны Николаевны полкъ.

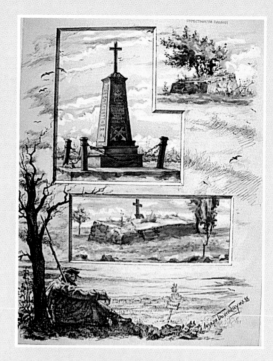

(Top) Illustrations from the album presented to the Tsar to commemorate Russian assistance (during the Russian-Turkish war) to the Bulgarians in their uprising against the Turks in 1877. This is just one of the many albums which were in the Emperor's collection, all are works of art in themselves.

(Above left) A photograph of Edward VII, with son George and the dog autographed: " 'Venus' [the dog], Papa, Georgie. 1892."

(Above) The menu from the the second wedding of Don Carlos of Bourbon-Siciliy and Princess Louise, daughter of Prince Louis Philippe of Orléans, on November 16, 1907 in Woodnorton. Don Carlos was the grandson of Ferdinand II of the Two Sicilies. Through his first marriage to the Infanta Mercedes he was the brother-in-law to Alfonso XIII King of Spain and Victoria Eugenia (daughter of Henry Prince of Battenberg). The Menu bears the signatures of titled Royalty of Europe.

(Left) A note from "cousin" Georgie, the Prince of Wales, wishing Alicky and Nicky a happy Christmas and thanking them for the lovely present.

(Right) A photograph of Heinrich of Prussia, brother of Wilhelm II and married to Irene, Alexandra Feodorovna's sister. It reads: "To darling Alicky from her devoted brother, Harry. March 1892".

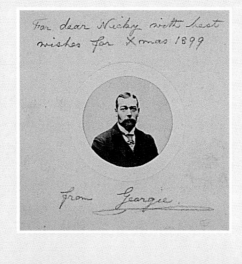

(Above left) A postcard and on the reverse side, a charming picture of Giovanna the daughter of King Vittorio Emanuele of Italy. Probably the father signed the baby's name on the photograph. The Tsar's family spent a holiday in Italy as guest of the King, and they used to write to each other friendly letters and postcards in French.

(Above) A victorian Christmas card from Queen Victoria inscribed: " To Nicky, from his affectionate Grandmama. 1899".

(Middle far left) A New Year dedication from *"Baby and Maud"*. Maud, the youngest daughter of Edward VII and Queen Alexandra, became Queen when her husband Prince Carl Christian of Denmark assumed the title of Haakon VII, King of Norway in1905. "Baby" became King Olav V of Norway.

(Middle left) A photograph with best wishes for Christmas 1899 from "Georgie". In1910 he would become King of Great Britain. (Far left) A photograph of Nikolai II inscribed: *"A sort of general, Nicky"*. Certainly it was given to his beloved Alix in 1894.

(Left) Alexandra, Princess of Wales, sister of the Dowager Empress Maria Feodorovna gave her nephew this photograph with the inscription: *"Fritle* [the cat] *and Alix, for Nicky dear.1879"*

(Top left) Grand Duchesses Olga, Anastasia, Maria and Tatiana, with the officers of the yacht on a picnic. The photograph was autographed by Grand Duchess Tatiana and it read: *"The island of lillies-of-the-valley. The yacht 'Standard' on the roadstead. June-July 1913"*.

(Top right) Departure from Sevastopol. Grand Duchesses Tatiana, Olga, Maria and Anastasia on board the Imperial yacht *Standard* during the voyage from Sevastopol to Yalta in1913.

(Above) Tsarskoye Selo, 1915. (From left to right) Tatiana, Olga, Alexei, Maria and Anastasia. In spite of the war, life continued. The Grand Duchesses are dressed in elegant summer outfits with bonnets and Alexei is wearing a soldier's outfit, even though he is too young to fight.

(Right) Emperor Nikolai II with his daughters in Byelovezh, 1913.

(Facing page) 1914. An official portrait of the Grand Duchesses. Seated: Tatiana. Standing: (from left to right) Maria, Anastasia and Olga.

Марія   Анастасія

Татіана   Ольга

Portrait of Alix, 1895. Alexandra always looked very solemn. Princess Marie Louise referred to this in her memoirs when she wrote: *"There was a curious atmosphere of fatality about her. I once said: 'Alix, you always play at being sorrowful: one day the Almighty will send you some real crushing sorrows and then what are you going to do?' "* (Facing page) A portrait of Alexandra Feodorovna signed *"Alix1896"*. (Ovals) Three regal portraits of the Tsarina.

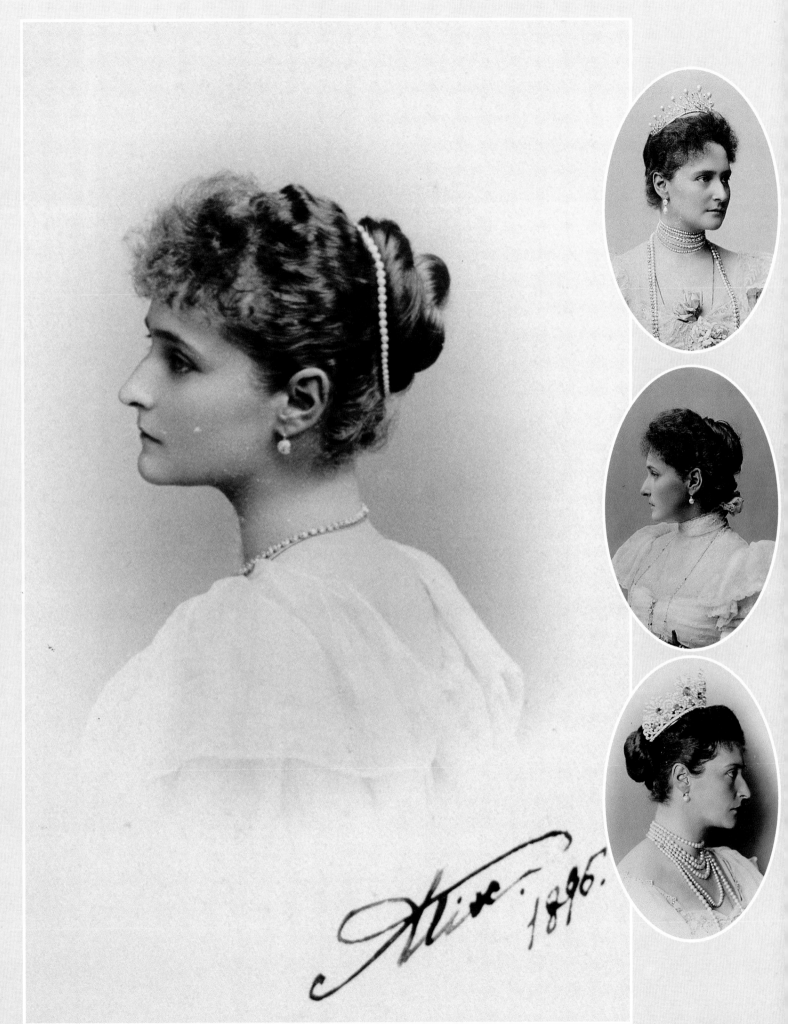

Alix. 1896.

your Nicolas

207

Nikolai & Alexandra

Chapter Eight

"WHY CAN'T I BE LIKE OTHER BOYS?"

atriarchal in its truest sense, founded on genuine respect for parents, deep piety, tender love and faithful friendship of all its members, the Tsar's family lived in a world of their own, peaceful and happy. A special part in such a family is reserved for an heir, whose arrival is anticipated with hope and excitement. In an imperial family the birth of an heir was of paramount national importance, and Nikolai and Alix spent ten years in hope and anxious expectation. In July 1903, the Imperial couple, accompanied by numerous members of the Imperial House, went to Sarov where the hierarchy of the Orthodox faith were gathered to witness the holy celebrations for the canonization of Seraphim of Sarov. The holy celebrations took place in the Sarov and Diveyev Cloisters and, so the legend goes, after the Empress' visit to the holy spring and the holy places one of the nuns predicted that she would give birth to a son.

The following year, 1904, was marked by Russia's failures in the war against Japan. The political situation in the country worsened and anti-government feeling increased. The general dissatisfaction took various forms, including extremist methods. On July 15, the Minister of Interior, V. K. Plehve, fell victim to revolutionary assassins. It was in these days, so grave for Russia, that the salute from the guns in the Fortress of Sts. Peter and Paul heralded the birth of the Heir to the Throne. The entry in Nikolai II's diary, dated July 30, 1904, reads: *"An unforgettable, great day for us on which so clearly the mercy of*

God has visited us. At 1.15 in the afternoon Alix gave birth to a son who was given the name of Alexei when praying [the name of the newlyborn was given during the prayer thanking God for the happiness granted]. *Everything had happened remarkably soon – for me at least. In the morning, as usual, I visited Mama, then I received a report from Kokovtsov and the artillery officer Klepikov wounded at Wafangou, and I went to Alix to have lunch. She was already upstairs, and half an hour later this happy event came about. I have no words worthy enough to be able to thank God for the consolation granted by Him in this year of hard trials. Darling Alix felt quite well. Mama came at 2 and sat long by my side before her first meeting with her new grandchild. At five I went to church service together with the children where the whole family had gathered. Wrote a mass of telegrams. Misha* [Grand Duke Mikhail Alexandrovitch, Nikolai II's youngest brother, after the death of Grand Duke Georgiy Alexandrovitch in 1899 and till the birth of Cesarevitch Alexei, was deemed, in accordance with the Law, Heir to the Throne] *arrived from the camp; he assures he has applied for 'resignation'. . ."* A small notebook carries complete information about the newlyborn: *"Weight: 4660 g; length: 58 cm; girth of head: 38 cm; girth of chest: 39 cm . . ."*

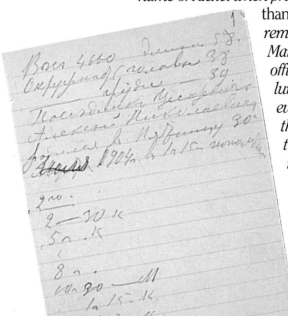

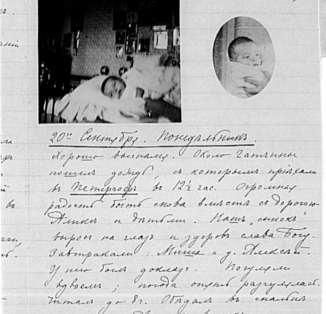

The new baby joined his happy parents and sisters as a little, sweet, warm "Sunbeam". He was named Alexei after Tsar Alexei Mikhailovitch, nicknamed "the Most Placid", whom Nikolai II particularly revered. A wet nurse was employed to suckle Alexei, but even while feeding, the Tsarina never left the nursery. She devoted so much time to her son – it was beyond her powers to leave her sweet beloved baby, even for a few minutes. The daily entries in Nikolai II's diary recorded the state of health of his wife and son. The entry of August 11, 1904, described Alexei's baptism in the church of the Grand Palace in Alexandria, Peterhof: *"The momentous day of our dear son's baptism. The morning was bright and warm. By 9 1/2, before the house the route along the sea was lined with golden carriages and by the Escort, Hussars and Atamans* [Cossack Chieftains], *a platoon of each. At five to ten the procession started off . . . The baptism began at 11 o'clock. Later I learned that little Alexei behaved very quietly. Olga, Tatiana and Irina together with other children came out for the first time and stood the whole long service excellently. The main godmother and godfather were Mama and uncle Alexei . . ."*

Within the Alexandria Palace, the Imperial home at that time, Cesarevitch Alexei was for Nikolai and Alexandra merely their , "Little Treasure", " Tiny", "Baby", "Babykins", "Babichka" or "Agounyoushka" (a nickname endearingly derived of the first sounds uttered by a baby), "Little Man", "Sunbeam". The first troubled entry in Nikolai II's diary appeared on September 8: *"At 11 o'clock went to the service with the children. Had lunch alone. Alix and I were perturbed with Alexei's navel bleeding which lasted intermittently till evening! We had to summon Korovin and the surgeon Feodorov . . . The Little One was amazingly quiet and cheerful! How hard it is to live through such moments of anxiety! . ."* No wonder exclamation marks recurred so often in the entry. What was it? The first sign of the heinous disease? But what if it was harmless? The parents were wracked with apprehension. The bleeding lasted for two days, and on September 11 Nikolai would thank God: *". . . for two days there had been no bleeding. How bright I became at heart".* The trouble seemed gone – the boy grew healthy and cheerful, putting on weight, and the parents became calmer. The pages of the Tsar's diary would soon be sporting photographs

(Top) The spread of the tiny notebook, preserved during the long decades of obscurity. The measurements of the newlyborn read: *"weight 4660 gms, length 58 cm , girth of head 38 cm, girth of chest 39 cm".* (Above) Nikolai's diary contains the first photographs of Alexei, probably taken by Nikolai. His diary records: *"September 20th, Monday 1904 . . . we came to Peterhof . . . it is a great joy to be together . . . our 'sonny' has visibly grown and is healthy, thank God."* Only a few days were to pass before their hopes would be crushed with the knowledge that Alexei was haemophiliac.

Portrait of Tsarina Alexandra
and the toddler Cesarevitch
Alexei.

of Alexei, probably the first-ever pictures taken of him – a little boy in his cot and held by a nurse or Nikolai himself, a baby with wide, inquisitive eyes. *"September 20. Monday. It's a great joy to be together with dear Alix and the children again. Our sonny has visibly grown and he is healthy, thank God . . ."* Only a few days were to pass before their hopes would be crushed. Horrified, Nikolai and Alexandra would find out that their son was incurably ill.

Any disease would create panic and anxiety in a child's parents. In Alexei's case it was haemophilia, the sinister disease when blood fails to clot normally, and so a trivial bruise or scratch can lead to fatal consequences. The Tsarina suffered worst of all, aware that she was to blame for Alexei's tragedy. The disease became especially appalling as the Heir began to crawl and toddle – the lively, fidgety child often tumbled which caused large, dark blue swellings on his arms and legs. Alexei was surrounded by numerous nurses ready to deter and protect their charge from every undesirable action. Maria Vishnyakova, bo'sun Derevenko, Nagorny the sailor and Sednev the footman were ordinary Russians entrusted with the care of the Tsar-to-be.

As Alexei grew, his education was taken up by Pyotr Vasilyevitch Petrov, tutor of Russian language and literature, and also by the Swiss Pierre Gilliard and the Yorkshireman Sidney Gibbs, who taught the Tsar's children French and English respectively. All those people were remarkable, first and foremost, for their humane qualities, which had won the trust, respect and confidence of the Tsar's Family.

The Cesarevitch's malady was kept secret even from the closest relations. Only a few knew about it. Gilliard spent seven years with the family before he learned about the disease. He did not suspect anything when he first saw the toddler Alexei, in February 1906: *"The Cesarevitch certainly was one of the handsomest babies one could imagine, with lovely fair curls, great grey-blue eyes under a fringe of long curling lashes and the fresh pink colour of a healthy child. When he smiled there were two little dimples in his chubby cheeks . . ."* However, some inexplicable anxiety that he noticed in the mother's eyes caught Gilliard's attention, as he wrote: *". . . Though every mother would tremble over her baby's life, but her* [the Tsarina's] *caress and the expression of her eyes that accompanied it, gave away, so clearly and so intensely, some latent restlessness that I was struck by it already then. Only long afterwards I was to understand the meaning of it".*

The most grim trial the family was to suffer came in autumn 1912. Nikolai II and his family were staying in Poland, in Skierniewice and Spala, traditionally favourite spots for Imperial hunting parties. There in Skierniewice Alexei sprained his ankle, causing profuse internal bleeding. He was taken to Spala and doctors Professor Rauchfus, Professor Feodorov and his assistant Doctor Derevenko were summoned to attend the child,

(Above) Alexei and his friends – cadets Vasya Agayev and Zhenya Makarov, sailing along the Dnieper in the vicinity of Mogilyov in 1916.
(Facing page) Tsarskoye Selo 1911. Alexei with his father wearing the simple uniform of a private soldier of the Imperial army. Like his father he was very fond of wearing a uniform and playing war games with friends, who were mainly the children of the servants at the Palace.

214

(Above left) Alexei on board the *Standard* enjoying the children of the officers playing the balalaika, a Russian instrument of Tatar origin. Nikolai's children enjoyed this instrument and some extracts from Maria and Anastasia's letters reflect this when they wrote from Tsarskoye Selo to Alexei in Mogilyov. Maria's letter read: *"My darling Alexei, just now Anastasia has taken out the balalaika to play, Tatiana is playing with Optima [the dog] . . ."*

Anastasia wrote to Alexei: *"My darling little Alexei, just now I am playing the balalaika, not too well . . ."* Finland 1906.

(Above) Ropsha. July 1908. The four year-old Alexei holding a spade and (left) sweeping the path. In spite of their casual look, these photographs were taken by a professional photographer and they were very much posed.

Facing page: (top) Cesarevitch Alexei. Tsarskoye Selo 1905. (Bottom left) Alexei dressed in a typical Russian outfit posing for the camera in St. Petersburg in 1907. (Bottom right) Alexei on board the Emperor yacht *Polyarnaya Zvezda* (Pole Star) in 1906.

215

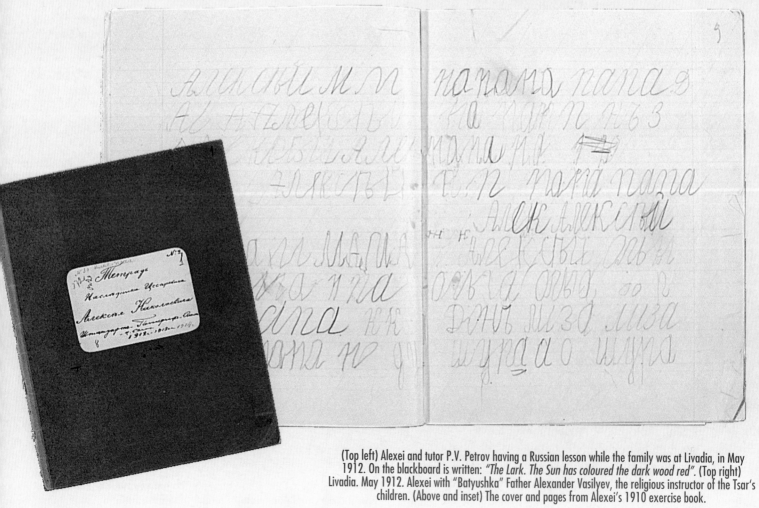

(Top left) Alexei and tutor P.V. Petrov having a Russian lesson while the family was at Livadia, in May 1912. On the blackboard is written: *"The Lark. The Sun has coloured the dark wood red"*. (Top right) Livadia. May 1912. Alexei with "Batyushka" Father Alexander Vasilyev, the religious instructor of the Tsar's children. (Above and inset) The cover and pages from Alexei's 1910 exercise book.

(Top left) Excerpts from the exercise book of Cesarevitch Alexei Nikolayevitch. Tsarskoye Selo. December 1912. The Genealogy of the Romanov House and the history of Mikhail Feodorovitch Romanov handwritten by Alexei: *"The Romanov House. I – Mikhail Feodorovitch 32 years; II – Alexei Mikhailovitch 31 years; III – Feodor Alexeyevitch 6 years; IV – Ioann (Ivan) Alexeyevitch V – 14 years . . ."* (Top right and above) Three water-colours by Alexei.

Ставка, 8 Ноября 1916 г.

Душка моя, родная,
милая, дорогая Мама.
Тепло. Завтра встану.
Жаловался! Умоляю...!!!!!!
Нечего фрррааать.!!! Въ
"Nain Jaune" тоже не везетъ!

Не надо !!! Скоро буду продавать
платье, книги и, наконецъ, ум-
ручку отъ голода.... Всѣ
Тебя цѣлуютъ въ руку !!!
Цѣлую много разъ и обни-
Поклонъ отъ Дюля и Котьки осаби и
зубговая. Да хранитъ васъ Богъ!
Алексѣй.

Массандра   Май 1912

(Above) Livadia 1912. Nikolai II and his son inspecting the Cossacks, the Imperial Escort, accompanied by Count Vladimir Borisovitch Fredericks. Facing page: (top left) Cesarevitch Alexei in a sailor outfit on board the Emperor's yacht *Standard*. (Top right) The Skerries 1910. Alexei during a walk in the wood. (Centre) The letter Alexei sent to his mother begging for his salary: *"My darling dear, sweet beloved Mummy. It's warm. Tomorrow I shall be up. The salary! Beg you!!!!!! Nothing to stuff myself with!!! In Naine Jaune also bad luck! Let it be!!! soon I shall be selling my dress, books and, at last, shall die of starvation"*. (Bottom left) Tsarskoye Selo 1911. Alexei stares solemnly at the camera in a rigid, upright military pose. (Bottom right) Under the supervision of bo'sun Derevenko the Cesarevitch and his cadet friends get to grips with the wonders of military drill, Massandra, May 1912.

(Above) Crimea.1912. Alexei in a horse-drawn carriage . Next to him are Father Vasilyev and Pyotr Petrov; in the background are Alexei's sailor-nurse Derevenko and Pierre Gilliard who is wearing a bowler hat. The basket resting on the carriage next to Alexei indicates they were having a picnic. All the Tsar's Family enjoyed long walk in the woods and here Alexei went with his three tutors. (Right) Alexei with the "Italian donkey", a gift from King Vittorio Emanuele III of Italy to the Tsar's children, during their visit to Italy in1909. Facing page: (top) Tsarskoye Selo. Alexei having fun in the snow. The boy in spite of his illness, loved to participate in all sports and family activities. Alexei wrote to his father on February 26,1916: *"My dear Papa, yesterday Fedotov and 5 sailors who were free worked at the snow tower. Today 9 people have worked. There will be a great surprise for your arrival. The ladder is ready. We are having fine weather. It is 8° of frost. I am coughing a little . . . Tell Goly my answer is yes* ["Goly" literally means naked and it was the nickname for General Voyeikov because he was bald] *God keep you! Loving you, Alexei."*
(Bottom left) Massandra. May, 1912. Heir Cesarevitch Alexei (fifth in the line from the left) at the drill under supervision of boatswain Derevenko and tutor Petrov. (Bottom right) Massandra (Crimea) 1913. Alexei with children, his fellows in games and classes, cooking at the stove.

Масандра

Май 1912.

221

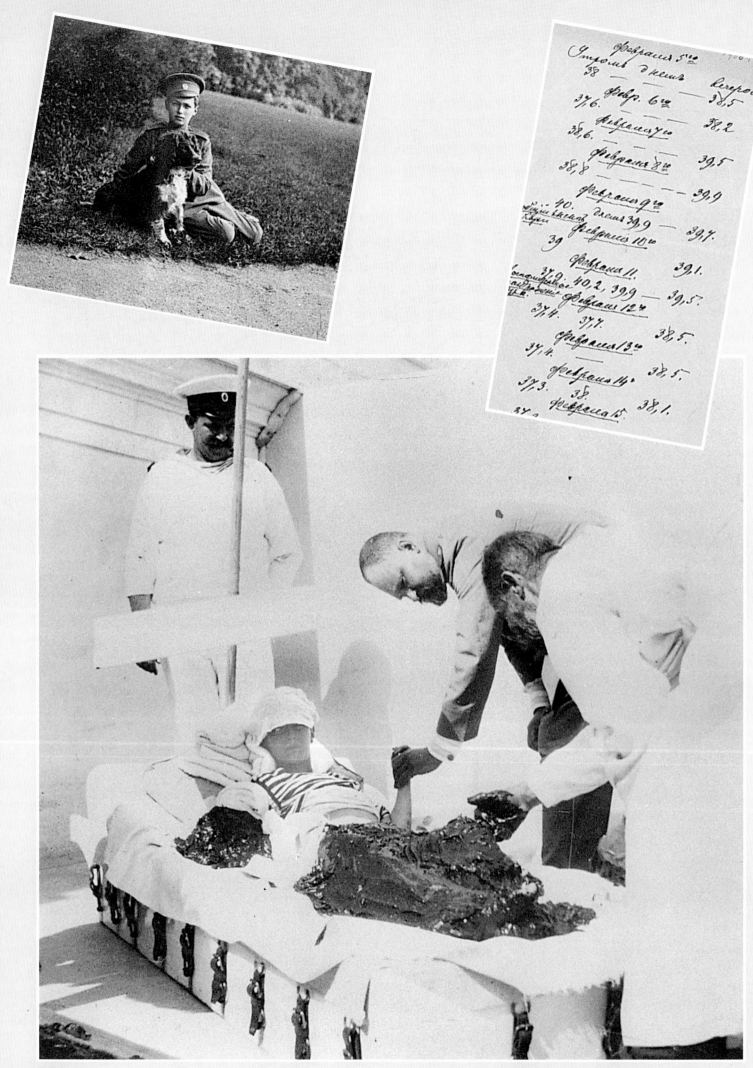

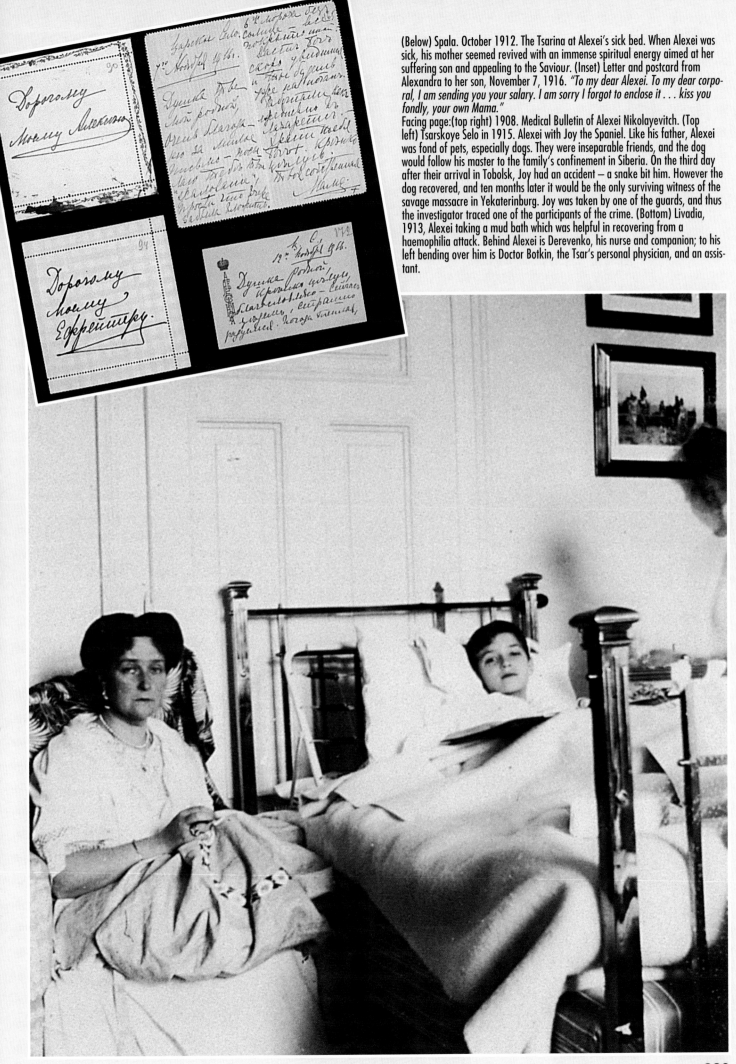

(Below) Spala. October 1912. The Tsarina at Alexei's sick bed. When Alexei was sick, his mother seemed revived with an immense spiritual energy aimed at her suffering son and appealing to the Saviour. (Inset) Letter and postcard from Alexandra to her son, November 7, 1916. *"To my dear Alexei. To my dear corporal, I am sending you your salary. I am sorry I forgot to enclose it . . . kiss you fondly, your own Mama."*

Facing page:(top right) 1908. Medical Bulletin of Alexei Nikolayevitch. (Top left) Tsarskoye Selo in 1915. Alexei with Joy the Spaniel. Like his father, Alexei was fond of pets, especially dogs. They were inseparable friends, and the dog would follow his master to the family's confinement in Siberia. On the third day after their arrival in Tobolsk, Joy had an accident — a snake bit him. However the dog recovered, and ten months later it would be the only surviving witness of the savage massacre in Yekaterinburg. Joy was taken by one of the guards, and thus the investigator traced one of the participants of the crime. (Bottom) Livadia, 1913, Alexei taking a mud bath which was helpful in recovering from a haemophilia attack. Behind Alexei is Derevenko, his nurse and companion; to his left bending over him is Doctor Botkin, the Tsar's personal physician, and an assistant.

together with Doctor Botkin. Alexei's health deteriorated to the critical stage and when his temperature ran as high as 39.6 °C on October 21, the Minister of the Court, Count Fredericks, told Nikolai II that it would be a mistake to conceal the state of the Heir's health any longer. Nikolai had to agree, and the first official bulletin was sent to St. Petersburg.

The boy seemed to be too weak to survive the physical suffering. Nikolai would describe the horrible days they lived through in a letter to his mother, Empress Maria Feodorovna. October 20, 1912: "... *The days between the 6th and the 10th were the worst. The poor little one suffered terribly. The pain seized him in spasms and recurred every quarter of an hour. His high temperature made him delirious night and day, he would sit up in bed and the slightest movement would cause him pain. He hardly slept at all, nor could he cry, he only groaned and kept repeating: 'God spare me'. I was hardly able to stay in the room, but I had to take turns with Alix for she was exhausted by spending the whole time by his bed. She bore the ordeal better than I did while Alexei was in a very bad state, but now, when thank God the danger is past, she feels the consequence of what she had suffered and it told on her poor heart*".

Slowly, the boy was pulling through to recovery, but even in days of remission Alexei still felt the latent presence of the disease. "I'd like to have a bicycle", he asked his mother. "Alexei, you know you can't!" "I want to learn to play tennis like my sisters do!" "You know, you don't dare to play." Such dialogues with his mother – recounted by Anna Vyrubova – reveal how very intently the boy, by nature lively and communicative, suffered. Once he burst out crying, long and bitterly, pleading: "Why can't I be like other boys?"

Pierre Gilliard, who was in charge of the child's education, determined to put an end to the excessive surveillance, justly maintaining that such close observation would distort his pupil's character. The Tsar and the Tsarina had to admit the wisdom of the tutor's reasoning, and the oppressive supervision over Alexei was considerably relaxed. Soon, however, the brilliant educational scheme mapped out for the Cesarevitch was to undergo a serious trial when a trivial, childish carelessness brought Alexei to the verge of a tragedy. "*One morning I found the mother sitting by her son's bedside*", recollected Gilliard. "*The inflammation spread, and the pain was worse than the day before. The Cesarevitch lay in his bed groaning piteously. His head rested on his mother's arm, and his small, deadly white face was unrecognizable. At times the groans ceased and he murmured the one word, 'Mummy', which expressed all his suffering, all his despair. And his mother kissed*

(Above) Livadia. Nine year-old Alexei stroking a little cat who was hiding in the bush. (Right) Alexei's pencil drawing with P.V. Petrov's note: "Livadia. October 1913. The head of the horse was drawn by the Heir and the rest by G.D.O.N. (Olga)" (Facing page) Germany. Friedberg, 1910. During the annual family holiday, Derevenko went riding with young Alexei, who was provided with a small seat. Derevenko and Nagorny were the sailor-nannies to Alexei. The faithful Nagorny was later to follow the family to their imprisonment. He was executed in Yekaterinburg, his loyalty to the Tsar 's family having been interpreted by the Bolsheviks as "a former sailor who had betrayed the revolution".

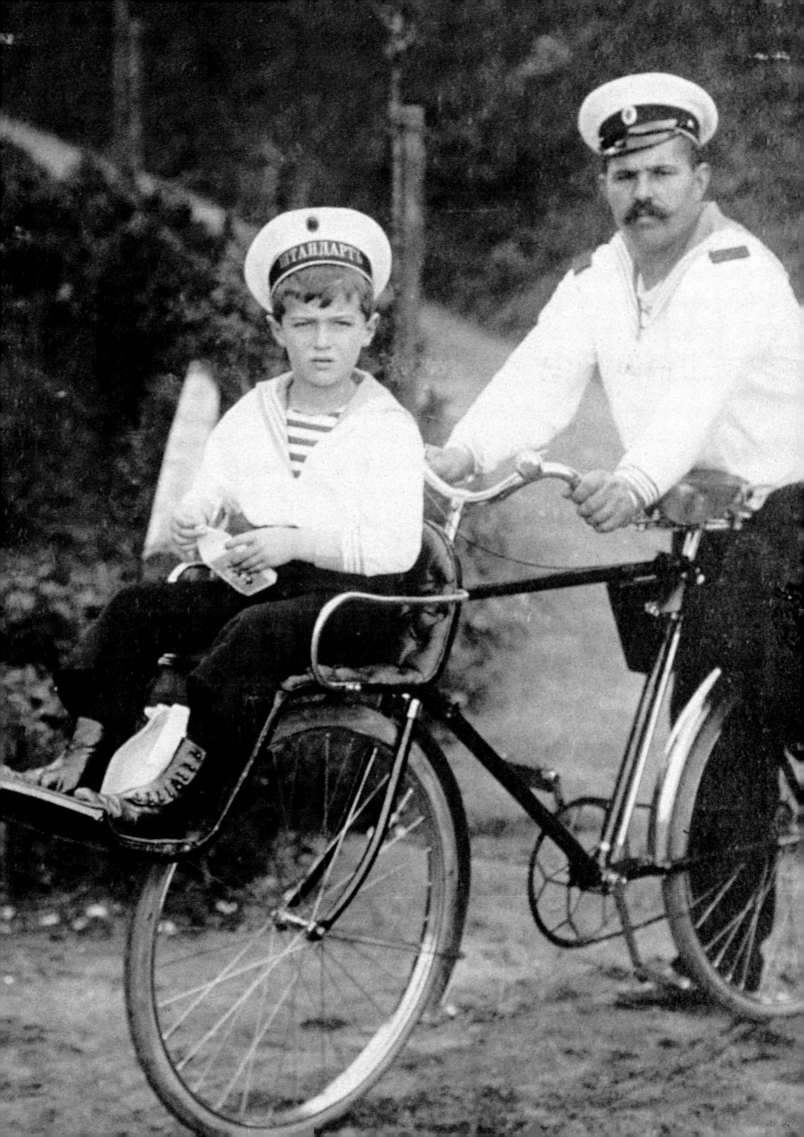

him on the hair, forehead, eyes, as if the touch of her lips would relieve him of his pain, and restore some of the life which was leaving him. Think of the torture of that mother, an impotent witness of her son's martyrdom in those long hours of anguish – a mother who knew that she herself was the cause of those sufferings, that she had transmitted the terrible disease against which human science was powerless".

The physical connection between a mother and her child, natural as it has always been, in the case of Alexandra and Alexei was beginning to acquire a mystic aura which bound them even tighter, making their lives even more interdependent. When Alexei was sick, his mother seemed revived with an immense spiritual energy aimed at her suffering son and appealing to the Saviour. But during the periods when Alexei's disease abated, Alexandra Feodorovna would collapse, exhausted. For days on end she lay on her couch.

For all the seriousness of the illness, it was virtually impossible to suppress the boy's natural temptation to run, jump and romp. Usually, when the disease was in remission, Alexei played games a lot, enjoyed strolls with his father, and often went canoeing with Nikolai or his sisters along the channels and lakes in Tsarskoye Selo. "When he was well, the palace seemed regenerated; it was as if a sunbeam excited everybody and everything", Gilliard noted in his reminiscences.

His relations with his sisters were friendly and devoted, but there was a special attachment between Alexei and Anastasia, the youngest of the sisters, nicknamed "Shvybzik", as she proudly called herself in the language of "Tarabar". They relished this invented language, and delighted in writing "mysterious" letters and exchanging them "in secret": "To Her Highness stupid Marie and Anostoie. Thanks for thesnakck I rekon well befightin. M. A. Alexei. 1914." (The spelling is deliberately distorted to convey their intentions from the original Russian). With all her sprightly energy and buoyant liveliness, good-humoured mischievousness and propensity for all sorts of jokes and pranks, Anastasia appeared for Alexei to be that zestful gulp of fresh air of which his haemophilia was trying to rob him.

Like all men of the Imperial Family, the Cesarevitch wished to dedicate himself to a military career. The boy enjoyed his father's stories about military service, manoeuvres and campaigns, and earnestly prepared himself for service to his Motherland. Military training was an important part of his education and by the age of thirteen Alexei had a good understanding of the workings of the rifle, the extended order and the fundamentals of reconnaissance. A special 'poteshnaya' team of boy-soldiers was recruited for military exercises, Alexei being its recognised ataman (chieftain). Alexei's favourite food was that of the ordinary soldier. Time and again, he would sidle up to the window of the Imperial kitchen and ask the cooks for a chunk of brown bread which he would then share with his pet dog, Joy.

Tsarskoï-Selo, 19 décembre 1915.

Cher Papa,
Hier j'ai dé-
jeuné en bas, j'étais
très content. Hier
Maman avait mal
aux dents, mais main=
tenant elle n'a plus

nal. J'ai commencé
avec Жиликъ deux
grandes forteresses,
j'espère que dans quel=
ques jours nous ferons
la bataille. Ce matin
dehors il y a trois de=
grès de froid, je sortirai
demain, je suis très

content, ура!!!!!
Salue grassouillet(cbklge)
et tout nu !!! et tout
le monde.
Je t'embrasse
ton
Alexis

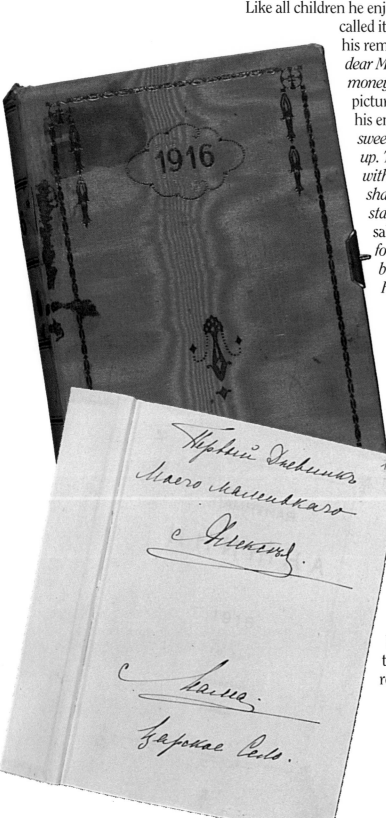

After the Tsar had become the Supreme Commander-in-Chief, the Heir would often stay with his father at the Headquarters and would accompany him in inspections of the troops. The Cesarevitch wore a common soldier's uniform, and was proud when he was created corporal. He liked to listen to his father's conversations with officers and soldiers. But like most boys, he was ready for pranks and mischief. Describing his relations with the foreign allies' representatives, he wrote to his mother: *"I scare the Belgian and begin talking with the Frenchman"* (October 10, 1915); or *"Today I, Papa, the Japanese, the Englishman and the Frenchman played with the water near the fountain. The Japanese and I were quite wet. I was sent to change my dress".*

Like all children he enjoyed having his own pocket money – "the salary" he called it. When the payments were delayed for some reason, his reminding was passionate, with vivid illustrations: *"My dear Mom. It rubbed today again. I have run out of money, please send me the salary. I beg you – it's me"* (a picture of himself kneeling). (June 6, 1916). Sometimes his entreaties were quite heart-rending: *"My darling dear, sweet beloved Mummy. It's warm. Tomorrow I shall be up. The salary! Beg you!!!!!! Nothing to stuff myself with!!! In Naine Jaune also bad luck! Let it be!!! Soon I shall be selling my dress, books and, at last, shall die of starvation "* (a picture of a coffin). But when "the salary" arrived, that was a feast! *"Very, very grateful for the letter and the 10 rou* [bles]. *Rich!! Drink barley coffee. Awfully glad that we shall meet soon!!! HURRAH!!!"* (November 9, 1916).

This lively child, ingenuous and sometimes mischievous as all children must be, was destined for a special role. *"He is ours, as our Friend* [Grigoriy Rasputin] *says so rightly and his life is so knitted to ours since all these years, he has shared our joys and sorrows and is quite our very own, and we are his nearest and dearest",* the Tsarina wrote to Nikolai, December 12, 1915, letter No 403. She urged her husband: *"For Baby's sake we must be firm as otherwise his inheritance will be awful, as with his character, he won't bow down to others but be his own master, as one must be in R[ussia] whilst people are still so uneducated".* (Alexandra's letter to Nikolai, No 464, March 17, 1916). However, as fate would have it, Alexei was not to fulfil his august predestination. The Bolsheviks executed him two weeks before his fourteenth birthday only because he was the Cesarevitch and the heir of a dynasty that posed a threat to the 'red' revolution.

Chapter Nine

GRIGORIY RASPUTIN: THE HOLY MAN FROM SIBERIA

Alexander Bokhanov

'HE LIVES FOR HIS SOVEREIGN AND RUSSIA, AND BEARS ALL SLANDERS FOR OUR SAKES'

(Above) The Heir to the Throne and only son of Nikolai II who was born a haemophiliac. (Facing page) Rasputin, the holy man who played such an important part in the life and destiny of the Tsar and Tsarina of Russia.

rigoriy Rasputin, the stigma and curse of the last Russian sovereigns, was at the same time their joy and hope. The incredible life story and destiny of a common Siberian *moujik* (peasant) who managed to attain staggering power and influence has seemed to conceal some fatal secret which has long whetted the world's imagination. Was he the "sexual maniac" who had seduced to his malignant will the dissatisfied metropolitan matrons; was it the state of Tsarina Alexandra's mind – "the hysterical woman susceptible to mesmerism"; was he a thread in a far-flung web of a foreign plot – "the Rasputin gang of Russia's enemies who had encircled the throne"? . . . and so on and so on, as the cheap fiction and pulp writers of the West and Russia itself fell prey to Rasputin fascination. But what was he really like?

Grigoriy, son of a well-off peasant Yefim Yakovlevitch Rasputin, was born in 1869 in the large Siberian village of Pokrovskoye, in Tyumen *uyezd* (district), Tobolsk province. He never went to school and was virtually illiterate. Whenever he had to sign anything, it was not an easy task for him to trace out his scribble of a signature. Later, with great difficulty, he learned to write some words, but he would never master the skill of writing properly.

The young Grigoriy was rowdy, drank, indulged in scuffles and several times

(Above) Rasputin and his followers at Melmanova's. Standing fifth from the left is Anna Vyrubova, on the far left is her sister Alya Pistolkors and her husband, Alexander Pistolkors (son of countess Hohenfelzen). Sitting first on the left is "Munya" Golovina, who acted as his secretary. She was helplessly in love with Felix Yusupov, and it was she who introduced the starets to his future assassin. Among the most eminent of his followers was the wife, by a morganatic marriage, of Grand Duke Pavel Alexandrovitch, Countess Olga Valerianovna Hohenfelzen. After having been allowed to return to Russia and eager to receive the title of "Princess", she sought the help of her sister Lubov Golovina and her niece Maria (Munya). They asked the *starets* for help. She met him in January 1914. Her impression of him was "strange but fascinating." Her husband did not approve of her meeting with Rasputin. As she admitted in her diary, she had several humiliating meetings with Rasputin, he spoke of his love, kissed and embraced her and then "took secretly 200 roubles". He did not help her. However her ambition would be realized, due to the protection of some members of the Imperial family, among whom was Dmitriy Pavlovitch, her step-son. There were other meetings with Rasputin, but "there is nothing special about him" she commented later.

was caught thieving, red-handed. Those who knew him at that time would point to his expansive nature; he had the reputation of working and playing hard. Early in the 1890s, this "tippler and womaniser" married a meek girl named Proskovia, who bore him two daughters, Maria (Matriona) and Varvara and a son, Dmitriy.

His life turned after his visit to a monastery in the Urals where he "perceived the divine grace". He gave up drinking, smoking, eating meat and began to test himself with severe fasting. Frantically, he would pray for hours on end. Later, he set out on pilgrimages to holy places. He visited a great number of cloisters in Russia and even undertook trips to Mount Athos in Greece and Jerusalem. In Pokrovskoye, there emerged a circle of his friends and relations, united by a kindred spirit. Under his house Rasputin dug out a cellar for an oratory where they collected to pray and to chant psalms and religious songs. By the time he appeared in St. Petersburg, Grigoriy would have a solid grasp of the Scriptures and would be able to keep up lengthy "God-pleasing" conversations on religious topics.

His immense willpower, natural wit and peasant's cunning were added to a miraculous intuition. All these features merged into an image of a vigorous, consistent person who could make a strong impact upon the weak, and those obsessed with hesitations and doubts, those who had found themselves in a *cul-de-sac* and powerless to solve their problems. His inborn qualities and a pious reputation, later to be dissipated in scandal, completed the fiendish image. And, as the twentieth century dawned, rumours of the extraordinary *starets* (holy man) and seer began to filter beyond the borders of the Tyumen district. Reverence of *starets* was a deeply ingrained, age-old tradition in Russia. It was one of the cornerstones of the Orthodox Christianity established on the vast spaces of the European plain, the Ukraine, the Urals and Siberia. A *starets* was neither a priest nor a monk, but he held immense moral authority for it was generally believed that through his experience he had perceived the invaluable Christian virtues. Seeking Absolute Truth, aspiring to Supreme Veracity and Divine Light were a general sentiment which possessed many Russians, those who lived in luxurious palaces and in decrepit shacks alike. These aspirations formed a sort of a magic crystal through which reality was viewed. To be able to perceive oneself and the world, to learn the truly "God-pleasing" mode of life, people turned to those who were reputed to be "the Divine candle on Earth"– the holy men, the *starets*.

The essence of this spiritual tradition was expounded by Feodor Dostoyevskiy when he wrote in his novel "The Brothers Karamazov": *"The starets is he who takes your soul, your will and makes them his. When you select your starets, you surrender your will and give it to him in utter submission, in complete self-renunciation. This temptation, this awful school of life is undertaken voluntarily, one dooms himself to it hoping, after long temptation, to overcome himself, to gain control over himself so that at long last he could achieve, through penance of all his life, perfect freedom from his own self, and could avoid the lot of those who had lived a whole life but had failed to find their own selves in themselves".* The mystery of the Rasputin phenomenon can be perceived only within the context of this popular conception of pious life which historically had been established in Russia.

Rasputin first appeared in St. Petersburg most probably in 1903, having by that time "won the heart" of the Kazan bishop Chrisanth who recommended him to the rector of the St. Petersburg Theological Academy, Bishop Sergius. The latter, in his turn, presented Rasputin to the professor, celibate priest Veniamin, and to the inspector of the Academy, Archimandrite Theophan. Rasputin mingled with the Orthodox hierarchy and the disciples of the academy for a long time, went through his "university" there,

(Above) Rasputin in a pensive mood. Like a character out of a Dostoyevskiy's novel Rasputin represented the incredible story and destiny of a common Siberian "moujik" who managed to attain staggering power and influence which has long whetted the world's imagination. (Left) The Tsarina in a photograph taken in 1915. (Below) Rasputin married a meek girl named Proskovia and they had three children, Maria (Matriona), Varvara and a son, Dmitriy.

(Top) A very impressive photograph of Rasputin, the *starets*. Neither a priest nor a monk he held immense moral authority among his followers.
(Left) The Prime Minister Stolypin and his family. Even Stolypin, not a man of spiritual character, invited Grigoriy to pray at the sick-bed of his daughter, maimed during the terrorists' attempt upon her father's life in the summer of 1906. (Above) Rasputin posing with Colonel Lomar and Major General, Prince Putyatin.

234

and his sagacious, prehensile wit and tenacious memory enabled him to pick up a lot from these contacts. *Starets* Grigoriy made a very strong impression on the famous preacher and pious pastor, Father Ioann of Kronstadt, who held immense moral authority in Russia at that time and who would give his blessing to the new "God-seeker".

Archimandrite Father Theophan, the confessor of Grand Duke Pyotr Nikolayevitch and his wife, Grand Duchess Militsa Nikolayevna, introduced the "Siberian *starets*" to the grand ducal chambers. It was only one more step from those parlours to the Tsar's palace. The fatal meeting was almost inevitable and it came about in Peterhof, on November 1, 1905. Nikolai noted in his diary: *"Had tea with Militsa and Stana. Met a man of God, Grigoriy, from Tobolsk province."*

It was a time of deep depression for the Tsar and Tsarina. The general situation in the country was rather sombre. The Manifesto of October 17, proclaiming political freedom, failed to pacify the country. Reports of disorder and violence came from all over Russia and in this dismal atmosphere there suddenly appeared one who brought comfort with his soothing conversation and prediction that all tumults and upheavals would soon be appeased. The first meeting did not impress the Tsar much; talking with men of God was not uncommon for him, and there had been some meetings that had deeply imprinted themselves in his mind; for instance, the prophecy of the *yurodivaya* (God's fool) Pasha of the Sarov Cloister – in 1903 she predicted the Russo-Japanese war and the murder of his uncle, Grand Duke Sergei Alexandrovitch.

For several years, meetings of the Imperial couple and *starets* Grigoriy were rare. Meanwhile, the fame of the Siberian holy man and prophet grew in St. Petersburg. Even the Prime Minister, Stolypin – not inclined to mysticism at all – invited Grigoriy to pray at the sick-bed of his daughter, maimed during the terrorists' attempt upon her father's life in the summer of 1906. But the sensational renown and the burgeoning popularity which Grigoriy would enjoy during the last years of the monarchy were still remote at this time. In fashionable salons, he cut an exotic figure, a sort of titbit for jaded guests.

As his fame spread, a trail of rumours drawn from his Siberian background were gaining ground. The aroma of "disturbing stories" about incredible erotic adventures and orgies fanned the lustful imagination of the petty bourgeoisie. It is not known how true they were. Some of those stories were recounted in public by "Grishka (slighting derivation of Grigoriy) the erotomaniac" himself. As his fame and influence grew, the unbridled *moujik* would revel in the ostentatious divulging of confidences. One of these stories set up an odious clamour when it was published in St. Petersburg newspapers and was presented as Grigoriy's confidential avowal: *"When in Siberia, I had a lot of admirers and among these admirers there were ladies close to the Court. They came to see me in Siberia and wanted to get nearer to God. One can get nearer to God only through self-abasement. So I took those fashionable ladies in diamonds and expensive gowns – I took them all to the bath-house (there were seven of them), made them undress and wash me".* A colourful, alluring spectacle of "fashionable ladies in diamonds and expensive gowns" washing a *moujik* tickled the imagination of Russian philistines. These titillating anecdotes shocked the public so much that they would remain part of the Rasputin mythology forever.

Rasputin's meetings with the Tsar's family became regular at the end of 1907. Most often they took place in No 2 Church Street in Tsarskoye Selo, half-a-mile from the Alexander Palace. It was a small stone house where Anna Vyrubova had settled. This "Ania's house" was to become something of a sanctuary where, during their outings, the Imperial couple would drop in – defying court convention – for a talk with the man who "expounded life". Soon the Tsar's children would join these gatherings: first the eldest, Olga and Tatiana, and then the rest. Very rarely would the Tsar and Tsarina privately receive Grigoriy in their chambers, but a series of scandalous stories put an end to meetings in the palace. The Tsar's children, with their deeply religious upbringing and infinite reverence for all that was dear to their parents, regarded the Siberian *starets* with sincere veneration. On June, 25, 1909, Olga Nikolayevna wrote to her father from Peterhof: *"My dear darling Papa. The weather is lovely today, it is very warm. The little Ones* [Anastasia and Alexei] *are running barefoot. In*

Alexandra was very critical of Dmitriy even before he committed, in her eyes, that dreadful act. On January 8, 1916, she wrote to Nikolai: *". . . Now are clean people round you and I only wish N.P. [Sablin] were of their number. We spoke long about Dmitriy – he says that he is a boy without any character and can be led by anybody. Three months he was under the influence of N.P. and held himself well at the Stavka [Headquarters] and when in town he kept himself like the others, and did not go to the ladies' companies – but out of sight – gets into other hands. He finds the regiment perverts, the boy, as their coarse conversations and jokes are hard. And before ladies too. And they drag him down . . ."*

The Tsarina had just learned that Rasputin had disappeared. Without her husband at her side to support her, dreading the worst and fearing for the life of Anna Vyrubova, she wrote to Nikolai: *"December 16, 1916 . . . We are sitting together-can imagine our feeling - thoughts - our Friend has disappeared. Yesterday A. [Anna] saw him and he said Felix asked him to come in that night. A motor wld fetch him to see Irina. A motor fetched him (military one) with 2 civilians and he went away. This night big scandal at Yusupov house - big meeting, Dmitriy, Purishkevich, etc. all drunk. Police heard shots, Purishkevich ran out, screaming to the Police that our Friend was killed. Police searching and Justice entered now into Yu [Yusupov's] house. Did not dare before as D. [Dmitriy] was there. The city governor has sent for D [Dmitriy]. Felix wanted to leave to-night for Crimea, [I] begged K. [Kalinin was a secret name designated by the Tsar and Tsarina in their private correspondence for Protopopov, then Minister of the Interior] to stop him. Our Friend was in good spirits but nervous these days . . . Felix pretends he never came to the house and never asked him. Seems quite a jam. I still trust in God's mercy that one has only driven him off somewhere. K. is doing all he can. Therefore I beg for Voyeikov. We women are alone, with our weak hands. Shall keep her [Vyrubova] to live here as now they will set at her next. Cannot and won't believe he has been killed. God have mercy. Such utter anguish (I am calm and cannot believe it). Thanks dear letters. Come quickly - nobody will dare to touch her or do anything when you are here. Felix came often to him lately . . ."*

235

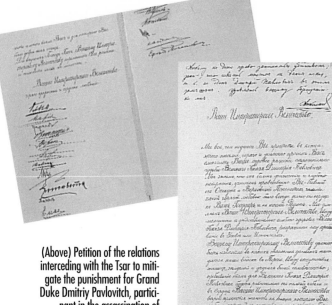

(Above) Petition of the relations interceding with the Tsar to mitigate the punishment for Grand Duke Dmitriy Pavlovitch, participant in the assassination of Rasputin, with instruction appended and hand written by Nikolai II: *"Nobody has got the right to commit an assassination, I know that many are conscience-stricken, for not only Dmitriy Pavlovitch is implicated in the crime. Your application surprises me. Nikolai ."*

"Your Imperial Majesty. We all whose signatures You will read at the close of this letter, fervently and strongly implore You to mitigate Your severe decision concerning the destiny of Grand Duke Dmitriy Pavlovitch. – We know that he is physically sick and deeply shocked, suppressed morally. You, – his former Trustee and Supreme Guardian, know his heart has always been filled with so much fervent love for You, Your Majesty, and for our Motherland. We entreat Your Imperial Majesty, in view of the young age and really poor health of Grand Duke Dmitriy Pavlovitch to allow him to stay in Usov or Ilyinskoye. Your Imperial Majesty must be aware of how hard are the conditions for our troops in Persia, because of lack of living quarters, epidemics and other scourges of the human race, should Grand Duke Dmitriy Pavlovitch be obliged to stay there, it would mean his complete ruin and in the heart of Your Imperial Majesty, there must emerge some pity for the youth whom You have loved, who since childhood has been happy to be much and often near You and to whom You have been as kind as a father. May the Lord exhort Your Imperial Majesty to change Your decision and temper justice with mercy. Fervently faithful to and fondly loving Your Imperial Majesty Olga, Maria, Kirill, Victoria, Georgiy, Andrei, Pavel, Maria, Yelizaveta (Mavrikievna), Ioann, Yelena, Gavriil, Konstantin, Igor, Nikolai Mikhailovitch, Sergei Mikhailovitch."

the evening Grigoriy will come to us. We all rejoice to see him again . . ."*

What spell took hold of the autocrat? Was it just the fluent quotations from the Scriptures that had impressed the Tsar so much? By no means! There were many people well-read in scripture; nor was there any lack of all sorts of prophets. Rasputin came as one of many, but he became the only one. The explanation of why this role fell to Rasputin demands further explanation. Vyrubova reflected that the Tsar and Tsarina "believed him as they believed Ioann of Kronstadt, they believed him awfully; and when they were in distress, when, for instance, the Heir was sick, they turned to him to pray for them". The Cesarevitch's illness seemed to have fatally chained the last sovereign's family to the notorious *starets* forever. Rasputin appeared at the Cesarevitch's sick-bed for the first time at the close of 1907. He said his prayers and the boy's condition improved. There were many more instances where Rasputin's intervention changed the course of the Heir's condition for the better. That fact is indisputable.

For all the outrageous rumours and gossip that swirled around Rasputin, the Tsarina saw only one side of the *starets.* For her, he was a true believer with a prayer on his lips, oblivious of his own self, caring for the destinies of common people and pleading for the miserable. During the whole period of their spiritual intercourse and "informal relations" the Tsar's "Friend" never asked for anything for himself. The Tsarina was extremely punctilious in such matters and she took it painfully whenever any of her retinue attempted to obtain certain favours and benefits for themselves. Amulets, small icons, girdles, embroidered shirts and handkerchiefs were all that the Tsar's family treated Grigoriy with. In his turn, he sent to his august patroness and devotee Easter cakes, Easter eggs, small icons, and – what always gave her utmost satisfaction – his blessing which he would give personally or by telegram. The Tsarina had her own experience of Grigoriy's miraculous healing abilities when several times he relieved her of migraines and alleviated heart spasms.

In Alexandra Feodorovna's life, Rasputin filled the role of teacher and confessor. She was convinced that he was an authentic messenger of God, their mascot, and his advocacy for them before the Throne of the Most High promised them hope for the future. Alexandra had met quite a lot of holy men, prophets, seers and miracle-workers, but believed that she and Nicky had had only two "real friends" – Monsieur Philippe and *starets* Grigoriy. The former predicted the birth of the Heir, the latter was the defender of the sovereigns' well-being.

In June 1915, Alexandra Feodorovna wrote to her husband: *"Hearken unto our Friend, believe him, He has your interest and Russia's at heart, it is not for nothing God sent Him to us – only we must pay more attention to what He says – His words are not lightly spoken – and the gravity of having not only His prayers, but His advice – is great".* Having been disappointed in people so many times, knowing from her own sad experience what slander and insidious rumours felt like, she took no heed of the reports about her mentor's misconduct and all the scandals in which he was alleged to have been involved. In her opinion, calumny inevitably accompanied pious people on their way on Earth, as she inferred: *"The wickedness of the world ever increases. During the evening Bible I thought so much of our Friend, how the scribes and pharisees persecuted Christ pretending to be such perfections (and how far they are from it now). Yes, indeed, a prophet is never acknowledged in his own country . . . He lives for his sovereign and Russia and bears all slanders for our sakes".* (April 5, 1916)

Conversations with "dear Grigoriy" brought peace and consolation to their souls, and that was what the last autocrat needed most of all. The Tsar once admitted in a private talk with Adjutant-General Dedyulin that Rasputin was "a good, simple, religious

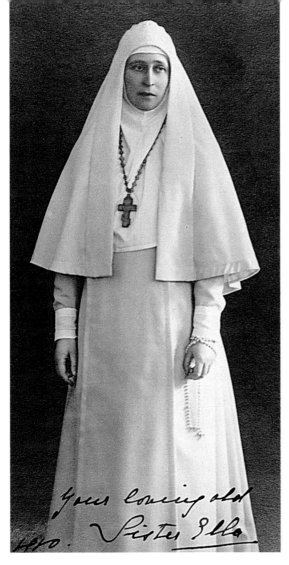

Russian man. In moments of hesitation and dismay I like to talk with him and after such a talk I always feel easy and calm at heart". Such confidences could not pass unnoticed. "Lord! What times have we arrived at?! What is doing with Russia?!" The world of Russian officials and gentry was horrified. Educated, refined society began to grumble.

The rows and scandal attracted the attention of the Dowager Empress. All her life Maria Feodorovna had lived under the pressure of the prophecy that she, as a young Cesarevna, had heard from an old clairvoyant woman: *"Your son will reign, will be climbing the mountain to attain wealth and great honour. Only he will never reach the top – stricken by a moujik's hand".* The rumours of Rasputin and his role wracked the Dowager Empress with sinister presentiments. But the Tsar and the Tsarina had already formed their own, unshakable opinion of Rasputin, and were adamant not to give in to their kin and society, who insisted that "the fiend incarnate" be banished from St. Petersburg.

The Tsar had sound reasons to ignore this pressure, which was complicated by Nikolai's very particular character – he would never comply with a decision which was imposed upon him. Then his stubbornness verged on obstinacy. He explained his decision to Count Fredericks: "Today they demand that Rasputin be driven away, tomorrow they would dislike someone else and would urge that he leaves". The Tsar's reproval to the palace superintendent Voyeikov (son-in-law of the Minister of the Imperial Court) was much sterner: "We may receive whom we wish".

Having become a focus of curiosity and admiration, Rasputin never cared to comply with existing standards of behaviour, and he blatantly disregarded the conventionalities of bourgeois society. He could not but understand that it was his very particular appearance and demeanour, coarse and strange, his ostentatious escapades that made him a source of lustful attraction for those people sated with luxury and comfort – and later he would deliberately exaggerate his peculiar behaviour. But he never gave up his habits.

General Beletskiy, who used to know Rasputin very closely, recollected: *"Rasputin never ate white or black meat and he hated it when someone smoked in his presence, he always ate little and seldom used a knife and fork; of wines he preferred madeira and sometimes red wine, he never drank sobering mineral waters, and to sober up he would drink either pure water or simple kvass* [a traditional refreshing Russian non-alcoholic beverage], *which he liked".*

Any account of the Rasputin phenomenon cannot be valid unless two major factors are given proper consideration: the message of his homilies and the characters of those involved in the Rasputin circle, notorious for their mysticism and pernicious influence. The core of Rasputin's prophetic speculations was formed of such vital religious and moral categories as Love and Submission. He asserted that only he, who had a heart filled with love for his neighbour, was a true Christian. Grand Duchess Tatiana, Nikolai II's second daughter, kept a notebook in which she recorded the *Staret's* maxims: *"Love is Light and it has no end. Love is great suffering. It cannot eat, it cannot sleep. It is mixed with sin in equal parts. And yet it is better to love. In love one can be mistaken, but he suffers, and through suffering he expiates for his mistakes. If love is strong – the lovers are*

Christmas.

— Prices are so high, sweetest! I have only one present for thee and it's the one thou hast chosen thyself!

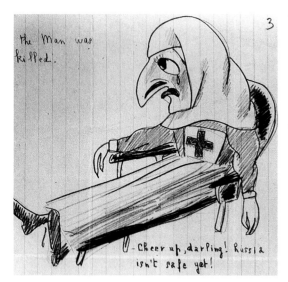

The Man was killed.

— Cheer up, darling! Russia isn't safe yet!

(Above right) Rasputin at his desk writing. (Above) These two caricatures of the Tsarina were made after Rasputin's murder in 1916, by Prince Vladimir Paley, son of Grand Duke Pavel Alexandrovitch and Countess Hohenfelzen. He was believed by some to be a promising young poet. He was murdered in Alapayevsk together with Ella. In the top cartoon, the words written in Russian read: *"Exile in Persia".*

happy. Nature herself and the Lord give them happiness. One must ask the Lord that He teach to love the luminous, bright, so that love be not torment, but joy. Love pure, Love luminous is the Sun. The Sun makes us warm, and Love caresses. All is in Love, and even a bullet cannot strike Love down".

However, love alone, Rasputin instructed, was not sufficient for a pious life. Only he could find a veritable path to God who would manage to overcome his pride, renouncing earthly bustle and weakness, who would learn to take quietly all trials sent from above to test the loyalty of his faith. For all the verbosity of his reasoning of love and resignation, he took sin very lightly, and diverging from the principles of Christian virtue, he believed that confession and repentance could earn absolution.

The major part of Rasputin's devotees were women who were reputed of "God knows what". Having implicitly taken all rumours of Grigoriy's sexual omnipotence as true, public opinion was unanimous – gathering in Rasputin's flat in Gorokhovaya Street were abnormal, sexually dissatisfied and mentally unbalanced women, and there they indulged in incredible, "fairly licentious dissipation". The gossip had it that he mesmerised his victims with his recitals of love, then he seduced them, and thereafter the victim was unable to free herself from his sorcery and remained faithful to him to the end. With minor variations, that was the gossip from the kitchen table to the professor's study.

The extent and number of Rasputin's alleged erotic conquests and sexual magnetism defied any possible reality. However, for quite understandable reasons, there could never be solid evidence for or against. But one important issue, which is often evaded, needs to be stated quite clearly – there were no intimate relations between the *starets* and the Tsarina, or her closest friend, Anna Vyrubova. Generally speaking, should the Rasputin phenomenon be regarded through the prism of the empire's decline, the sexual motive does not appear significant at all.

On June 29, 1914, in the village of Pokrovskoye, a peasant woman Khionia Guseva, Rasputin's former devotee, attempted to end the life of the *starets,* by stabbing him in the stomach. Rasputin was gravely hurt, and for several days he was on the verge of death, but, as he would later describe to the Tsarina, he said his prayers, the Lord listened unto them and saved him for her well-being. Grigoriy returned to the capital after the outbreak of the world war, late in August 1914. On August 22, the Tsar remarked in his diary: *"After dinner saw Grigoriy, for the first time after his wounding".* During the months that followed the *starets* would acquire the status of the Tsarina's mentor – paraphrasing Dostoyevskiy's maxim, he had "completely taken her will and made it his".

During the war the relationship between the Imperial couple and Rasputin became more intense. On October 17, 1914 – a day of dismay and commotion – the Tsar received the report about the treacherous attack of the Turkish and the Germans against the Russian fleet in the Crimean ports. In the evening, the Tsar reflected in his diary: *"Was in a furious mood about the Germans and the Turks because of their vile behaviour on the Black Sea! Only in the evening, under the influence of the soothing talk with Grigoriy my soul restored balance"*.

Soothing and cheering talks with Rasputin were a seance of soul-healing. The Tsar and Tsarina's need for them would become addictive. But important as they were, spiritual talks were but a part of the monarch's life, and it needs to be emphasised that this sort of leisure was quite common in Russian pious families. They talked, then prayed before going to bed, and in the morning the Tsar's life took its normal course: a short morning prayer and then endless meetings, receptions, journeys, reports, papers. Nikolai's love for talks of Good and Evil, Love and Submission, and the Purpose of Life by no means implied that he would listen to Grigoriy's opinions on matters of state and politics. For all his sincere respect of "dear Grigoriy", the Tsar was far from being a blind follower of his advice and visions, especially in matters of state. Thus, sharing his plan concerning the Duma and the rearrangement of the Cabinet, he noted in a letter to the Tsarina of November 10, 1916: *"Only, please, don't mix in our Friend! It is I who carry the responsibility and I want to be free to choose accordingly"*. That was the Emperor's indisputable right.

Rasputin's influence on the Tsarina was much stronger. As if under a spell, she implicitly believed that her family's well-being depended on his prayers. This extraordinary man was so whole-heartedly devoted! He had so often saved the "Baby" (Alexei) from inevitable death. Who else was capable of that? His prayers also safeguarded her beloved Nicky! What was more, he came "from the earth", he knew the people's needs, and the Tsar should act so as to make the life of common people better. As for the opinion of society, it could be ignored – they were forever interfering in matters of government with so little knowledge about it. How aptly Grigoriy put it about the aristocrats, that their education only stinted life, leaving no place for the natural! *"The major half of this education,"* Rasputin declared, *"makes the man a stuffed dummy, takes away simplicity. Why so? Because, first of all, he is not allowed to talk to a common man. And what is the common man like? 'Cause he cannot foreign phrases say, but speaks plainly and lives a plain life, and it feeds him and develops his spirit and wisdom"*.

In the opinion of staunch monarchists, the Tsar's family mixed with an indecent man, and this connection, as well as the scandalous demeanour and mode of life of the "Tsar's Friend", disrupted the halo of "divine infallibility" which had always surrounded the tsars. Attempts to "open His Majesty's eyes" and explain the danger of the situation had been undertaken before the war. Itching to collect as much damaging evidence as possible, Rasputin's enemies picked up every slipshod piece of gossip, caring not about its reliability. When at last this "black collection" was presented to the Tsar, very often many of the "facts" proved counterfeit. Similarly, Rasputin's former supporter, Grand Duke Nikolai Nikolayevitch, got into an awkward situation having presented a scandalous summary of surveillance on Rasputin, with a detailed report of carousing, meetings with prostitutes and

(Above) A drawing of Rasputin made while he was recovering after the attempt on his life in 1914. On it he wrote: *"What's tomorrow? Thou art our guide Lord how many in life are thorny ways."*

The Tsar's family and especially the Empress were shocked at the grave news. Alexandra sent several telegrams to the "dear Friend" and to his family: "FILLED WITH INDIGNATION. SHARE YOUR GRIEF. PRAY WITH ALL HEART. ALEXANDRA." (June 30). "THOUGHTS, PRAYERS ARE AROUND. OUR GRIEF IS UNSPEAKABLE, HOPE FOR THE LORD'S MERCY. ALEXANDRA" (July 2).

In the late summer of 1915, Grigoriy introduced his wife and two daughters to Alexandra Feodorovna. The meeting took place in Vyrubova's house. According to Rasputin's reckoning, his relations, common Russian peasant-women, would create a positive impression on the Empress and help enhance his image as an exemplary family man. Moreover, it was important as it would help repair his reputation shaken by rumours of his indecent behaviour. It was a perfect move. The impression was most favourable. On August 27, 1915, Grand Duchess Olga wrote to her father: *"... Visited Ania, there we met the wife and daughters of Grigoriy Yefimovitch. He is so simple and nice ..."*

other actions highly inconsistent with piety. The Tsar doubted the authenticity of the report as he soon found out that one of the evenings when Rasputin had allegedly been implicated in a restaurant debauch was spent by Grigoriy in Tsarskoye Selo in a long talk with the Tsar and Tsarina, which lasted into the morning. Nikolai II was a pedant. He was annoyed at negligence and inexactitude in matters. He hated gossip and trusted only solid evidence – or his heart. The lack of cogency in the anti-Rasputin material resulted in a consistently hostile reaction against all denunciations in general.

But the Imperial House was wracked with anxiety. In Russia, the Tsar had always been far beyond the judgement of the crowd, nobody had ever dared to discuss his actions in public, even more severe was the veto on any mention of his private life. Now that all vetoes were removed, things went from bad to worse. Should gossip travel only in fashionable salons, that would be trouble enough, but the rumours proliferated even among common people and in the army. The prestige of power and the might of power have always been indissoluble. Why couldn't "Nicky" understand that? Could it be true that he had been mesmerised by Rasputin? Questions arose, but they would remain unanswered. Even his relatives could not explain the "unintelligible" behaviour of the Tsar.

The prospect of standing aloof, idly waiting for a denouement, did not satisfy society. The monarchy and the monarch were in danger, action was needed. The hysterical

refrain "Something has to be done" was hammered out, especially in aristocratic circles, by those whose destiny, origin and position were inseparable from the dynasty. The plans "to save His Majesty" were numerous, all of them hinged on a dream to eliminate Rasputin's influence. But as the old Russian saying goes, no sooner had the plans been hatched, than they died.

But one was to be successful. The scheme and its realization were associated with the name of Felix Felixovitch Yusupov, Count Sumarokov-Elston. He was descended from one of the most elite aristocratic families and was reputed to be an aesthete, music lover and an extreme Anglophile. Felix was born in 1887 and received a brilliant education, first at the classical gymnasium and then at Oxford University. For a long time he sought the hand of Grand Duchess Irina Alexandrovna, born in 1895, daughter of Grand Duchess Xenia, Nikolai II's sister and Grand Duke Alexander Mikhailovitch. She was the favourite niece and god-daughter of the Tsar and the favourite grand-daughter of Dowager Empress Maria Feodorovna. The assassination plot was hatched in November 1916. One of the accomplices was Nikolai II's favourite and cousin, Grand Duke Dmitriy Pavlovitch – the young man became an enthusiastic supporter of his friend's plot. The other was Vladimir Mitrofanovitch Purishkevich, an outstanding right-wing political figure, member of the State Duma for the Bessarabian province.

The realisation of the "action" was scheduled for the night of December 16 /17. Yusupov took Rasputin in an automobile to his palace on the Moika embankment, the ostensible purpose of the visit being Rasputin's meeting with Irina, Felix's wife. Here it was first attempted to poison the "hateful *moujik*" – without success – and then he was shot with a revolver. Rasputin's corpse was taken in the Grand Duke's automobile far from Yusupov's palace and thrown under the ice in the river. The assassins agreed to categorically deny all possible accusations. However, all their subterfuges were in vain. Already on December 17 the Tsarina wrote to her husband: *We are sitting together – can imagine our feelings and thoughts – our Friend has disappeared. Yesterday A.* [Vyrubova] *saw him and said Felix asked him to come in the night. A motor would fetch him to see Irina. A motor fetched him (military one) with 2 civilians and he went away . . . Cannot and won't believe He has been killed. God have mercy!"*

Great as the shock was for the Tsarina, she nevertheless preserved her self-control in public. The Minister of the Interior, Protopopov, who came to see her with a report, recollected: "Sad but calm, she expressed hope that the prayers of Grigoriy Yefimovitch, who had died as a martyr, would save their family from the danger of the hard time they were to live through".

As the Empress insisted, it was decided to bury Rasputin in Tsarskoye Selo, though many of the court were strongly opposed to it.

Fearing a possible public scandal, they had assumed that the coffin would be sent to Grigoriy's birthplace, the village of Pokrovskoye. Yet it was resolved that the body be buried in a quiet spot in Tsarskoye Selo, the site where Anna Vyrubova was building the Seraphim Asylum, under the altar of the future church. The secret burial ceremony took place on December 21. Nikolai II recorded in his diary: *"At 9 o'clock drove with all the family past the building of the photographer's* [studio] *and* [turned] *right to the field where we witnessed a gloomy picture: the coffin with the body of the never-to-be-forgotten Grigoriy, murdered on the night of December 17 by the bigots in Yusupov's house, had already been lowered into the grave. F.*[ather] *Al. Vasilyev read the burial service, after which we returned home. The weather was grey with 12 degrees of frost".*

Rasputin's murder could have no effect: the course of events was inexorable. The 74 days between Rasputin's death and Nikolai II's abdication witnessed the approach of the denouement. Everybody was apprehensive of the imminent catastrophe, nobody could prevent it. All that was left for the sovereign was to pray and trust in the Lord's mercy.

Rasputin's body was not to rest in peace long. On March 22, 1917, a group of revolutionary soldiers disinterred the coffin and burned the remains. The ashes were scattered to the wind.

(Above) 1913-1914. Alexandra Feodorovna and Dmitriy Pavlovitch in earlier years. The assassination of Rasputin caused friction among the Tsar's relatives. Reading the letter Nikolai wrote to Alexandra, during the arduous period of the war, one can understand the great spiritual support Rasputin provided for the Emperor of Russia. Here he mentioned the soothing words of their "friend": *"February 28, 1915 . . . This time I start with such a peace in my soul, that even astonishes me. Does it come from having talked with our Friend* [Rasputin] *last evening, or is it the paper that Buchanan gave me, Witte's death or perhaps a feeling of something good going to happen at the war . . . wish I could have stayed with you. I was so happy to have spent two days at home — perhaps you saw it, but I am stupid and never say what I feel . . . and never to sit quietly together and talk!*
In the afternoon I can never remain at home, such a yearning of getting into the fresh air — and so all the fresh hours pass and the old couple is very rarely together . . ."
(Left) Tsarskoye Selo. 1908. Rasputin with the Imperial family. Standing are Anastasia, Alexei, Olga ,Rasputin and Alexandra Feodorovna. Sitting are Maria, Tatiana and nurse Maria Vishnyakova.

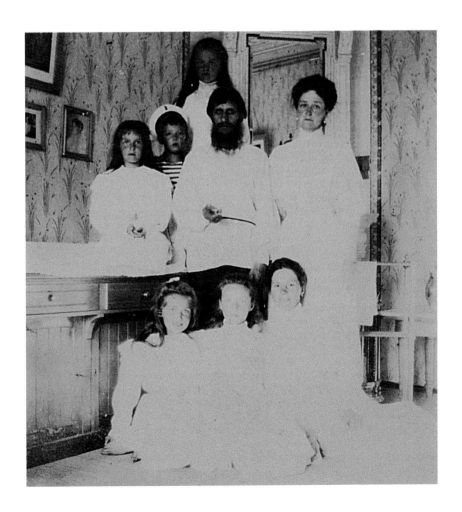

Chapter Ten

THREE HUNDRED
YEARS OF
THE HOUSE OF
ROMANOV

Vladimir Oustimenko
Zinaida Peregudova

A NEW DYNASTY RISING OUT OF THE TIMES OF TUMULT

Kostroma. The monument
erected in the memory of
Ivan Susanin.
(Facing page) Portrait of Nikolai
II by the famous Russian artist
Valentin Serov (1865-1911).

On December 11, 1912, on the first page of his lined exercise-book, the eight year-old boy, who was the heir to the Russian throne, started his records, his hand unsteadily forming letters: *"The Romanov House , Mikhail Feodorovitch. 32 years."* Tsar Mikhail Feodorovitch Romanov became the first tsar of a new dynasty, and his ascendancy to power in 1613 would put an end to the Time of Tumult, one of the most distressful periods in Russian history. The death of the cruel and powerful Tsar Ivan the Terrible resulted in the Russian crown being fought over by numerous claimants, all implacable rivals.

The ascendant *boyar* (aristocracy in old Russia) parties of the Godunovs, Shuiskiys, Vorotynskiys and Trubetskoys exhausted one another in political and military tussles, and they eventually abandoned the battlefield, leaving it to countless rogues who vied to be successors to the Russian throne. They were all replaced and superseded by the Poles. On August 27, 1610, Moscow swore allegiance to Wladislaw, son of Sigismund III of Poland. There seemed to be no power able to rescue this vast country from devastating internal dissension, popular disorder, plunder and violence.

From the abyss of chaos there emerged a great hope for the unity of the Russian people. It was given a tremendous impetus by the necessity of safeguarding the Orthodox faith from encroachment by the Roman Catholic Poles. Prince Dmitriy Pozharskiy and a citizen of Nizhniy Novgorod, Kozma Minin, stood at the head of the anti-Polish movement. It was not only a struggle against religious oppression that inspired the uprising – Pozharskiy dreamed of a Russian tsar who would rule out all discord and soothe internal dissension. That was the most cherished aspiration of the long suffering Russian people who had to bear the ravages of the Tumult. "Without a sovereign we will not survive for long, for there is no one to care for the realm and no one to provide for God's servants," the people of Rus (name of ancient Russia) used to say .

Hetman Gonsevski, having been defeated in the battle of Moscow, soon afterwards the Poles were driven away from Russia. Now the main problem had to be faced. In January 1613, the *Zemsky Sobor*, then Russia's national assembly, convened to elect the tsar. First and foremost, it was resolved not to elect any bogus foreigners. Then the contenders were to be nominated. The claims by Princes Shuiskiys, Trubetskoys and Vorotynskiys, the surviving descendants of the Rurik dynasty, which had been ruling Russia hitherto, were rejected in the fear that their candidacies may have led to a recurrence of the dreaded Time of Tumult.

After endless disputes suddenly the name of Misha (pet-name for Mikhail) Romanov came up. He was a sixteen year-old youngster who had lived together with his mother in the village of Domnino not far from Kostroma. The Romanovs had been separated and exiled by Tsar Boris Godunov. The baby Mikhail had lived with aunts for several years before the mother and son were allowed to live together. The nomination of the young *boyar* whose family had not been involved in the disreputable turmoil that had wracked Russia, won the sympathies of the entire assembly.

The eight year-old Cesarevitch Alexei recorded this event in his history exercises: *"Before he was elected to reign Mikhail Feodorovitch had lived with his mother in the village of Domnino. At that time a band of Poles was scouring about the countryside. They wanted to ruin Mikhail. The Poles wanted to get to the village, but they did not know the way. There was a thick forest around. So they demanded that the village elder show them the way. Ivan Susanin saw what they were after. He sent his son-in-law Sabinin to Domnino to warn Sister Martha of the danger. And he himself led the Poles through the forest. He brought them to a thicket in the very heart of the forest so that it was impossible to find a way out. Susanin stopped and said: 'Nobody will get out of here.' So the Poles sabred him to death . . . but they, too, all perished."*

Meanwhile Sister Martha and her son moved to the Ipatyev monastery near Kostroma, where they would find refuge. In March 1613 a deputation arrived "to notify them of the election and to submit a humble petition to Mikhail Feodorovitch and his mother, Sister Martha." It was not an easy task to persuade the young boy to accept the proposal. Both Sister Martha and her son were against it, and "the youngster responded to the deputies with great ire and tears". Fearing for the future of her son, Martha reproved the deputies that in a time when "a chain of treasons around the throne" were being com-

(Above) View of the Ipatyev Monastery in Kostroma, built in the 16th – 18th centuries. The Ipatyev Monastery (of St. Hypatius and St. Trinity) was founded about 1330 and it was there that the first Romanov Tsar, Mikhail Feodorovitch and his mother took refuge to escape from the Poles.
(Facing page) Portrait of Her Majesty Empress Alexandra Feodorovna painted by Pyotr Sokolov (1821-1899).

(Above) Moscow, 1913. View of the Winter Palace. The Tercentenary celebrations began on February 21, 1913 from the Winter Palace. A national festival all over Russia, at 8 a.m., a 21-gun salute from the Towers of the Fortress of Sts. Peter and Paul's heralded the beginning of the celebrations. Facing page: (top) Aboard the steamer *Mezhen*. With the officers are Anastasia, Maria, Olga, Tatiana and, sitting on the chair, Alexei. The Tsar's family left Nizhniy Novgorod on May 18 on the way to Kostroma. An historic and ancient city in Russia, Kostroma dates back to the 12th century, when it was the centre of an apanage principality which joined the Moscovite estate in the 13th century. Its historical monuments, monasteries, cathedrals and churches refer to the 16th-17th centuries. The Royal children look very happy. Their enthusiasm during this great celebration was shared with the Russian people in every town and "kremlin" they visited. (Bottom) May 19, 1913. The view of Kostroma from the steamer.

mitted, it was "difficult even for a born sovereign to rule in the Muscovite State". But the deputies assured her that the people of the Muscovite State had been "punished" and had "come to a union". After much persuasion, Mikhail relented, and Sister Martha blessed him with the icon of Our Lady of Feodor. Ever since, the icon was considered patrimonial, and in 1912 Nikolai II would erect a cathedral dedicated to the icon in Tsarskoye Selo, near the Alexander Palace. Inside the cathedral there was a "grotto chapel" where Tsarina Alexandra Feodorovna used to pray in private.

In 1613, within the walls of the Ipatyev monastery, the reign of the Romanov dynasty began and was to last for three centuries. The dreadful Tumult was over, and gradually, order was established and consolidated. It took an incredible effort for Russia to overcome the grim times which had seemed insurmountable, and now the realm was striving towards grandeur. There were many more great challenges to be met and glorious pursuits to accomplish. That was what this little boy with big sad eyes may have been thinking about, while he painstakingly traced every letter in the names of his ancestors, the Russian monarchs.

"The 15th tsar of the Romanov dynasty, Nikolai Pavlovitch, reigned for 30 years; Alexander II Nikolayevitch, 26 years; and Alexander III Alexandrovitch, 13 years." On December 21, 1912, this exercise in history would be concluded with the record: *"XVIII. Daddy. Nikolai II Alexandrovitch."* And the tutor, Petrov, would give his pupil a mark: "Good". The Cesarevitch's next exercise was the story of Tsar Mikhail Feodorovitch's accession to the throne . . .

The celebrations of the Tercentenary of the Romanov House were coming and Russia was preparing for the festivities while Cesarevitch Alexei was assiduously learning the history of his forefathers. He was to continue the succession of the Russian monarchs and become the 19th Tsar. But the boy was most unlikely to have been thinking about that. "Dear Daddy" would be governing Russia for many years to come. Even in a nightmare, he

(Top) May 19, 1913. The Volga Embankment in Kostroma. The citizens came out to welcome the Tsar and his family. (Insets) From left to right the Map "Plan of Place" where the feat of Ivanin Susanin was accomplished. Water colour from the album dedicated to Ivan Susanin by Mihai Zichi: "Death of Ivan Susanin". Cover of the album dedicated to Ivan Susanin's exploit as he gave his life for the first Romanov Tsar. The album features the village of Domnino where Susanin lived and the Monastery near Kostroma.
Facing page: (Top) Nikolai II, Maria, Anastasia, Olga and Tatiana meeting the people in Kostroma. (Bottom) The Royal Family leaving the Cathedral of the Ipatyev Cloister. May 1913.

could not have dreamt of the fatal events of a July night in 1918.

The festivities began on Thursday, February 21, 1913, a day of celebrations all over Russia. At 8 a.m., a 21-gun salute from the towers of the Fortress of Sts. Peter and Paul heralded the beginning of the celebrations. The weather favoured the occasion; the day was fine and sunny. The services in the churches were followed by the declaration of the Manifesto issued by His Imperial Majesty to mark the Tercentenary of the Romanov House. The closing phrases of the Manifesto appealed to the Lord: *"May the Lord's benediction upon us and our dear subjects not grow scantier than it is now. May our Lord the Omnipotent, strengthen and glorify the Russian Land and grant us strength to hold high and steady the glorious banner of our Fatherland".*

The Imperial procession to the Cathedral of Our Lady of Kazan was a lavish, picturesque sight. Ahead of the procession rode the *Sotnia* (Cossack squadron) of His Imperial Majesty's Own Escort, the horsemen dressed in red Circassian coats. Behind them, in an open carriage, travelled His Majesty the Tsar with the Heir Cesarevitch, Grand Duke Alexei Nikolayevitch seated next to him. Alongside rode the Escort Commander, Prince Trubetskoi. The Dowager Empress and the Tsarina travelled in a luxurious carriage with a high coach-box, drawn by four white horses in traditional Russian harness, a postilion and Chamber Cossacks standing on the footboard. The four Grand Duchesses came in

a *barouche* drawn by a pair of horses. Another Cossack *Sotnia* brought up the rear of the procession. The noise in the streets was unabating – coach wheels rumbled, horses' hoofs clattered, banners dipped and fluttered, music played, church bells peeled and people exultantly cheered their Tsar.

The service in the Cathedral of Our Lady of Kazan was held at midday. Anna Vyrubova remembered that the cathedral was jammed with courtiers and invited guests. *"I saw from a distance the kneeling Tsar and the Heir who would time and again look at something above. Later they told me that they were watching the doves hovering in the dome"*.

Later that day there was a great reception in the Winter Palace. The ladies were wearing traditional Russian gowns. *"Though she was very tired"*, recollected Vyrubova, *"Her Majesty looked amazingly beautiful in her blue velvet Russian gown, wearing a tall kokoshnik* [a traditional tiara-shaped headdress for married women in old Russia] *and a veil beaded with pearls and diamonds. There was a pale blue ribbon of the Order of St. Andrew across her breast, and the Grand Duchesses were wearing the Order of St. Catherine on a scarlet ribbon"*. The ball was magnificent and crowded. The following evening Their Imperial Majesties and Her Imperial Highness Olga Nikolayevna graced the Mariinskiy Theatre's opera performance of Glinka's *A Life for the Tsar* with their presence. The opulence of the evening dresses and the pageantry of the theatre decorations were dazzling. Among those present were the Emir of Bokhara and the Khan of Khiva, wearing their national costumes, and accompanied by their resplendent entourages. Starring in the performance were the leading ballerinas Pavlova, Preobrazhenskaya, Kschessinska and

Festivities in Kostroma. May 20, 1913. (Top) Everywhere the Imperial Family went, they were welcomed by a huge crowd. The turmoil which was to follow, the war and the revolution, could not be foreseen in these very rewarding moments. (Inset) Alexandra Feodorovna and Cesarevitch Alexei in the carriage.

Kostroma, May 19. (Above) The Tsar visited the officers' assembly and the Church of Christ's Resurrection and, seen here, the new building of the Red Cross community and the local exhibition.

(Left) May 21. The Steamer *Mezhen*, with the Imperial family on board, leaving Kostroma on the way to Yaroslavl. A large crowd of people are waving to the Imperial Family. Nikolai described their departure from Kostroma in his diary, May 20: *"The people standing on the bank formed a dense wall, some even up to their knees in the water . . ."* From Yaroslavl they took a train for the next part of their itinerary to the old Russian towns of Rostov the Great, Petrosk, Pereyaslavl— Zalesskiy and Sergiev Posad, then to Moscow for four days of celebrations. They finally went to Tsarskoye Selo on May 28.

Gerdt, singers Nezhdanova, Zbruyeva, Kostorski, Yershov, Sobinov and Figner. Napravnik conducted the orchestra.

The four days of celebrations in St. Petersburg were a dense schedule of receptions, meetings and balls. Summing up his impressions, Nikolai II wrote in his diary: *"Thank Lord God who shed his grace upon Russia and us all so that we could decently and joyously celebrate the days of the tercentenary of the Romanov's accession".*

The Easter of 1913 saw the continuation of the celebrations. On May 15, 1913, the Imperial Family started on a tour of old Russian towns to trace the route taken by the first Romanov Tsar three centuries before. The family visited Vladimir and Suzdal (where they went to see the burial place of Prince Dmitriy Pozharskiy in the Spasso-Yefimovsky monastery). On May 16, Nikolai admitted in his diary: *"With delight and interest* [I] *inspected the wonderful treasures kept in the vestries, and the churches of ancient Russian architecture. On our way there and back people came out from villages with icons.* [I] *was not tired at all. The impressions were so strong and good."* The next stops on their pilgrimage were Bogolyubovo and the town of Nizhniy Novgorod, where they visited the burial place of Kozma Minin, the other hero of the anti-Polish libera-

(Above) Moscow. In front of the Upper Shopping Centre (known at present as GUM — Moscow's main supermarket built in 1893, on the eastern edge of Red Square), a canopy was erected during the Tercentenary celebrations. (Left) May 22. After leaving Kostroma, on the way to Moscow, they stopped in Rostov the Great to visit the Assumption Cathedral. Facing page: (Top) Moscow, Kremlin: Alexandra and Nikolai parading, followed by their children. (Inset) Pilgrimage of Russian Towns. A photograph kept in the Family's album. In the top right corner is written "Pereyaslavl–Zalisskiy".

(Above) Moscow, May 24, 1913. The Triumphal Gates: Imperial Ceremonial entry. The first Triumphal Gates were made of wood and erected at Tverskaya Zastava (Post) in 1814 to greet the victorious Russian troops returning from France after the Napoleonic campaign. In 1827-1834 the wooden construction was replaced by a monument of stone by architect Osip Bovet. The Gates were adorned with sculptures by Vitali & Timofeyev. In keeping with Stalin's reconstruction plans for Moscow, the Gates were dismantled and restored in 1966 in Kutuzovskiy Prospect, far from the place where they used to stand. Facing page: (top) Moscow, Kremlin. The Tsar, the Tsarina and in front, held by a Cossack, Cesarevitch Alexei. (Below) Moscow. Another day of celebrations and Alexei, preceded by the military and the members of the Church, carried by a robust and strong Cossack.

tion movement. The Tsar was present at the ceremony of laying the foundation for the monument to Minin and Pozharskiy. All along the route of the Imperial Family's journey, people of all classes came out with bread and salt, the traditional Russian welcome, to salute their Tsar.

In Nizhniy Novgorod the Romanovs boarded the steamer *Mezhen* to sail down the Volga river. From the deck the passengers were to see a marvellous sight – the town and steamers on the river were brightly illuminated, and in the fields bonfires blazed. Music was playing constantly, and shouts of "hurrah" resounded from the banks of the river. As the steamer put out, the church bells rang out, and a polyphonic chorus broke spontaneously into the Russian folk song, "Down the Mother Volga river."

On May 19, they reached Kostroma, the memorial place of the Romanovs. The streets were crowded with people and Archbishop Tikhon welcomed the Imperial Family with the renowned icon of Our Lady of Feodor. The days were crowded with meeting delegations and sightseeing: they visited cathedrals, the Romanov chambers in the Ipatyev monastery, and the New Romanov Museum. One of the ceremonies was dedicated to laying the foundation of the Romanov House Memorial. Then they sailed to Yaroslavl, where they took a train for the next part of their itinerary – the old Russian towns of Rostov the Great, Pereyaslavl–Zalesskiy and Sergiev Posad, the seat of the Troitse-Sergievskaya Lavra (of St. Sergius and St. Trinity), the Orthodox monastery of the highest rank.

The celebrations came to a climax in Moscow, where the Tsar's train arrived at the Alexander Station on May 24. Moscow looked particularly magnificent in those days.

1913. Tercentenary Celebrations in Moscow. (Top) Yelizaveta Feodorovna dressed in her monastic clothes with her nieces in the carriage. Next to her is Olga, sitting across are Tatiana, far right, Anastasia in the middle, next to her is Maria. (Inset) On May 26, for the celebration of the Dynasty of the Romanovs, the Tsar paid a visit to the Novospasskiy Monastery; Ella's community. After the liturgy they went down to the Crypt to bow to the tomb of their ancestors.

"People's greetings in the streets were reminiscent of the Coronation ceremonial entries", Nikolai II noted in his diary. The church bells were booming as they had three centuries before when Mikhail Feodorovitch entered the capital. One side of the route was lined by troops, glamorous in their full dress uniforms, the other by crowds of cheering people. The head of the procession was the Cossack *Sotnia* of His Imperial Majesty's Own Escort; then, astride on a golden chestnut horse, rode the Tsar, followed by the brilliant Court entourage. The Tsarina and the Heir Cesarevitch travelled in a carriage, and the Grand Duchesses came in an open *barouche.* The Cesarevitch was sick in those days and whenever the family had to walk, a robust, strong Cossack carried the boy in his arms.

The terse entries in Nikolai II's diary were a minutely detailed report of the crowded schedule of receptions, ceremonial meals, services, worship of the relics and sightseeing. On the last day of the celebrations in Moscow, Monday, May 27, the exhausted, yet very happy Tsar admitted in his diary: *"Finally* [I] *sat on my feet because of tiredness."*

The fortnight of the celebratory journey was over. Russia seemed to have recovered after the upheavals of 1905-1907, and it looked as though the Romanov dynasty was to reign for centuries. But Fate decreed otherwise. Like a mortally sick patient who sometimes seems revived for a short period before he relapses into agony, the feasting empire irretrievably approached its collapse. The Dynasty would manage to make only five more steps towards their quadricentenary and the progress would be tragically cut short in the dirty basement of the Ipatyev house in Yekaterinburg . . . What a macabre coincidence of the names: the Ipatyev monastery saw the birth of the Romanov dynasty and the Ipatyev house saw its annihilation.

256

(Above) Moscow, the Kremlin. After visiting the "Hall of Facets", as always, the Tsar described the event in his diary: *"May 25, 1913. A lovely day with a breeze. The entry began at 11. In St. George's Hall* [in the Kremlin], *Samarin presented* [me] *with a coffer and the address on behalf of all the nobility. The Red Porch was a beautiful sight with a sea of heads. The liturgy was served at the Assumption Cathedral. Then we kissed the relics and made our first worship of St. Ermogen's tomb. . . . The whole family lunched together. At 3 p.m.* [I] *went to the Chudov Monastery with my daughters where, in the Patriarch's Sacristy, we saw the most interesting collection of church things from the last three centuries . . ."* (Left) Moscow, May 26. Visiting the Novospasskiy Monastery is Victoria Melita, with Alexander Mikhailovitch behind her. The Tercentenary was a significant event in the life of the entire Imperial Family. The only member of the family who was denied participation in the celebrations was Nikolai's only surviving brother Grand Duke Mikhail Alexandrovitch, who had been dismissed from his office and forbidden to return to Russia after having married the twice divorced Madame Wulfert in 1912.

257

(Above and right) May 20, Kostroma. Laying the first stone for the monument commemorating the Tercentenary of the Romanov Dynasty. Nikolai noted in his diary: *". . . each of us laid a stone with our names"*, then Tsarina Alexandra visited the Bogoyavlenskiy nunnery with the children.

Facing page: (top) The Imperial Family visited the Assumption Cathedral (a monument of old Russian architecture, it was built in 1160 and reconstructed in 1189) in the old Russian Town of Vladimir. Situated on the river Klyazma, it was founded by Prince Vladimir the Monomakh in 1108.

(Bottom) The Tsar went to the Governor's House where he received local officials, foremen and peasant representatives of volosts (small rural districts). In the background, wearing dark tunics and crosses on chains, the foremen and the peasants watched the Tsar as he sampled the food intended for them.

(Above) The People's House where Nikolai went on the last day of the winter celebrations of the Tercentenary of the Romanov House on February 24. He met students of various educational institutions.

(Left) The Icon of Our Lady of Feodor. The original Icon is kept in the Ipatyev Monastery in Kostroma. When, in 1912, a cathedral dedicated to this Icon was built in Tsarskoye Selo, a replica of the Icon was specially made for it.

Facing page: (Top) Tsarskoye Selo. The Cathedral of Our Lady of Feodor. To the right of the photograph is the seat for the Tsar's family.

(Bottom) The cover of the menu of the ceremonial dinner in Kostroma, May 20, 1913, commemorating the Tercentenary of the Romanov dynasty, designed by Yeguzhinskiy, featuring the first Tsar Mikhail Romanov and Nikolai II and bearing the dates 1613 and 1913.

261

THE WAR THAT NOBODY WANTED AND EVERYBODY FEARED

A portrait of Nikolai and Alexandra signed and dated:"Mama, & Papa. 1917".

(Facing page) Emperor Nikolai II and Grand Duke Nikolai Nikolayevitch (1856-1929). During World War I, from July 1914 until August 23, 1915, the Grand Duke was Supreme Commander-in-Chief. After his dismissal, he went to the Caucasus as Governor General as well as becoming Commander-in-Chief of the Caucasian Front. Soon after, Nikolai II assumed the responsibility of Supreme Commander-in-Chief and he appointed the brilliant General Alexeyev as Chief of Staff. During the "abdication" crisis both Grand Duke Nikolai Nikolayevitch and General Alexeyev felt the only way to prevent bloodshed in Russia was for the Tsar to abdicate. Grand Duke Nikolai stayed in the Crimea until 1919, when he left Russia with the Dowager Empress Maria Feodorovna and settled in France where he died in 1929. He was buried with the full military honour due to an Allied Army Commander-in-Chief.

ars come in all shapes and sizes – just and ignoble; hot and cold; prolonged attrition and *blitzkrieg;* fought over vast expanses and local conflicts waged from village to village and town to town; wars of aggression and wars of liberation. Wars can also be absurd – which was the case for the war which broke out on July 15, 1914, when the mighty Austria-Hungary declared war upon the small state of Serbia in a prologue to what became the First World War. In the fire of that savage slaughter the old, great monarchies of the Romanovs, Habsburgs and Hohenzollerns died. Having long posed as protector of the Slavs, Russia started mobilisation on July 17. From this moment on, the war became a deadly clash of imperial ambitions. The course of events had been inexorable and rumours had circulated since spring. In June, after the assassination of the heir to the Austrian throne, Archduke Franz Ferdinand, war was imminent.

Russia became entangled in a war which nobody wanted and which everybody had feared. Its aims were abstract, intelligible only to a very narrow circle, and the appeals to vindicate the Empire's prestige, to annex the straits in the Black Sea and to erect an orthodox cross upon St. Sophia's Cathedral in Constantinople could not inspire enthusiasm in the people. The majority of Russia's population did not have the slightest idea where

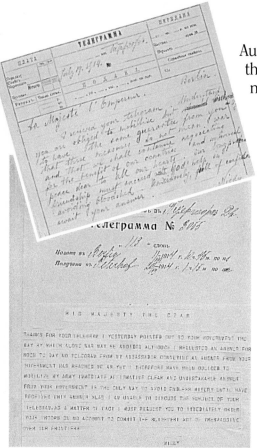

Austria-Hungary or Germany were situated and why the Russians had to fight them. The Russian peasant knew nothing about the Dardanelles and he would never understand why he had to go to war and risk his life for them.

Early in July 1914, as usual at this time of the year, the Tsar and his family went on a voyage to the Finnish fiords on board the imperial yacht *Standard*. The weather was hot, and stifling heat was interspersed with pouring rain. Nikolai II was not to admire the picturesque landscape and relax with the serene joys of family life: since the end of June one piece of bad news had followed another. The assassination of the Austrian Archduke – whom Nikolai and Alix had known very well – and the attempt upon the life of "dear Grigoriy", disrupted the mental equilibrium of the Imperial couple, but very soon they learned that God had listened to their prayers and their friend's life was out of danger. In the international arena, however, the perilous clouds became quite dense. The Russian autocrat was indignant at the appalling deed in Sarajevo. It was obvious that the assassination was the result of a plot, and its threads extended to Belgrade, the capital of the friendly Serbia. Nevertheless, the Tsar would never have the friendly Slav state defeated and annexed. The Russian Foreign Ministry's feverish work and Nikolai II's intensive private correspondence with Kaiser Wilhelm (Willy) during the three weeks immediately after the assassination were futile. No compromise was achieved.

Nikolai II did not wish for war. The bitter experience of the Russo-Japanese campaign made it absolutely clear that any armed conflict would inevitably lead to suffering, deprivation and death on a very large scale. In his heart of hearts, he was opposed to violence, and whenever he was brought to face it, he would painfully regret it.

The Tsar was also apprehensive of the fact that any military failure was fraught with the peril of a revolutionary outburst and a recurrence of the nightmare that had haunted them in 1905-1906. He knew very well that there were too many obstacles in the way of a speedy, victorious military campaign: the recently initiated modernisation of the Russian army had just begun to have effect. The technical equipment and ammunition supplies of Russia were inadequate compared to those of Germany. Of all those facts, Nikolai was perfectly aware. But to commit a betrayal, letting the friendly country be torn to pieces and thus losing his prestige both in Russia and throughout the world, such a decision was out of the question. The Tsar deemed it his duty to rise to protect the Slavs and Russia, and his duties as a sovereign were sacred to him. He would not shrink from them. Circumstances decreed that he choose war, and he did.

Recounting a private conversation with the Tsar, Grand Duke Konstantin Konstantinovitch described in his diary the events which preceded the war: "*On July 19, the day of St. Seraphim, who is especially revered by His Majesty, on his way to a night-service, he learned from Count Fredericks, with whom for promptness Sazonov [Minister of Foreign Affairs] had spoken, that Pourtalès [the German Ambassador] had visited him [Sazonov] with Germany's declaration of war upon Russia. Pourtalès handed over to Sazonov a paper which contained both answers of the German government, for the event of Russia's favourable and unfavourable answer concerning the cancellation of mobilisation. I do not know what moved the Ambassador, confusion or distraction. So, war was declared upon us. His Majesty summoned the British Ambassador and worked with him from 11 p.m. till 1 a.m. His Majesty can quite easily, as he explained to me, write in English, but they may have encountered some technical terms of which he was not sure. Buchanan is a sluggish brain and a slowcoach. Together with him His Majesty drew up the longest telegram to the British King. Tired, soon after 1 a.m. he went to have a cup of tea with the Empress who was waiting for him, then he undressed, took a bath and went to the bedchamber. He was about to open the door when Teteryatnikov, the valet, overtook him with a telegram. It was from Kaiser Wilhelm; again (having already declared war against us) he appealed to His Majesty's peace-loving sentiments imploring him to stop*

(Top) Handwritten telegram from Nikolai II to Wilhelm: "Sa Majesté l' Empereur. Berlin. I received your telegram. Understand you are obliged to mobilise but wish to have the same guarantee from you as I gave you, that these measures do not mean war and that we shall continue negotiating for the benefit of our country and universal peace dear to all our hearts. Our long tried friendship must succeed, with God's help, in avoiding bloodshed: anxiously, full of confidence await your answer. Nicky." July 19, 1914.
(Above) Kaiser Wilhelm's answer to Nikolai's telegram: "Peterhof. His Majesty the Czar. Thanks for your telegram. Yesterday pointed out to your Government the way by which alone war may be avoided. Although I requested an answer for noon today, no telegram from my Ambassador conveying an answer from your Government has reached me as yet. Therefore have been obliged to mobilize my Army. Immediate, affirmative, clear and unmistakable answer from your Government is the only way to avoid endless misery. Until [I] have received this answer, alas, I am unable to discuss the subject of your telegram, as a matter of fact, I must request you to immediately order your troops on no account to commit the slightest act of trespassing over our frontiers. Willy." August 1, 1914.

(Above) 1915. Alexei on the train to Headquarters. The education of the Cesarevitch was taken care of even when he went to the Headquarters to stay with his father.
Seen here with Alexei on the way from Stavka to Mogilyov are his tutors, Pierre Gilliard, Vladimir Voyeikov, Sidney Gibbs, Pyotr Petrov.
Vladimir Voyeikov was Count Fredericks' son-in-law and he held the post of Palace Superintendent. He was not a tutor but taught mathematics to the Cesarevitch, while the boy was staying in the Stavka. Alexei followed his father during inspections and reviews, and sometimes he had to spend several hours on his feet, standing or walking. It was not very easy for the boy, but he never complained. (Left) Nikolai II and Alexei at army Headquarters. They had taken a stroll and were taking a rest in a trench.

Добрании 4ᵉ сотни на Ставку. 1916г.

(Above) Tsarskoye Selo, 1916. Emperor Nikolai and Alexei receiving the report from the Commander of Cossack sotnia (squadron) 4. It was a painful decision for Alexandra Feodorovna to be separated from her "Sunlight" and "Sunbeam" as Alexei spent time with his father at the Stavka, but she justly maintained that the presence of the Cesarevitch by Nikolai's side would strengthen her husband's spirit and build up the people's sympathy to their sovereigns, and at the same time, dispel the spiteful rumours of the Heir's handicaps. She knew that nobody could help admiring the angelic features of her son's face, his good humour and buoyancy. Rasputin also encouraged the Tsarina in this opinion. (Right) May 1916. The Tsar's family arriving at the Headquarters. Alexandra had the powers to receive reports and act on matters of state on behalf of her husband when he was away at the front. Nevertheless the family tried to be reunited as often as possible, even for a short period. In those days, Alexandra and the children were a great comfort to Nikolai, who felt so isolated with the burden of war and, as his nature commanded, he felt that ultimately he, alone, was responsible for the great tragedy that had befallen the Russian people.

military actions. There was to be no reply ..."

The Kaiser's perfidy being notorious, Nikolai did not trust a single word. The die was cast; the vast empire was put on a war footing; the Tsar appointed the supreme military leadership and Grand Duke Nikolai Nikolayevitch assumed the responsibilities of Commander-in-Chief; General Yanushkevitch, Professor of the Academy of the General Staff who had acted as Chief of Staff before the war, was confirmed in his office. Though His Majesty did not interfere with commanding the troops directly, he nevertheless regularly visited the *Stavka* (Headquarters) then located in Baranovichi and inspected the troops.

The military campaign opened with Russia's brilliant offensive in East Prussia. But inadequate preparation combined with incompetent leadership turned early success into defeat. His Majesty took the failure very hard; it was then, he would admit later, that he "for the first time felt his old heart". The actions on the South-Western front were much more successful. The Russian Army dealt the Austro-Hungarians a series of crushing blows; the Austrians surrendered such important citadels as Lvov, Galich, Przemysl. The advanced Russian units broke off to the western frontiers of Austrian Poland. This brilliant military operation, renowned as the Great Galician battle, might have been decisive both for Russia and its allies. But the desperate resistance of the German soldiers, abetted by the sad inefficiency of services in the Russian rear and, particularly, the "munition famine" undermined prospects for a speedy victory. The wheel of fortune turned; the Russian troops were forced to retreat all along the front line; the Tsar had to shuttle from Tsarskoye Selo to Baranovichi. One of these visits, in May 1915, resulted in Grand Duke Nikolai Nikolayevitch's request "to replace him with a more competent person".

The situation at the front took a dramatic turn for Russia. By September 1915 about four million men had been lost, wounded or taken prisoner. The gravity of the situation was exacerbated by the disagreements between the Council of Ministers and the Headquarters, the Commander-in-Chief constantly attempting to intervene in the civilian government of the country. Nikolai II undertook drastic measures which, though they were misunderstood by many of his subjects, saved Russia from utter defeat. On August 23, 1915, the Tsar issued the edict: *"This day I assume command over all land and navy forces engaged in the theatre of war operations. With firm trust in God's help and unshakable confidence of final victory, we shall do our sacred duty of defence of our Motherland to the end, and we shall never have the Russian Land disgraced".*

Nikolai II had always been convinced that in times of military trials his place was at the battlefield. In September 1904, at the height of the Russo-Japanese war, the Tsar wrote from St. Petersburg to his mother, who was staying in Denmark: *"My conscience is often troubled by my staying here instead of sharing the dangers and privations of the army. I asked Uncle Alexei yesterday what he thought about it: he thinks my presence with the army in this war is not necessary – still, to stay behind in times like these is very upsetting".* Then, he was not to fulfil his intention. Now, in this war, when the peril was even more desperate, he could act as his heart urged him.

The government and the State Duma were perturbed. The ministers predicted catastrophe for Russia, but the Tsar stood firm in his decision. His determination provoked the Council of Ministers to plead in a letter trying to dissuade the Tsar from his decision. Only Prime Minister Goremykin and Minister of Justice Kokovtsov did not sign the letter. "I'm a man of the old school, and for me His Majesty's edict is Law. The situation at the front being catastrophic, His Majesty deems it sacred duty of the Russian Tsar to be with the troops, and either he shall win together with them, or he shall perish", Goremykin reproved his colleagues.

The talented General Alexeyev was appointed Chief of Staff at the Headquarters of the Supreme Commander-in-Chief, which was relocated to Mogilyov. After his dismissal, Grand Duke Nikolai Nikolayevitch went to the Caucasus where he was to assume the

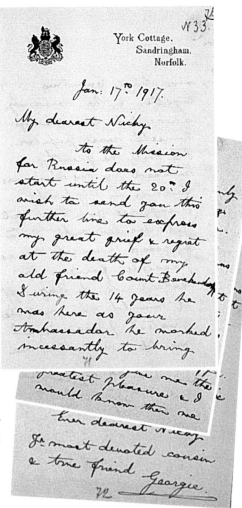

(Above) A letter from George V to Nikolai II: York Cottage. Sandrigham. Norfolk. "Jan. 17 1917. My dearest Nicky, As the Mission for Russia does not start until the 20th I wish to send you this further line to express my greatest grief & regret at the death of my old friend Count Benckendorf. During the 14 years he was here as your Ambassador he worked incessantly to bring our two Countries together & he certainly succeeded in making himself most popular. He will be greatly missed by his numerous friends in Britain. I suppose you have not yet decided who is to succeed him, if it was possible for you to select U. de Sazonoff it would give me the greatest pleasure & I would know that we had such a real friend who would do everything to maintain and increase the most friendly relation which so happily exists now between Russian and England. I hope you do not mind my having suggested him. With best love to Alix. Ever dearest Nicky, yr. most devoted cousin and true friend. Georgie"
In the darkest days of 1917-1918 Nikolai II must have anguished over why no help was coming from the British King, "his devoted cousin and true friend".

responsibilities of Governor-General, as well as becoming Commander-in-Chief of the Caucasian Front. The co-operation of the 47 year-old Tsar and the newly-appointed Chief of Staff, one of the most gifted officers of the Russian Army, restored Russia's strategic situation. By the summer of 1916, the Russian army was 240 divisions strong as against the 140 divisions at the beginning of the war. The proper organization of the rear services meant sufficient ammunition and food supplies. The preparations were under way for decisive battles against Germany in the spring of 1917. Surveying the scene at the close of 1916, Winston Churchill was to write: *"We may measure the strength of the Russian Empire by the battering it had endured, by the disasters it had survived, by the inexhaustible forces it had developed, and by the recovery it had made"*.

Soon after Nikolai II had assumed the responsibilities of the Supreme Commander-in-Chief; his son, Cesarevitch Alexei, who had just turned eleven, arrived at the Headquarters, and stayed several months with his father. Alexandra Feodorovna had brought herself to allow him this journey for she knew what substantial moral support for the Tsar the presence of his beloved son would be. The Heir was delirious with pride and delight. He would follow his father everywhere, thus learning to perceive the severe truth of war experience.

In Mogilyov the Cesarevitch had two friends – cadets Vasya Agayev and Zhenya Makarov – and a team of boy-soldiers to have drills and play with. The team was made up of local children, from whom he would pick up a lot of expressions which may have shocked the court. But the parents did not seem to mind . . .

In October 1915, Alexei was awarded the Medal of St. George, and in May 1916, he was promoted to corporal, and so he took his first step up in his military career. On September 30, 1916, the Cesarevitch was awarded the Serbian Gold Medal which, however, he received with embarrassment. As he commented to his mother: *"My darling Mama. Yesterday the Serbian general Yurishich, the Ambassador and the suite stayed with us for dinner. They presented Papa with the Serbian Military Cross, and I was given a gold medal with the inscription 'For Bravery'. I deserved it in my battles with the tutors"*. Colonel Nikolai Alexandrovitch Romanov and corporal Alexei Nikolayevitch Romanov, the Tsar and the Cesarevitch, father and son, marched together, measuring long miles of soldiers' roads, both possessed by an ardent wish for an end to the tremendous insanity of war.

The front having become a trial and a second home for the men, the infirmary became a second home for the Tsarina and her daughters. Her Majesty organized an evacuation centre in Tsarskoye Selo of about eighty-five infirmaries in Peterhof, Pavlovsk, Luga and in Tsarskoye Selo itself. Alexandra Feodorovna and the elder girls, Olga and Tatiana, attended special courses and received the red cross and war time nursing certificates. They got up early; they went to bed late, sometimes long after midnight. The two younger girls, Grand Duchesses Maria and Anastasia, were also engaged in caring for wounded and invalid soldiers. "Like all surgery nurses, Her Majesty handed over sterilized instruments, cotton wool and bandages, she took away the amputated limbs, dressed gangrenous wounds, and

(Above) Tsarskoye Selo, December 31, 1915. Letter from Olga to her father: "My warmest wishes to you for the New Year. God keep you. We are going to the New Year party at the local military infirmary. The weather is cold and I've got a cold. As usual we visited the infirmary in the morning. Everything is all right there. Do you recognize the paper you and Mama gave me as the New Year present? Now I finish. Again and again I wish you, my dear Papa, all the happiness. I love you so, I hold you tight in my arms. Yours Yelisavetgradets. I send my regards to Silayev and Mordinov." Olga was patroness of the 3rd Yelisavetgradsky Hussar Regiment and signed the letters with her regimental name.

(Above) Mogilyov. The winter of 1916. Alexandra Feodorovna and the four Grand Duchesses have just left the Imperial train. They have come to visit the Tsar. Ladies were not allowed to come to the Stavka, therefore the Tsarina and the girls were allowed to stay there just for a short time and their accommodation had to be on the Imperial train. Nikolai wrote a letter to his mother on July 1914, explaining the awkward situation, when he refused to receive the lady who had brought Maria Feodorovna's letter to him: " *I did not receive the lady because I never receive ladies. I sent Valya* [nick name of Prince Vasily Alexandrovitch, the Hof-Marshal, member of the Emperor's suite] *Dolgorukov to the station to explain to her the reason for my refusal.*"

(Left) 1914. Baranovichi railway Station. The officers and the soldiers, waiting to embark for the front. In the background, behind a wagon, in the middle, is a row of men looking on, waiting to be caught by the photographer's lens.

269

never showed the slightest aversion for ordinary work, staunchly enduring the odours and heinous sights of a military hospital in war-time", recollected Anna Vyrubova.

In her letters to Nikolai, Alexandra wrote about the wounded she took care of, about their horrific mutilations and sufferings. She took their pain close to her heart: "... *This morning we were present (I helped as always giving the instruments and Olga threaded needles) at our first big amputation (whole arm was cut off). Then we all had dressings (in our small hospital), very serious ones in the big hospital. I had wretched fellows with awful wounds ... scarcely a 'man' any more, so shot to pieces, perhaps it must be cut off as it's so black, but [we] hope to save it – terrible to look at, I washed and cleaned and painted with iodine and smeared with vaseline, and bandaged all up – it went quite well – and I feel happier to do the things gently myself under the guidance of a d.[octor]. I did three such ... One's heart bleeds for them, I won't describe any more details as it's so sad, but being a wife and mother I feel for them quite particularly ..."* (November 20, 1914).

A series of letters traced her very special attachment to a young soldier, still a boy, who, as she wrote, *"kept begging for me"*, and was *"gradually getting worse"*. When he died, the Tsarina was overcome with grief: *"I came home with my tears. The elder sister cannot either realize it ... Never did he complain, never asked for anything, sweetness itself – all loved him and that shining smile ... Another brave soul left this world ..."*

There has been a lot of speculation about the Tsarina's "interfering in the affairs of State" during the war. However, a close analysis of her letters to Nikolai II reveals that there were no ambitious aspirations which allegedly moved Alexandra, except her intense desire to help "her beloved Nicky": *"I do so yearn to make it easier for you – and the ministers all squabbling amongst each other at a time when all ought to work together and forget their personal offences and have as aim the welfare of their sovereign and country – it makes me rage. In other words it's treachery, because people know it, they feel the government in discord and then the Left profit by it. If you could only be severe, my Love, it is so necessary, they must hear your voice and see displeasure in your eyes. They are too accustomed to your gentle, forgiving kindness."* (June 10, 1915).

"... By the by, did you settle anything about a senator to inspect the railways and coal depots and see to set all moving, because it is a shame – in Moscow one has no butter and here still many things are scarce and prices very high, so that for rich people

ЗАЩИТНИКАМЪ
ОТЕЧЕСТВА!

ВОЙНА ОБЪЯВЛЕНА
La guerre est déclarée

№1

(Top) 1915. Alexei and Pierre Gilliard in the carriage; standing on the side is Kolya the son of Doctor Derevenko. Like his father, Alexei loved the outdoors – the cold weather, the snow. (Above) August 1914. The Tsar, Olga and Alexei are looking with interest at the first German machine gun which fell into Russian hands. At that time, the Russians had the upper hand militarily. (Left) Front of a postcard Alexei sent to Tatiana: *"The War Has Been Declared"*. *"Dear Tatiana, I shall be waiting for letters from you. God keep you. Loving you, Alexei."* Facing Page: (top) Spring 1916. A stop en route to Mogilyov. The Grand Duchesses had a chance to meet some peasants and their children. Olga and Anastasia are seen here playing with the little ones. Later, Tatiana took the trouble to write the name of the children in her album. Petty bourgeoisie disapproved of this behaviour, and interpreted it as "lack of taste" or "a wish to show the modesty of the Imperial family during the war time". The local "ladies" were irritated by the Duchesses "common, tasteless" outfits, which "even a provincial girl would not dare to wear". (Bottom) Front and back of a postcard Tatiana sent to her father in the New year of 1917. *"My dear Papa, God bless this New Year and I hope it will bring you peace and quiet. I kiss you as fondly and tenderly as I love you. Your Tatiana"*.

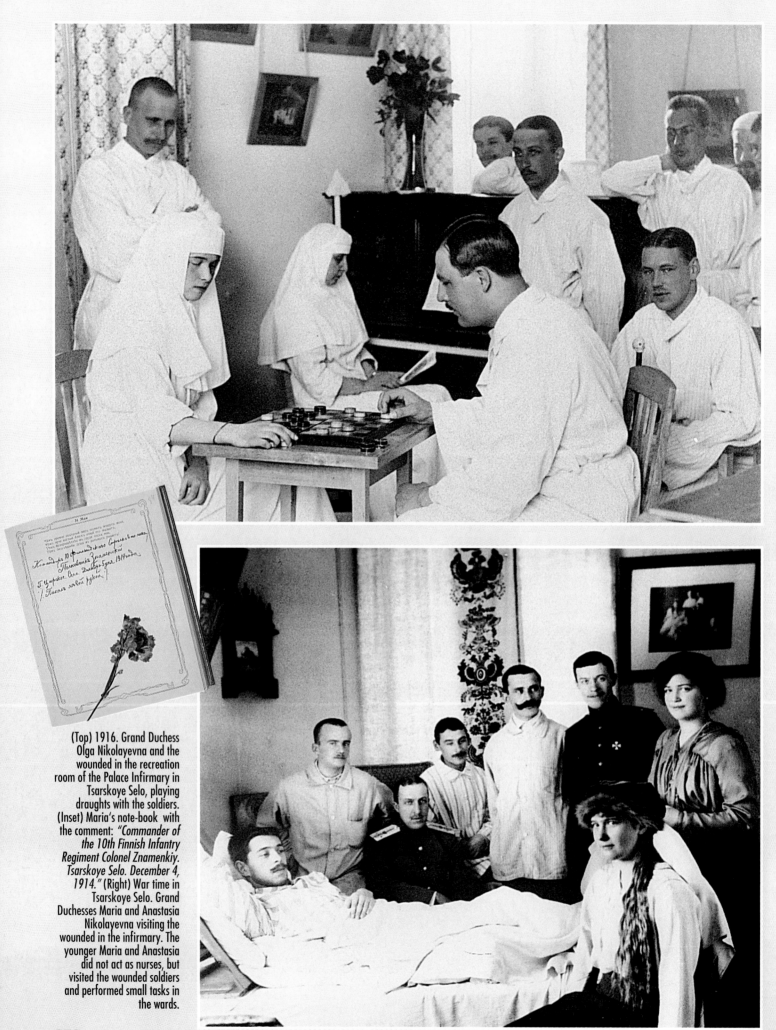

(Top) 1916. Grand Duchess Olga Nikolayevna and the wounded in the recreation room of the Palace Infirmary in Tsarskoye Selo, playing draughts with the soldiers. (Inset) Maria's note-book with the comment: *"Commander of the 10th Finnish Infantry Regiment Colonel Znamenkiy. Tsarskoye Selo. December 4, 1914."* (Right) War time in Tsarskoye Selo. Grand Duchesses Maria and Anastasia Nikolayevna visiting the wounded in the infirmary. The younger Maria and Anastasia did not act as nurses, but visited the wounded soldiers and performed small tasks in the wards.

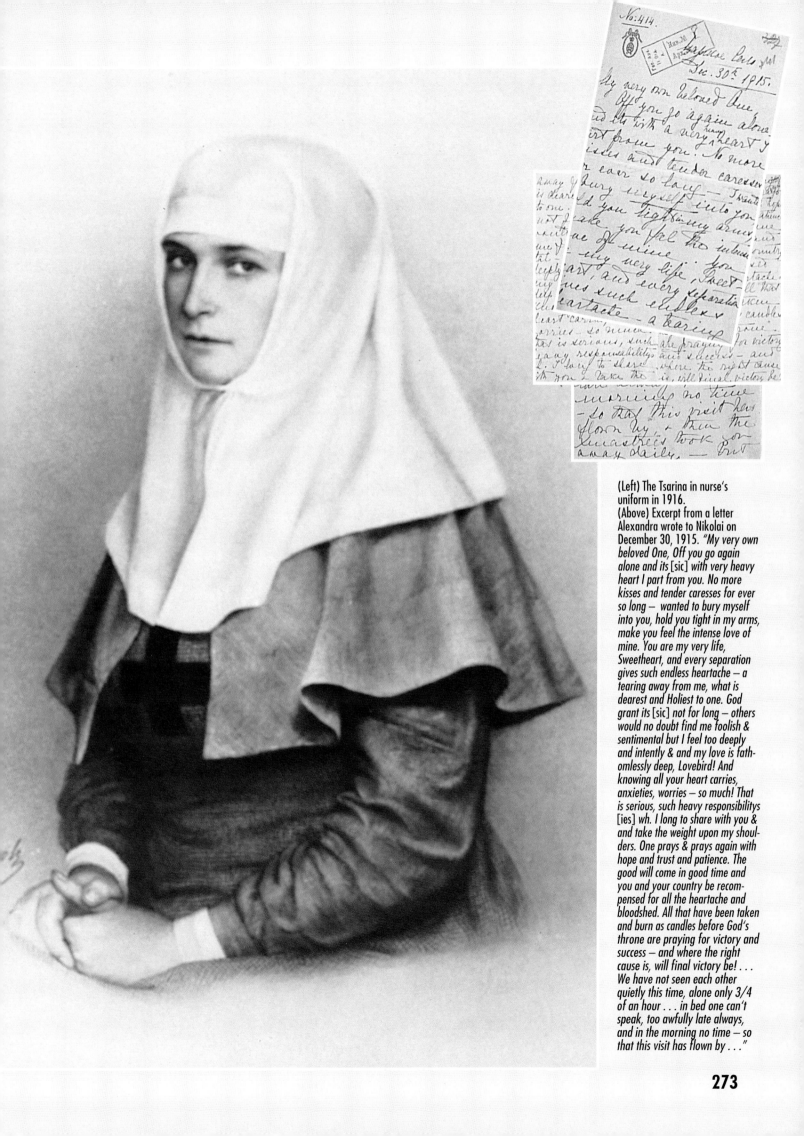

(Left) The Tsarina in nurse's uniform in 1916.

(Above) Excerpt from a letter Alexandra wrote to Nikolai on December 30, 1915. *"My very own beloved One, Off you go again alone and its [sic] with very heavy heart I part from you. No more kisses and tender caresses for ever so long — wanted to bury myself into you, hold you tight in my arms, make you feel the intense love of mine. You are my very life, Sweetheart, and every separation gives such endless heartache — a tearing away from me, what is dearest and Holiest to one. God grant its [sic] not for long — others would no doubt find me foolish & sentimental but I feel too deeply and intently & and my love is fathomlessly deep, Lovebird! And knowing all your heart carries, anxieties, worries — so much! That is serious, such heavy responsibilitys [ies] wh. I long to share with you & and take the weight upon my shoulders. One prays & prays again with hope and trust and patience. The good will come in good time and you and your country be recompensed for all the heartache and bloodshed. All that have been taken and burn as candles before God's throne are praying for victory and success — and where the right cause is, will final victory be! ... We have not seen each other quietly this time, alone only 3/4 of an hour ... in bed one can't speak, too awfully late always, and in the morning no time — so that this visit has flown by ..."*

273

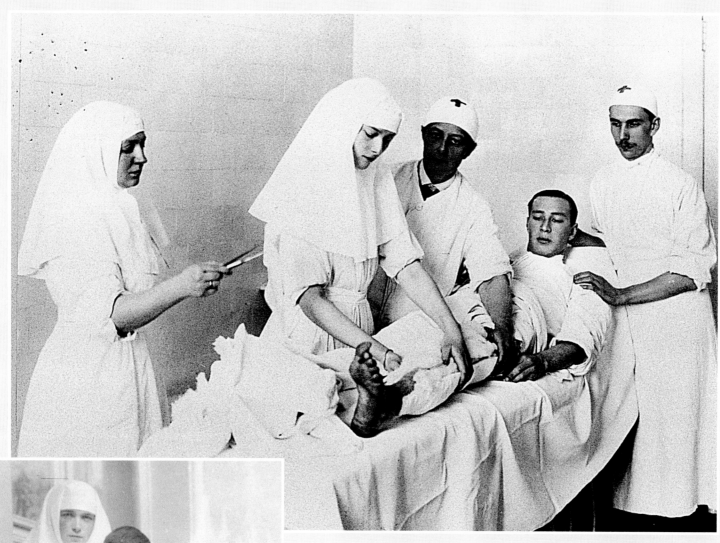

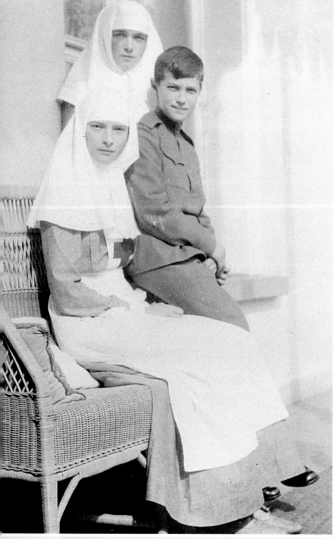

(Top) Tsarskoye Selo. 1916. The Infirmary. From left to right: Princess Gedroits (doctor of medicine, Head Physician of Tsarskoyelsky Palace Hospital for the wounded), Grand Duchess Tatiana, Doctor Nedelin and nurse Chebotaryova, taking care of a young wounded soldier. (Left) Tsarskoye Selo, 1915. Grand Duchesses Olga and Tatiana Nikolayevna are having a break and posing for the photographer with brother Alexei. (Above) From left to right. In the second row, sitting, dressed in the Red Cross uniforms are Alexandra Feodorovna, Olga and Tatiana. Standing at the back are Maria and Anastasia.

(Left) The Imperial family on board the yacht *Standard* in 1915. From left to right: Tatiana, Anastasia, Olga, Alexei, Nikolai II, Alexandra Feodorovna and Maria, posing with the officers and crew.

(Below left) 1916. The grounds of the hospital at the Tsar's Headquarters: the Tsarina with Olga and Tatiana pictured with the doctors, nurses and hospital staff. Alexandra and her daughters were dedicated to their hospital duties and the news of what was happening at the front sometimes took second place. Alexandra's work as a nurse during the war was an example of selfless service to her people. It appeared normal among aristocratic ladies to hold some honorary but 'non tiring' office in all sorts of charitable commissions and public foundations, which provided them a chance to show off and to establish some useful contact. The Tsarina's neglect of conventionalities by becoming a "common nurse" was misinterpreted as a "beau geste", a "cheap method of seeking popularity", and simply "mauvais tone".

(Below) Like her sisters, Olga was patroness of a Regiment. Here she is seen in a 1911 photograph taken with officers of the 3rd Yelisavetgradsky Hussar Regiment.

(Above) Tsarskoye Selo,1915. Alexei in a joking mood wearing a dressing gown, slippers and a hat. Like all children Alexei was aware of the war, but times of fun were always to be taken advantage of. (Above right) Near Mogilyov, on the Dnieper river, Nikolai enjoys a cigarette, relaxing after a long walk. As he himself said — he had that yearning to get into the fresh air — so much more during the war, when so much pressure was put upon him. The camera has captured the gentle expression in his eyes and the tender smile. Nikolai had a lot of charm, he had a very gentle nature incapable of harming anybody personally. The war to him was an act of cruelty towards those young soldiers dying at the front. (Right) 1916. On the Dnieper, in the environs of Mogilyov, the Tsar watches as Cesarevitch Alexei with his friends, cadets Vasya Agayev and Zhenya Makarov, play on a hay stack.

(Left) Tsarskoye Selo, 1915. Cesarevitch Alexei in military uniform. Alexei had charming manners like his father, he was self confident and had an air of pride that suited a future Tsar of Russia.
(Inset below) Dedication from Alexei: *"A papa et Mama pour Noël d' Alexis. Tsarskoye Selo. December 25, 1914."* (Poem: *"La petite hirondelle"*)
(Inset bottom) Alexei wrote to his mother: *"In the train we played a lot "Nain Jaune" and I won a lot of money. I thank everybody for their salutations. Send me my money, please. My cold has completely gone. I have started my lessons again, this morning. God bless you, your small, Alexei."*

(Above) Documents kept by Nikolai II of Official Ranks bestowed on him by the British Kings. In 1908 King Edward VII appointed Nikolai Honorary Admiral and in 1916, during the war, King George V gave him the Rank of Field-Marshal.

(Right) The convoy of cars has stopped in the forest and Nikolai II, looking tired, but with a kind expression is talking to the soldiers. Photography played an important role in recording the events in the life of the Tsar's family and the camera was always there, whether to capture the children having a picnic in the woods or the images on the war front. Away from his family he kept in touch all the time with Alexandra, even about matters of state. In a letter of November 10, 1916, he wrote: "Many thanks for your dear letter. When you get this one you will have heard from St. [urmer] about the changes which are absolutely necessary now. I am sorry about Prot. [opopov], a good honest man, but he jumped from one idea to another and could not decide for himself to stick to one opinion. I remarked that fr. the very beginning. People say he was not normal some years ago fr. a certain illness (when he went to Badmayev), It is risky having the Minister of Interior in such hands at such times. Old Bobrynskiy need also replacing. If one can get a strong and energetic man in his place, then I hope the food supplies question will be rightly settled without breaking the existing system. While these changes go on the Duma will be shut for 8 days, else they would say one does it under their pressure. In any case Trepoff will try and do his best. He comes back on Sunday. I think, with a list of names, wh. we have spoken about it with St. [umer] and him. Only please don't mix in our Friend [Rasputin]! It is I who carries the responsibility and I want to be free to choose accordingly..."

even it is hard living. This is all known and rejoiced at in Germany as our bad organization, which is absolutely true". (November 10, 1915).

"... It continues still for 2 months that we may have disagreeable rows and stories in towns – and I understand it, as it's shameful making the poor people suffer so and the humiliation before our allies!! We have got everything in quantities, only they won't bring it, and when they do, the prices for all become unattainable". (February 1, 1916).

"... Yes, I am more Russian than many others, and I won't keep quiet. I begged them to arrange ... that food, flour, butter, bread, sugar should be weighed out beforehand in the shops and then each buyer can get his parcel much quicker and there won't be such endless tails – all agreed it's an excellent idea – now why did not they think of it before?" (September 20, 1916).

Despite all this, many still suspected the Tsarina's motives, gossip spread that she was in contact with her relatives in Germany and received letters from her brother "Ernie" – which was untrue, but inevitably rumours of plots and intrigues dogged all her efforts. She bore all the slander with equanimity, immersing herself in helping others. "You are so staunch and enduring, I admire you more than I can say", Nikolai admitted in his letter, December 4, 1916.

And through everything, they gained courage and hope from their "fathomless", reciprocal love:

"... Me loves you so, so deeply! My thoughts and prayers are nearly always around you and especially in the evening when we are generally together! I hope this time not to be away long and that nothing will worry you. God bless you and the dear girlies. I kiss you ever so tenderly and love you without end ... " (Nikolai to Alexandra; November 24, 1915.)

"... Others would no doubt find me foolish and sentimental – but I feel too deeply and intently and my love is fathomlessly deep, Lovebird! And knowing all your

heart carries, anxieties, worries – so much! That is serious, such heavy responsibilities which I long to share with you and take weight upon my shoulders. One prays and prays again with hope and trust and patience. The good will come in due time and you and your country [will] be recompensed for all the heartache and bloodshed. All that have been taken and burn as candles before God's throne are praying for victory and success – and where the right cause is, will final victory be! One longs just a bit quicker for some very good news to quieten the restless minds here, to put their small faith to shame".
(Alexandra to Nikolai; December 30, 1915.)

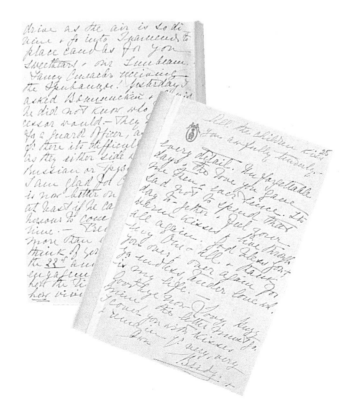

(Above left) 1915-1916. Nikolai II and a barefoot Alexei on the bank of the Dnieper river. Alexei loved the time he spent at the Army Headquarters with his father. Nikolai, contrary to his own upbringing, acquainted his son with the duties of a future Tsar. (Above) A regimental menu, dated April 23, 1916, portraying Emperor Nikolai on horseback and the heir to the throne Cesarevitch Alexei Nikolayevitch standing near by. (Left) Excerpt from a letter from Alexandra to Nikolai written on April 6, 1916.

". . . Precious one, more than ever shall I think of you to-morrow, the 22nd anniversary of our engagement – dear me, how the time flies and yet how vividly one remembers every detail. Unforgettable days & the love you gave me then & ever since. Its sad not to spend the day together & and feel your warm kisses & and live through all again. God bless you my One and all & thank you over & over again for your endless, tender love wh. is my life. Goodbye now Lovy, Huzy mine, the letter must go. I cover you with kisses & remain y. very, very Own Bridy. All the children kiss you awfully tenderly."

279

Chapter Twelve

'IT IS NOT THE AUTOCRATIC POWER THAT I'VE TREASURED, BUT RUSSIA . . .'

" . . . He is about to be struck down. A dark hand, gloved at first in folly, now intervenes. Exit Tsar. Deliver him and all he loved to wounds and death. Belittle his efforts, asperse his conduct, insult his memory: but pause then to tell us who else was found capable"
Winston Churchill, "The World Crisis, 1916-1918".

(Above) Nikolai II's Manifesto of Abdication .
(Facing page) Portrait of Nikolai II presented to Shulgin, on December 12, 1912.
In March 1917 Shulgin with Guchkov, accepted the Act of Abdication from the Tsar in Pskov.

Russia entered the fateful year of 1917 in a chaotic state, caught up in anxious expectation of the imminent unknown. All and everything cried out for change. The intelligentsia's opposition demanded the democratisation of the country after the Western model, insisting on the realignment of State powers and the introduction of a constitutional monarchy or – even more radically – a democratic republic. The majority of the State Duma's members accosted the Tsar urging him to satisfy the "general public's" demands, or else they "would resound out of the excruciated breast of the whole Russian nation", as Feodor Rodichev, a constitutional democrat, exclaimed.

Workers and peasants were turned against employers and landlords, driven by the growing poverty and chaos, and incited by the propaganda of illegal revolutionary organizations. The aristocratic deputies waited for the palace revolution, hoping it would halt the Tsarina's interference in government affairs. And even some members of the Imperial House, according to Vladimir Voyeikov, the palace superintendent, joined the ranks of

Настоящій снимокъ съ изображеніемъ ЕГО ВЕЛИ-
ЧЕСТВА ГОСУДАРЯ ИМПЕРАТОРА ВСЕМИЛО-
СТИВѢЙШЕ пожалованъ Члену Государственной
Думы *В. В. Шульгину*,
имѣвшему счастье представляться ЕГО ИМПЕРА-
ТОРСКОМУ ВЕЛИЧЕСТВУ 12 Декабря 1912 года.

Начальникъ Канцеляріи
    Генералъ-Лейтенантъ *Мосоловъ*

(Above) Diary of Nikolai II on his abdication day. On Monday, February 27, 1917 he wrote: *"Several days ago disturbances broke out in Petrograd; regretfully they were joined by the troops. It gives a loathsome feeling to be so far and to receive scrappy, bad news. I have listened to some reports. In the afternoon I went for a stroll along the road to Orsha. The sun was shining. After dinner I resolved to go to Tsarskoye Selo and at 1 a.m. I went to the station. Tuesday, February 28. I went off to bed at 3.15, having had a long talk with N.I. Ivanov, whom I sent to Petrograd with the troops to re-establish order . . ."* Events precipitated, on Wednesday, March 1. Nikolai's diary entry: *"At night we turned back from Malaya Vishera, as it was found that Ljuban & Tosno have been occupied by rebels".* Thursday, March 2: *"This morning Ruzskiy arrived and he read me the never-ending conversation he had had with Rodzyanko. He believes that the situation in Petrograd is such that the ministry formed by the Duma is allegedly impotent to do whatsoever because they are combated by the soc. [ial] dem. [ocratic] party in person of the workers' committee. It is necessary that I abdicate. Ruzskiy has referred this conversation to the Stavka, and Alexeyev to all the Commanders-in-Chief. About 2.30 everybody's reply arrived. The result is, that in the name of the salvation of Russia and to keep forces at the front calm, I have to decide and take this step. I have assented. The Stavka have sent a draft of the manifesto. In the evening Guchkov and Shulgin arrived from Petrograd, with whom I had a talk, and to whom I handed the manifesto signed and modified. At 1 a.m. I left Pskov, the recent experience lying heavy on my mind. There is treason, and cowardice and deceit all around".*

282

active fighters against the tsarist regime, which they labelled an incompetent and corrupt tyranny, pretending they cared for "the people", whom they really regarded as "uncultured and barbarous, requiring the rule of force".

Most people were discontented with not only Alexandra Feodorovna, but the Tsar himself; his prestige had suffered a headlong decline. Reluctance or inability either to make reformatory concessions or to act decisively and quell the opposition by force, lost him the support of both the left and right. The Tsar was aware of the need for reforms, but he believed their implementation during the circumstances of war untimely. In a private conversation with Adjutant General Ivanov, Nikolai commented: *"It is not the autocratic power that I've treasured, but Russia . . . I'm not certain that any change in the form of governing might bring peace and prosperity."*

The representatives of Russia's allies, Britain and France, did not stand aloof from the fundamental Russian dilemmas of "What to do?" and "Who's to blame?". The Allies' Commission, which arrived in Petrograd in January 1917, came to the conclusion that political reform was imperative. As Grand Duke Alexander Mikhailovitch recollected: *"the most grievous thing was that I got to know that the British ambassador at the Imperial Court, Sir George Buchanan, had countenanced the plotters: he fancied that such a conduct would be the best way to protect the Allies' interests and that the succeeding liberal Russian government would lead Russia from victory to victory. He realized his mistake no longer than 24 hours after the triumph of the revolution. Tsar Alexander III would have thrown such an ambassador out of Russia . . . but Nikolai II put up with everything".*

Nikolai and Alexandra also suffered the questioning of their competence and even their loyalty. The Tsarina, due to her German origins, was accused of pro-German sentiment and even betrayal of Russia's interests, which widened the gulf between the Tsar's family and Russian society. Lewd and obscene pamphlets circulated, crudely denouncing the Imperial couple. A sense of loneliness and fatal submission to his destiny was seizing the soul of the last Russian Tsar. To many he gave the impression of a man withdrawn into himself, lost in his own thoughts. The former Chairman of the Council of Ministers, Vladimir Kokovtsov, noticed: *"His Majesty's look was an expression of helplessness. A forced and melancholy smile did not leave his face, and several times he told me only: 'I am quite sound and cheerful, but I have to sit motionless a great deal, and I am so used to regular exercise' . . . A kind of morbid look did not leave his face, and he kept on looking at me, as if seeking encouragement . . . "*

At this difficult time the mounting misunderstanding between the Dowager Empress Maria Feodorovna and Alexandra Feodorovna burdened the Tsar's mind further. The antipathy was deeply rooted, and exacerbated by differences in the dispositions, interests and tempers of the two women. Charming, radiating joy and peace with her whole aspect, adoring balls, parties and festivals, the Dowager Empress had won all hearts by her courtesy and affability – the exact antithesis of her daughter-in-law, who was inclined to meditation, religious mysticism and was always sad and worried, with unceasing spiritual torment written on her face. Rasputin and his scandalous legend had split them once and for all. Both Maria Feodorovna and Alexandra Feodorovna, each in her own way, meant well for their son and husband, their country and their subjects. Both had a grave foreboding of an impending catastrophe.

The same Kokovtsov remembered Maria Feodorovna's words: *". . . I think you'll understand, for I fear for the future and dark thoughts are possessing me. My daughter-in-law does not like me, thinking that I am somehow jealous of her power. She does not understand, I have but one wish – that my son be happy, and I feel that we are approaching some disaster with relentless steps and that His Majesty listens only to flatterers and does not see that there is something forming under his feet. Something he does not see yet, and I feel it, instinctively, but can't make out what exactly we are in for . . ."* Meanwhile, the political crisis in the country was approaching its climax. The disruption of food supplies aggravated the people's frustration. The bread-queues in the capital were getting ever longer and more embittered with every passing day; meanwhile, grain was rotting in goods vans along the whole of the snowbound Siberian track and on the railways of the South-Western territory. The fuel and raw material shortages were bringing production to a standstill, and unemployment grew daily. The Petrograd garrison, 200,000 strong and consisting mainly of recruits and reservists, sloppily drilled and ill-trained, was too unreliable a support in case of riots – and the crack Guards units, loyal to the throne, were fighting at the front.

On February 20, a wave of strikes and demonstrations broke out in Petrograd, and at the same time the revolutionary underground sensed their moment approaching. Yet the authorities and the Tsarina believed that the situation was under control. Alexandra Feodorovna displayed considerable equanimity and strength of mind. Nursing her children, ill with measles, she often came down from the nursery to the ground floor of the palace to cheer up and reassure the loyal men of the Tsarskoye Selo garrison.

On February 23-26, mounted and foot police dispersed demonstrators in Petrograd, the army blocked approaches to the city centre, and on February 26 the demonstrators were met with gunfire. But on February 27, things came to a head – "troops mutinied"; they disobeyed the order to shoot at the demonstrators. Military and civil authorities had lost control of the situation. On February 27, Chairman of the State Duma, M. Rodzyanko, sent two telegrams to the Tsar, urging him to immediately "form a government that would enjoy the confidence of the whole population". At this moment there was still a chance that Nikolai II would keep the throne. But, on the evening of February 27, the old government fell and, strictly speaking, two powers took over in the city – the Interim Committee of the State Duma and the Petrograd Soviet of Workers' and Soldiers' Deputies. Later, on the night of March 1-2 they reached an agreement to form a Provisional Government.

On February 27, the Tsar would reflect in his diary: *"Several days ago disturbances broke out in Petrograd; regretfully, they were joined by the troops. It gives a loathsome feeling to be so far and to receive scrappy, bad news . . . After dinner I resolved to go to Tsarskoye Selo as soon as possible, and by night I took the train".*

On February 28, in the Tsar's absence, the Chief of Staff, General Mikhail Alexeyev, came to an agreement with the Interim Committee of the State Duma. On the night of March 1, the Tsar's train was stopped 150 miles from Petrograd at the station of Malaya Vishera, under the pretext that rioters had captured the next stations. All his attempts to reach Tsarskoye Selo by another route were hindered. The way to the capital was barred, and the Emperor was ordered to go to Pskov, where the Headquarters of the Northern front were located.

(From top to bottom)
Alexander Guchkov member of the Third State Duma.
Mikhail Rodzyanko Chairman of the Duma.
Vasiliy Shulgin. Some of the key figures involved in the abdication of the Tsar of Russia, Nikolai II and his brother Grand Duke Mikhail Alexandrovitch.

On March 1, the abdication still remained uncertain, but the development of events, the mounting anarchy in the city, the excited state of the troops, brought the leaders of the Interim Committee of the State Duma to the decision that to maintain control of the situation it was necessary to take extreme measures – to demand that the Tsar abdicate in favour of 13 year-old Cesarevitch Alexei, with Grand Duke Mikhail Alexandrovitch acting as Regent.

Responding to General Alexeyev's urging, the Commanders-in-Chief of the fronts – including Commander-in Chief of the Caucasian front, Grand Duke Nikolai Nikolayevitch – came out in favour of the abdication. On the afternoon of March 2, these telegrams were delivered to the Tsar and they convinced him that abdication was unavoid-

(Above) Tsarskoye Selo, 1914. Nikolai II on the balcony of the Alexander Palace, and Alexandra Feodorovna in happier times aboard the yacht *Standard* in 1913. The strong bonding and love that existed between these two people never weakened. Nothing seemed to alter their feelings. Their love for each other gave them comfort in troubled times and now the final act – the abdication – of that eroded power had come . . . Alexandra was alone in Tsarskoye Selo nursing the sick children. Far away from her beloved Nicky, who had to face the greatest turmoil of his life all alone, she wrote to him pouring out words of love just like 23 years ago: *"March 2, 1917. Beloved, precious Light of my life. Gramotin and Solovyov* [officers of the Escort] *are going off with two letters, hoping one at least can reach you to bring you and get news. It is more that madning* [maddening] *not being together – but* [our] *soul* [s] *& heart* [s] *are more* [united] *than ever – nothing can tear us apart, tho' they just wish this. That's why they won't let you see me until you have signed a paper of theirs – resp.* [onsible] *min.* [instry] *or constitution. The nightmare is that having no army behind you, you may be forced into it – but such a promise is "null" when once will be in power again – They meanly caught you like a mouse in a trap – unheard of in history & kills me the vileness & humiliation. The young men will tell clearly the whole situation wh.* [ich] *is too complicated to write . . . Forgive this wild letter, Apr.* [Count Apraksin], *Res.* [Resin, Major-General] *whole time disturb and my head goes round . . . Lili* [Dehn] *always with us . . . A,* [nna Vyrubova] *she send prayers . . . Bless & kiss you without end . . ."* Nikolai's diary entry. Monday, March 6: *"This morning I was so happy to receive two letters from dear Alix and two from Maria, brought by the wife of Captain Golovkin."*

able. In his telegram, addressed to Rodzyanko – which was never sent – Nikolai wrote that there was nothing in the world he wouldn't sacrifice for the welfare of Motherland Russia and for the sake of the Motherland he was abdicating the crown in his son's favour. But the prospect of parting with his sick son, the boy being obliged to live with the Regent's family, was unacceptable to the Tsar. After discussing the matter with Professor Sergei Feodorov, Nikolai became firm in his decision that he would be unable to part with his son.

When, late in the evening of March 2, the representatives of the Committee of the State Duma, Alexander Guchkov and Vasiliy Shulgin, entered the brightly illuminated salon-carriage, Nikolai II received them calmly, having resolved to hand over the Throne to his brother Grand Duke Mikhail Alexandrovitch. Vasiliy Shulgin described in detail the signing of the Manifesto of Abdication: *". . . After a few moments the Tsar came in. He was wearing the uniform of one of the Caucasian regiments. His face expressed absolutely nothing more than one could have seen at any other time. He greeted us amiably rather than coldly, holding out his hand . . . I was afraid that Guchkov would say something spiteful and ruthless to the Tsar, but this did not happen. Guchkov was speaking for a rather long time. He did not touch on the past. He gave an account of the present situation, trying to ascertain what abyss we had fallen into. He spoke without looking at the Tsar, his right hand on the table, his eyes cast down. He did not see the Tsar's face and probably this way it was easier for him to say everything he intended.*

"When Guchkov finished, the Tsar began to speak, his voice and manners being calmer and somehow more matter-of-fact than Guchkov's slightly pompous speech . . . in a quiet voice, as if speaking about a most ordinary matter, the Tsar said: 'Yesterday and the whole of today I was thinking it over and I came to the decision to abdicate. Till three in the afternoon I was ready to abdicate in my son's favour but then I realised that I could not part with my son'. After a short pause he added, in the same calm manner: 'I hope you will understand it'. Then he continued: 'That's why I have resolved to abdicate in favour of my brother'. We expressed our agreement to the abdication in favour of Mikhail Alexandrovitch. After that the Tsar asked if we could assume certain responsibility, give a certain guarantee, that the act of abdication would really appease the country and wouldn't cause any further aggravation. To this we answered that, as far as we could foresee, we were not in for any complications. I did not remember exactly when the Tsar stood up and went to the next carriage to sign the act. Approximately at a quarter-to-twelve the Tsar re-entered the carriage. In his hands he held sheets of a small size. He said: 'Here is the Act of Abdication, read it'.

"We started reading in a low voice. The document was written beautifully,

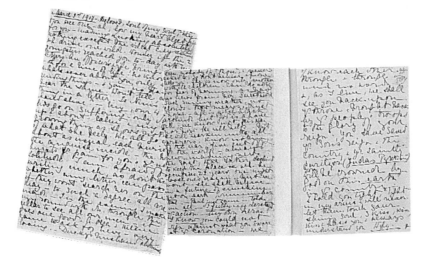

with nobleness. I felt ashamed of the paltry text we had drafted before. It came about between 11 and 12 o'clock on the night of 2nd to 3rd of March".

"Manifesto of Abdication of Nikolai II
Headquarters.
To Chief of Staff

In days of great struggle against the foreign enemy who has for almost three years coveted to enslave our country, the Lord God has chosen to send down on Russia a new severe trial. The internal popular disturbances which have begun, threaten to have a disastrous effect on the further conduct of this persistent war. The destiny of Russia, the honour of our heroic army, the good of the people, the whole future of our dear Fatherland demand that whatever it costs the war be brought to a victorious end. The cruel enemy is straining his last effort, and already nigh is the hour when our valiant army together with our glorious allies will be able to finally crush the enemy. In these days, decisive for the life of Russia, WE deem it Our duty of conscience to facilitate for OUR people a close union and consolidation of all national forces for the earliest attainment of victory, and in agreement with the State Duma, WE consider it right and proper to abdicate from the Throne of the Russian State and lay down the Supreme Power. Not wishing to part with OUR beloved son, WE hand over OUR inheritance to OUR brother Grand Duke MIKHAIL ALEXANDROVITCH, and give OUR blessing to HIS Accession to the Throne of the Russian State. We bequeath it to OUR brother to rule over the matters of the State in full and inviolable union with the representatives of the people in legislative institutions, on the basis which will by them be established, having taken an inviolable oath thereof. In the name of our dearly loved country we call on all faithful sons of our Fatherland to fulfil their sacred duty to HIM, by obedience to the Tsar at a moment of national trials, and to help HIM, together with the representatives of the people, to bring the Russian State on to the road of victory, prosperity and glory. May the Lord God help Russia.

Nikolai
Pskov,
March 2, 1917 3.05 p.m. "

Describing the events of this day in his diary Nikolai would conclude: "*. . . At 1 a.m. I left Pskov, the recent experience lying heavy on my mind. There is treason, and cowardice, and deceit all around".* At 1 a.m. on March 3, the sovereign set out for Mogilyov, to the Headquarters, where final arrangements were to be made. Soon after 4 a.m. Rodzyanko phoned Ruzskiy. He declared that the text of the Manifesto was unacceptable, and that the reign of Mikhail Alexandrovitch "was absolutely inadmissible", and that his abdication would therefore be "rather desirable and helpful". On March 3, having failed to become the new Russian Tsar, Grand Duke Mikhail Alexandrovitch renounced the throne. Mikhail's renunciation ended the monarchist order in Russia, bringing the three century –

After the abdication Alexandra wrote to Nikolai II: "*March 3, 1917. Beloved, soul of my soul, my own wee one – ah, how my heart bleeds for you – madning [sic] knowing absolutely nothing except the vilest rumours wh. drive one wild. Wonder if the two young-sters reached you to-day with my letters. An officer's wife, brings this. Oh for a line of life! No knowledge whatsoever about you, only heart rending things – and you no doubt hear the same. Won't tell anything in a letter. Is Nini's husband alive? – my, [Lord] our own 4 invalids go on suffering – only M. [aria] is up & about – calm – my help growing thin as shows nothing of what she feels. We all go up and about as usual, one buries the anguish inside – the heart bursts fr. [om] pain for you and your utter solitude. I am afraid of writing much, as don't know whether any letter can pass, if they won't search her on the way – to such a degree all are mad. In the evening I make my round with M. through the cellar to see all our men – it does one good . . . Such sunny weather, no clouds – that means, trust and hope – all is pitch black around but God is above all; we know not his way, nor how He will help – but he will hearken unto all prayers. Know nothing of the war, live cut off fr. [om] the world – always new, madning [sic] news – the last, that Father [Nikolai II] decline to keep the place wh. he occupied 23 years. One might lose one's reason – but we won't – she shall believe in a future of sunshine yet on earth, remember that. – Paul [G. D. Pavel Alexandrovitch, Nikolai's uncle] just came – told me all – I fully understand y.[our] action – my own hero! I know you could not sign against what you swore at y. coronation – We know each through & through & need. no words &, as I live, we shall see you back upon y. throne, brought back by y. people & troops to the glory of your reign. You have saved y. son's reign & the country & your saintly purity & (Judas Ruzsky) you will be crowned by God on this earth in y. country. I hold you tight, tight in my arms & will never let them touch your shining soul. I kiss, kiss, kiss & bless you & always understand you. Wify ."* Nikolai upon receiving her letter, entered in his diary: *Tuesday, March 7, "I have received two more letters from dear Alix, deliv-ered by two officers of the Escort . . . After tea [I] began to pack. Had dinner with mama and played bezique with her."*

(Right) 1915. Grand Duke Mikhail Alexandrovitch reading in his study. (Above) The Abdication Manifesto of Grand Duke Mikhail Alexandrovitch . *"A heavy burden has been laid upon Me by the will of My brother, who has handed Me the Imperial All-Russian Throne in the year of unprecedented war and popular disturbances. Inspired by the same thought that permeates the nation, that the well being of our Motherland is the supreme good, I have taken the firm decision to accept Sovereign authority only in the event that such will be the desire of our great nation which, by means of a national referendum, through its representatives in the Constituent Assembly, shall determine the form of policy and the new fundamental laws of the Russian State . . . calling on the Lord to give us His blessing, I request all the citizens of the Russian Empire to submit to the Provisional Government, created at the initiative of the State Duma, and endowed with full authority, until the Constituent Assembly, which shall be convened in the nearest possible time, on the basis of the universal, direct, equal and secret vote, with its decision concerning the form of government, give expression to the people's will. MIKHAIL"* Nikolai's diary, as always, was written in a simple straightforward manner.
Friday, March 3: *"Had a long and sound sleep. Woke when we had long passed Dvinsk. The day was sunny and frosty. Spoke with my people about yesterday ['s events]. Read a lot about Julius Cæser . . . I arrived in Mogilyov at 8.20. . . All the ranks of the headquarters were waiting at the platform. Received Alexeyev in [my] carriage. At 9 1/2 moved to the house. . . I've learnt Misha [G.D. Mikhail Alexandrovitch] abdicated . . . God knows who had put it in his mind to sign such a foul! In Petrograd disorders ceased – I wish it went on like this further on."*

long history of the Romanov dynasty to an end.

Mogilyov was as quiet and peaceful as ever. Nothing seemed to have changed in the small provincial town. But events had had their effect here as well. Under way were preparations for swearing of allegiance to the Provisional Government. General Alexeyev ordered that monograms "N" be removed off the epaulettes of uniforms. One of the generals, who had been recently fairly close to the Tsar, began to unpick the monograms off his coat himself, but he was rather ungainly at that. So he asked his courier, a Preobrazhenskiy regiment veteran, for help. "Mikhailov, help me remove the monograms off the epaulettes". "No, I cannot, spare me. I could never agree to do that, and God save me from watching it", the old soldier replied, his eyes cast down.

The day before leaving for Tsarskoye Selo, in the evening, on March 7, Nikolai issued his last, handwritten, order to the Army and Navy: *"For the last time I address You, Beloved Forces. For two and a half years you have been hourly on hard military service. I appeal to you, my dearly beloved troops, urging you to defend our dear country from the mortal enemy. Russia is being united with her valiant allies by one common aspiration for victory. This unprecedented war must be concluded to the utter defeat of our enemies. Those who are thinking of peace, wishing for it – are betrayers of their Fatherland, traitors. I know that every honest soldier realizes it and thinks so. Fulfil your duty as you have been doing hitherto. Do your utmost to defend our great Russia. Obey your commanders. Any relaxation of order [discipline] in the service will abet the enemy.*

"I am fully confident that your hearts will never cease to infinitely love our Motherland. May the Lord God bless your further exploits, and may the Holy Martyr, St. Georgiy the Victorious, lead you from victory to victory". Pathetically, the order never reached its destination.

On Wednesday, March 8, His Majesty bade farewell to all the servicemen of the staff. His simple, calm words touched the hearts of even the most battle-hardened and experienced officers. Many cried openly. Suddenly, His Majesty interrupted the ceremony and hurriedly made for the exit. At about 4 p.m. the train which had been sent for Nikolai

(Top) 1914. Nikolai on horseback at the Headquarters.

(Left, inset and below) The text of the last appeal of Nikolai II to the forces after his abdication: *"For the last time I address You, Beloved Forces. For two years and a half you have been hourly on the hard military service. I appeal to You, dearly beloved troops, urging you to defend our dear Motherland from the enemy . . ."* (March 1917).

(Above centre) The last officers' menu. On the last day a few of his faithful friends and officers gave a farewell dinner for Nikolai. Among the ones who signed the menu were Prof. Feodorov, Kirill Noryshkin; Vasiliy Dolgorukov. That night, March 8, Nikolai entered in his diary: *"The last day in Mogilyov. At 10 1/4 signed my farewell order the armies. At 10 1/2 I went to the orderly-house to say goodbye to all ranks of the general headquarters and departments. At my place [I] bid farewell the officers and the Cossack of the Escorts and the Composite regiment. My heart nearly broke. At 12 p.m. I came to Mama's carriage and had lunch with her suite and stayed there with her till 4.30. Bid farewell to her, Sandro* [G.D. Alexander Mikhailovitch] *Sergei* [Mikhailovitch, Inspector-General of the Artillery], *Boris* [Vladimirovitch, Major General of the Suite] *and Alec* [Prince Alexander of Oldenburg]. *Poor Nilov* [Adjutant–General, Admiral, nicknamed ' 'Little Admiral] *was not allowed to go with me. At 4.45 I left Mogilyov, a crowd of people came to see me off, it was touching. 4 members of the Duma accompany me on the train! Turned to Orsha and Vitebsk. The weather is frosty and windy. Hard painful and dreary. How painful, agonising and sad."* (Right) Officers' dinner menus, which Nikolai treasured in his albums. He always enjoyed the time spent with Army friends and these meetings were always conducted in a very informal and relaxed atmosphere.

(Right) Nikolai II and the Cesarevitch. The great love the Tsar had for Alexei never faltered. Nikolai II's manifesto read: *"Not wishing to part with OUR beloved son, WE hand over Our inheritance to OUR brother Grand Duke MIKHAIL . . . "* Before reaching this decision, Nikolai had spoken to Doctor Feodorov – Alexei's illness was incurable, there was no certainty that he could have lived till old age. He had to be taken care of. The instability of power was felt by everyone in society. Lies and gossip deformed the mentality of even virtuous monarchists. The liberal-aristocratic circle of Russia's "succourers" hatched various plans, all them elaborate as well as absurd. At last all decided on a scheme: Nikolai abdicates in favour of his son, Alexei, Grand Duke Mikhail acting as a Regent. Meanwhile, the real power was to pass into the hands of various activists, to the satisfaction of all the people populating the vast Russian Empire. How little they knew their Tsar who had been ruling for over 22 years, to imagine that he might emigrate, leaving behind his beloved son, whom he treasured above all on earth. Many were amazed at the Tsar's self-possession in this pathetic moment of his life. Had he burst into hysterical cries and moaning, it might have been understandable to petty, ambitious people. The Tsar's renowned lack of thirst for power was acutely felt and proved crucial. Persuaded that his abdication was necessary for the good of the country, Nikolai did not think of struggling for power. Of course it was stressful for him, but having lost the throne, he managed to preserve what was dearest to him – his darling Alix and children. Nikolai's diary entry on March 5: *" . . . Bid farewell to poor C. [Count] Fredericks and Voyeikov, whose presence seems for some reason to irritate everybody here; they have gone to his [Count Fredericks'] estate in Penza prov. [ince]. At 8 we went to dine with Mama".* Dowager Empress Maria Feodorovna specially arrived in Mogilyov from Kiev to stay with her "poor Nicky" in those grave days. She never reproached him for anything, her only wish was to morally support her son. In her telegrams from Mogilyov to Xenia, who was staying in Petrograd, Maria Feodorovna wrote: *"Happy to be with him in this gravest moment"* (March 5); *"Thanks God we are together. We think a lot about you. Hope that you and your children are well. The weather is also desperate . . ."* (March 6). On March 8 mother and son parted, neither of them suspecting that they would never see each other again.

arrived with deputies of the State Duma on board. Its chief, Commissar Bublikov, handed over to General Alexeyev the Provisional Government's decree on the arrest of the former Tsar. General Alexeyev might have refused to announce the decree, ceding the privilege to Bublikov. But Alexeyev preferred to do it himself. "Your Majesty shall consider yourself somewhat under arrest", he said to Nikolai. The latter made no reply, he grew pale and turned his back on Alexeyev.

The train started off. Standing at a compartment window was a calm man, his face pale, bidding his mute farewell to all those who had quite recently addressed him as "Your Imperial Majesty". Later that evening, the former Tsar recalled these events: *"The last day in Mogilyov. At 10 1/4 signed the farewell order for the armies. At 10 1/2 . . . bid farewell to the officers and the Cossacks of the Escort and the Composite Regiment – my heart nearly broke! At 12 went to Mama in the railway carriage, had lunch with her and her suite and stayed with her till 4 1/2. Bid farewell to her . . . Poor Nilov was not allowed to come with me. At 4.45 left Mogilyov, a touching crowd of people saw me off . . . The weather is frosty and windy. Hard, painful and dreary".*

Later, many Russians would question these decisions. What made the Emperor abdicate? Was the abdication in his brother's favour, omitting the heir apparent, Cesarevitch Alexei, legal? Was there a conspiracy, a malicious intent in the decision of generals and public figures, forcing Nikolai II to abdicate? Did they, in that dreadful time, reason that it was the only way to appease the rising tide of the revolution?

It was generally believed that the main motive behind the Tsar's abdication was the desire to avoid bloodshed. Pierre Gilliard thought that the Tsar was confronted with a dilemma: to abdicate or to make a desperate attempt to go to Petrograd with those troops remaining faithful to him; but this would have meant civil war in the enemy's presence . . . Nikolai had no hesitations. A participant in these events, Vasiliy Shulgin, was of the same opinion: *"Not to abdicate . . . meant to flood Petrograd with blood. Who could do this*

then? Where was that man and those people?"

But who knew at that time how much innocent blood would be shed on Russian soil? Very soon, in Tobolsk, the former Tsar would regret his decision. Could the successors of autocracy succeed where Nikolai II failed?

"Men gifted and daring, men ambitious and fierce; spirits audacious and commanding – of these there was no lack. But none could answer the few plain questions on which the life and destiny of Russia turned. With victory in her grasp she fell upon the earth, devoured alive, like Herod of old, by worms."

Winston Churchill, The World Crisis 1916-1918".

(Above) Nikolai at the window of the Imperial train. The very same train on which he renounced the Russian throne.

(Left) 1899. Document sent by the American people of Pennsylvania about "The Hague Treaty" This document reads: *"We the undersigned, sovereign citizens of the United States of America, without regard to race, creed, or political affinity, desire to express our hearty sympathy with the Czar's noble effort for the cause of God and humanity. Appreciating the difficulties that confront him at home and abroad, we admire the high noble courage . . . "*

From May 18 to July 29, 1899 at Nikolai's initiative a peace conference took place in Le Hague. 26 Nations including America and China participated. A major achievement was obtained with the creation of the Permanent Court of Arbitration. In 1914 Nikolai pleaded with Wilhelm II, to no avail, to co-operate with him to resolve the Austro-Serbian dispute, taking it to the Hague.

(Far left) A telegram Nikolai, by now a broken man and his heart in turmoil, sent to his beloved Alexandra on March 4, 1917. *"Telegram No. 3. Tsar Headquarters — Tsarskoye Selo. To her Majesty, Thanks darling. At last your telegram came during this night. Despairing being away. God bless you all. Love very tenderly. Nicky."*

Chapter Thirteen

THE LAST ACT
OF THE
ROMANOV
TRAGEDY

Vladimir Oustimenko
Lyubov Tyutyunnik

TSARSKOYE SELO, TOBOLSK, YEKATERINBURG: THE ROAD TO CALVARY

"And then, pointing at the crucifix, Her Majesty said: "Our suffering is nothing. Think of the torments our Saviour underwent to redeem us. Should Russia need it, we are ready to sacrifice our lives and everything . . ."
M.K. Diterichs. "The Murder of the Tsar's Family and the Members of the Romanov House in the Urals".

"A year shall come for Russia of dread things
When in the dust shall fall the crown of kings.
The mob shall loathe what once they loved,
While blood and death
Shall be the people's daily bread."
Mikhail Lermontov (1814-1841). "Prophecy"

Once Nikolai was back in Tsarskoye Selo with his family, his diary entries gave a daily account of their life under house arrest. *"Friday, March 10: '[We] slept well. In spite of the conditions we found ourselves in, the thought that we are together raises our spirits and comforts us . . . In the morning [I] received Benckendorf, then looked through, tidied and burnt my papers. Stayed with the children till 2 1/2. Went for a walk with Valya Dolgorukov accompanied by the same two ensigns who were more polite today. Enjoyed working in the snow. The weather was sunny. Spent the evening together."* (Facing page) The ex-Tsar, working in the garden, clearing the snow. He seemed already, in an enduring but industrious way, to be adapting to his new conditions.

ow difficult it is to grasp the essence of the phenomenon when a lump of crystal, solid and intact, suddenly bursts into kaleidoscopic fragments. This mysterious process is known under the conventional term of "fatigue". Eroded with fatigue, remote stars and whole galaxies become exhausted and perish; people get weary of this world and forsake us, and mighty civilisations wear out and self-destruct. They die and pass into oblivion, superseded by ravenous barbarians. In that winter of 1917, Russia seemed to be overtaken by fatigue; she indulged in a malignant ecstasy of self-mutilation, burning down everything which had primordially constituted her flesh and spirit.

Having been left behind by events, the former Tsar felt lost – forced from power, but not allowed the status of a private citizen. It was this which kept him restless, aggravated by a vexatious anxiety for the destiny of his family. The situation in Tsarskoye Selo was extremely tense and dramatic. Four of the children were seriously ill, and only Grand Duchess Maria Nikolayevna was "up and about". So critical was the state of Alexei's health that rumours began to spread in the capital about the Cesarevitch's death. The tutor Gilliard recollected: *"In those days of mortal anxiety, hearing nothing from His Majesty, the Empress was driven to desperation at her sick child's bed, and her anguish was worse than anyone could imagine. It strained her to the limitations of human endurance, it was*

her last trial from which she elicited the amazing, luminous tranquillity which would support her and all her family till their day of doom".

It was in those days that hosts of inebriated daredevils began to ramble from Petrograd all over the suburbs. Tsarskoye Selo was one of the destinations of their crusade. A horde of about ten thousand armed people moved to the Alexander Palace, and soon only several hundred feet separated this savage rabble from its fence. Two companies from His Majesty's Composite Regiment, joined by the sailors of the Garde Equipage, and guards of the Escort and the Cavalry Battery, faced the attackers. But those five hundred could have been easily swept away by the rioters. A sinister shadow of carnage hung over the Palace.

But hardly had the skirmish, which included both rifle-shot and invective, erupted, when it was cut short. All eyes were fixed on the doors from which emerged the Tsarina, resolute and cool. "I'll go to them not as Her Majesty, but as a common nurse of my children", she said calmly as she left the Palace. The Empress was bare-headed, wearing a simple house dress. She was holding her daughter Maria by the hand, and so the two ladies, accompanied by the brave old Hof-Meister, Count Apraksin, walked straight to the soldiers.

"Courageous and calm, she went along the rows of soldiers, and her voice sounded soft and soothing, yet persistent, as she exhorted them not to shed their brothers' blood, not to aggravate animosity and tumult because of her, because of her children and family", recounted one of the witnesses. Tragedy was prevented. Now that Alexandra had seen that the revolutionary mob was prepared to tear apart herself and her children, she was stricken by an acute awareness of the peril that threatened the Emperor, her beloved, adored husband.

The Tsarina's telegrams and letters, full of anxiety, despair and hope, were following the lost Tsar's train. *"Beloved, soul of my soul, my own wee one ah, how my heart bleeds for you maddening knowing absolutely nothing except the vilest rumours wh. drive one wild . . . Oh for a line of life! No knowledge whatsoever about you, only heart-rending things and you no doubt hear the same."* At last, on Saturday, March 4, Nikolai received the Tsarina's first telegrams. *"Thanks, darling. At last your telegram came during the night. Despairing being away. God bless you all. Love very tenderly. Nicky."*

On that same day, her letters reached the Tsar. *"It made me very happy when I received two letters from dear Alix in the morning"*, he wrote in his diary. The first of the letters was written on March 3, when the abdication act was promulgated. Fraught with the Tsarina's anxiety, it still bore support and encouragement which Alix never failed to render her Nikolai. *". . . Paul* [Grand Duke Pavel Alexandrovitch, Nikolai II's uncle] *just came and told me all. I fully understand your action my own hero! I know you could not sign against what you swore at your coronation, we know each other through and through and need no words and, as I live, we shall see you back upon your throne, brought back by your people and troops to the glory of your reign. You have saved your son's reign and the country and your saintly purity and (Judas Ruzskiy) you will be crowned by God on this earth in your country. I hold you tight, tight in my arms and will never let them touch your shining soul. I kiss, kiss, kiss and bless you and always understand you. Wify."* The second letter, dated March 4, was numbered 653.

This is the last of the Tsarina's letters, of those known and preserved, the last page of their great, tragic novel . . . *"Sweet, beloved Treasure - the lady* [Golovkina, wife of one of the officers of the Life-Guards Finnish regiment] *leaves today instead of yesterday,*

Nikolai's diary entry on Tuesday, March 21, 1917: *"This afternoon, unexpectedly, Kerenskiy, the current Min*[ister] *of Justice arrived.* [He] *Went around all the rooms, asked to see us, spoke with me for five minutes, introduced the new palace superintendent and then left. He ordered to arrest poor Anya* [Anna Vyrubova] *and take her together with Lili Dehn to the city. This happened between 3 and 4 p.m., meanwhile I was out for a stroll. The weather was nasty just like our mood . . ."*
Thursday, March 23: *"It became a fine day after 2 p.m. and a thaw. In the morning took a short stroll.* [I] *have tidied up my things and books and have started to put aside everything I would like to take with me if we shall have to go to England . . . Spent the evening as usual."*
March 25. Annunciation: *"In inconceivable conditions* [we] *spent this holiday – under arrest in our own house and without the remote possibility to communicate with Mama and our kin. At 11 a.m. I went to the liturgy with O.* [lga] *and T.* [atiana] *. . ."*
Monday, March 27: *"We began fasting, but, for a start, it brought us no luck. After the liturgy Kerenskiy arrived and asked to limit our meeting only to meal times and to sit separately from the children; he needed this allegedly to appease the illustrious Soviet of Workers' and Soldiers' Deputies! We had to submit to avoid any form of violence . . ."*
Saturday, April 1: *"I forgot to enter it that yesterday we parted with 46 of our servants who at last were allowed to leave the Alexander Palace and reunite with their families in Petrograd . . ."*

(Facing page) View of the Alexander Palace, the family home, where the Tsar and his family were kept under house arrest.

(Left) April, 1917. Tatiana and Alexei in the park near the Alexander Palace.

(Bottom left) April 28, 1917. Tatiana and soldiers of the guard. Monsieur Gilliard wrote under this photograph: *"Creating a kitchen garden in the Alexander park in front of the palace during our captivity. Tatiana Nikolayevna is carrying peat on a wheelbarrow with one of the guards who has decided to work with us."*

(Bottom right) April 30, 1917. Nikolai's family and courtiers laying out a kitchen garden. In the background we see the women and in the foreground Doctor Derevenko looking straight at the camera and Nikolai on his left, digging. The same evening Nikolai wrote in his diary: *"The weather was excellent. Before the liturgy [1] took a stroll. At 2 p.m. we all went out together with many of our people wishing to work in the garden. With great zeal and even with enthusiasm we started digging and without realizing we worked till 5 p.m. The weather was most enjoyable. Read before and after dinner."*

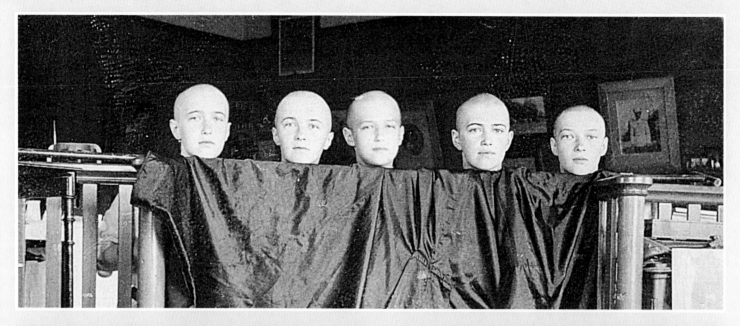

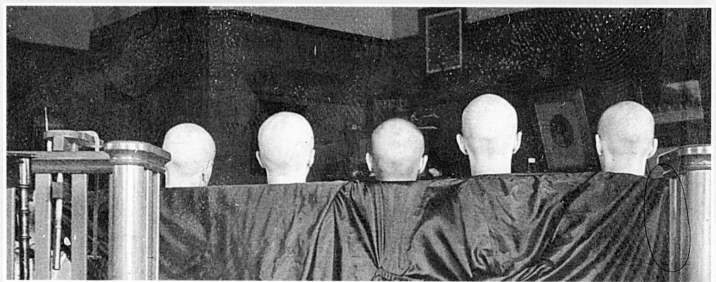

(Left) 1917. Olga and Alexei photographed by Pierre Gilliard with the inscription: "O.N. and A.N. 'On the Children's island'."

Facing page: (top) The Imperial children had measles and to avoid the hair falling out and not growing back properly they had their heads shaved. Obviously, they took it all with good humour, but the picture acquires a certain bleakness in the light of their fate. From left to right, Anastasia, Olga, Alexei, Maria and Tatiana.

(Bottom) Tatiana and Anastasia rowing on the lake of Alexander Palace.

On Monday, May, 1 Nikolai wrote in his diary: "A lovely, warm day . . . At 12 gave Alexei a lesson of geography . . . Yesterday we learnt about Gen. Kornilov's dismissal from his office of Commander-in-Chief of Petrograd military district, and this evening about Guchkov's resignation, both for the same reason of irresponsible interfering with the orders of the military administration of the Sov. [iet] of Work. [ers'] Deputies . . . What Providence keeps in store for poor Russia? May the Lord's will be upon us!"

Saturday, May 6: "I have turned 49. My thought especially flew to dear Mama. It is painful not to be able even to write to each other. I know nothing of her, except silly, disgusting articles in newspapers . . ."

Nikolai's diary Saturday, May 13. "A sunny day with a cool breeze. Took a one hour stroll with Alexei. In the afternoon worked well in the garden. Saw the canoes and a boat brought to our pond. Tatiana and Alexei took the occasion and went boating . . . in the evening read aloud the book 'Le Parfum de la Dame Noir' . . ."

Sunday, May 14. "In a different situation we have spent the 21st anniversary of the Coronation! . ."

Monday, May 22 : ". . . At last it began raining wh. lasted till 8 p.m. Marvellous fragrance came through the windows. Today is an anniversary of the beginning of the offensive by the armies of the South-Western Front. What state of spirit it was then and what it is now".

Wednesday, May 31: ". . . After tea together with Benckendorf I removed the seal from the cabinet in Papa's study and looked through all papers and things that were there . . ."

Saturday, June 3: "After morning tea unexpectedly Kerenskiy arrived in his motor. He did not stay long with me: asked to send to the investigation committee some papers or letters dealing with internal policy . . ."

so [I] *have occasion to write again. What relief and joy it was to hear your precious voice, only one heard so badly and one listens now to all conversations. And y. dear wire this morning before 1. Baby leant over the bed and tells me to kiss you. All 4 are lying in the green room in the dark, Marie and I are writing, scarcely seeing anything with the curtains drawn* [because of the children's measles]. *This morning only read the manifesto* [of Nikolai's abdication] *and later another from M.*[ikhail Alexandrovitch]. *People are beside themselves with misery and adoration for my Angel* [Cesarevitch Alexei]. *A movement is beginning amongst the troops. Fear nothing from Sunny, she does not move – does not exist. Only I feel and foresee glorious sunshine ahead . . . Live with you, love and adore you. Kiss and embrace so tenderly fondly. God bless and keep you now and ever . . . God on high will help and new Worship of the Cross coming. Hold you tight. Y. very own Wify".*

(Above) June 1917. Nikolai with Alexandra on one of her rare outings, due to her poor health. On June 9, Nikolai wrote in his diary: "It is exactly three months since my arrival from Mogilyov and we live like convicts. The pain is not having news from dear Mama and for the rest I don't care . . . Alix did not go out. Before dinner just five of us went for a stroll."

Saturday, June 10: "During the night and until 3 in the afternoon the stuffy heat was unbearable. This evening at about 11 we heard a shot, after a quarter of an hour the chief of the guard came and informed us that the sentry had fired because it seemed to him that from the children's window one was sending signals with a red lamp. After having inspected the position of the light and the movement of Anastasia's head, who was sitting next to the window, one of the non-commission officers who had come in together with him [the chief of the guard] understood what was happening and having apologised they left."

Sunday, June 11: "Yesterday Teteryatnikov left, and Chemodurov [the Tsar's valet who would follow the Tsar's family to exile in Siberia] came to replace him . . ."

Monday, June 26. ". . . Our good superintendent Col. [onel] Kobylinskiy asked me not to stretch out my hand to shake with the officers in front of strangers . . . Before there were several instances when they did not reply . . ."

Friday, July 7: "In the morning went for a walk with Maria, Valya [Dolgorukov] and the entire escort of the guards of the 3rd rifle regiment . . . in the evening I glued the photographs of our life 'under arrest' into my album."

On the morning of March 8, the new commander of the Petrograd front, General Kornilov, accompanied by Kobylinskiy, the new chief of the Tsarskoye Selo garrison, arrived in Tsarskoye Selo. "Your Majesty", the general addressed the Tsarina, "I'm entrusted with the grave task of explaining to you the resolution of the Council of Ministers of the Provisional Government, that from this moment you must consider yourself under arrest . . ." Alexandra Feodorovna took it with dignity. What really mattered for her about Kornilov's visit was the news that Nikolai was soon coming to Tsarskoye Selo.

Next morning Nikolai arrived in Tsarskoye Selo. The motor took him from the station to the Alexander Palace. His diary does not betray what must have been a very emotional reunion. Thursday, March 9: "At 11.30, quickly and safely, I reached Tsarskoye Selo. God, how different everything is – the street and the park around the palace are full of sentinels, inside young recruits – I went upstairs to see dear Alix and the children. Maria is in bed with the measles . . . As we are not allowed out* [on March 8, without any sanction of the law-court, Nikolai had been put under arrest] *I went with Valya Dolgorukov to work in the garden . . ."* Now they were together again, and it brought peace to their souls. But every day of captivity was to be marked with new, spiteful reminders of their changed position. Once Anna Vyrubova witnessed a shameful scene when the revolutionary soldiers "pushed His Majesty with their fists and even with rifle butts as if he had been a criminal, and they called in raised voices: " *'Look here, Sir Colonel, you can't go there, come back, we tell you!' Absolutely calmly, His Majesty looked at them and returned to the Palace".* Alexei's toys were taken away and broken; they destroyed the ice-slopes, the favourite and only entertainment for the children and grown-ups; they shot at the tame goats; they carried off things from the Palace; the instances of abuse were numerous. However, as the guards got to know the family, their respect returned.

Their daily routine was simple: they got up at 8 a.m., then there was morning tea. From 11 a.m. till noon and from 2.30 till 5 p.m. they were allowed to take a walk. In the evening His Majesty used to come to the daughters' room and he read aloud Russian classics while the Tsarina and the girls did some needlework. All the members of this united family, except for the Tsarina who was often unwell, did a lot of hard work, clearing the alleys of snow and twigs, felling old trees and storing up fire-wood. When it became warmer, they were busy laying out a kitchen garden, and soon they were joined in their

Summer 1917. Tatiana and Anastasia, with one of their pet dogs. The two girls, along with the rest of the Tsar's family, by now had been under house arrest for several months, and their facial expressions, that of Tatiana in particular, betray some of the stress and anxiety they must have experienced.

At this time the family was allowed to take walks and here the two girls seem to be enjoying the beautiful, natural environment; they could not have imagined what horrors life had in store for them. They are both prettily dressed in typical summer clothes and are still wearing their jewels. They had probably gone picnicking or picking wild flowers on this beautiful summer's day. The only hint of menace in this beautiful setting is the presence of the guard . . .

Four pet dogs followed the Tsar's family to exile in Siberia: Joy the Spaniel, Jemmy the Lap-dog, Ortino the Pekingese and a Bulldog. The fate of the latter two is unkown to us. Joy survived the massacre. Anastasia's Jemmy was the one which was shot together with the family. Its corpse was found by Sokolov during the searches of 1918, in the same shaft, together with the Tsarina's finger and Botkin's jaw.

Friday, July 28. ". . . After breakfast I learnt from Count Benckendorf that they will send us not to the Crimea, but to one of remote provincial towns, three or four days journey eastwards! . . And we all had so much wished we could stay long in Livadia!"

Sunday, July 30. "Alexei has turned thirteen today. May the Lord grant him health, strength of spirit and body in these grave times . . . After lunch [we went] to prayers for which they brought the icon of Our Lady of the Signs, [it] was especially heart-warming to pray to her saintly image together with all our people ."

July 31–August 1. "Our last day in Tsarskoye Selo. The weather was lovely . . . After dinner we were waiting when they would appoint the hour of our departure, which was forever postponed. Suddenly Kerenskiy came and declared that Misha [G.D. Mikhail Alexandrovitch] would soon come. Indeed, about 10 1/2 p.m. dear Misha came accompanied by Ker. [enskiy] and the guard's chief. It was nice to see him, but it was uncomfortable to talk in the presence of the strangers. When he left, the rifle-men of the guards started to carry our luggage to the rounded drawing-rooms. Sitting there were the Benckendorfs, the maids-of-honour, the maids and the servants. They kept our departure such a secret, that the motors and the trains were ordered only after the hour of our departure had been appointed. We were exhausted to a colossal extent! Alexei felt sleepy – now and again he tried to go to bed, and then got up. Several times they made false alarms, we put on our coats, went out on the balcony, and then returned into our rooms. It dawned already. We had some tea at last, at 5 1/4 Ker. appeared and said that we could go . . . We left Tsarskoye Selo at 6.10 a.m."

August, 1. "We occupied a good sleeping-car of international class. I went to sleep at 7.45 and slept till 9.15. It was dusty and stuffy in the carriage – 26 [degrees]. Went out for a walk with our rifle-man in the afternoon, picked flowers and berries. We have our meals in the restaurant, the delicious food is cooked by the cuisine of the East- Chinese Railway."

August 4. "Having passed the Urals we felt it was much cooler. We passed Yekaterinburg early in the morning . . . We dragged on incredibly slowly – so as to arrive in Tyumen late – at 11 1/2 p.m. There the train came very close to the quay, so we just had to descend to embark on a steamer. Ours is called "Rus". They began to load which lasted through the night. Poor Alexei, again he went to bed God knows when. The rumbling tumbling never ceased and it kept me sleepless. Put off from Tyumen at about 6 a.m.

August 6. ". . . We have reached Tobolsk . . . There were a lot of people on the bank – it means, they knew about our arrival . . . Valya [Dolgorukov], the commissar and the superintendent went to inspect the houses intended for us and for the suite. On their return we learnt that the lodgings are empty, without any furniture and dirty, and we cannot move there. So [we remained] on board the steamer . . ."

Sunday, August 13. ". . . At 10.30 we went to our new lodgings with the children. We have taken the first floor . . . We went to visit the house which will accommodate the retinue . . . We went to see the so called orchard, an ugly kitchen-garden, and went to see the kitchen and the guard-house. They all look old and desolate . . . I have put my things in my study and in the dressing room which I am sharing with Alexei. . ."

Monday, May 1. It was a very hot day and the Tsar's children had worked very hard in the kitchen garden; (top) from left to right are Olga, Alexei, Anastasia and Tatiana, taking a rest. That evening, Nikolai read to them the book, started earlier, the Sherlock Holmes classic, "The Hound of The Baskervilles" by Sir Arthur Conan Doyle. (Above left) Working in the garden, posing to look at something on the ground are Nikolai, Prince Dolgorukov and, in the foreground, is the faithful Nagorny. (Above right) Tsarskoye Selo, June 1917. By the lake, in the grounds of the palace, Pierre Gilliard with Alexei. Alexei's hair is very short, having been shaved when the child was ill with measles. Facing page: At the time of their arrest in the Alexander Palace the Tsar's family had the comfort of being surrounded by familiar faces and friends. Here posing for the camera are from left to right: Prince Dolgorukov, Pierre Gilliard, Countess Hendrikova, Baroness Buxhoeveden, Countess Benckendorf, Count Benckendorf and Doctor Derevenko; sitting is Schneider. (Bottom) Nikolai enjoying a cigarette. He seemed to have lost weight and his face showed some strain. At this time there was a small ray of hope in his heart that things could make a turn for the better.

(Above) Alexander Feodorovitch Kerenskiy, one of the leaders of the February revolution. On March 7, 1917, the Provisional Government presided over by Prince Lvov, passed the resolution in accordance with which the Emperor Nikolai II and his spouse were placed under arrest. However, not only were the former Tsar and Tsarina deprived of freedom, but their children also found themselves in captivity, which could have no legal justification at all. The Minister of Justice, and from July 8 — Chairman-Minister of the Provisional Government, Alexander Kerenskiy was one of the politicians involved in organizing the Romanovs' arrest and their subsequent exile in Tobolsk. This fierce enemy of the Romanovs and the monarchy would later avoid requital for his deeds. For decades afterwards, knocking about the world, this failed political braggart would try to prove to the public, both orally and in writing, that the death of the Tsar's Family was not his fault and that his one and only aspiration was to save them from the crowd's wrath. The inconsistent Russian Cromwell sought to rescue his historical image, but the truth is crystal clear: Kerenskiy failed to keep a single promise he had made to the Tsar. In September 1917, Nikolai wrote from Tobolsk to his sister Xenia, then staying together with her family and mother, Dowager Empress Maria Feodorovna, in Ai-Todor, Grand Duke Alexander Mikhailovitch's Crimean estate: *". . . I also hoped that they would send us there and we would be locked up in Livadia. At least [we could be] nearer to you. So many times Kerenskiy promised me this . . ."* With the entire government authority vested in him at that time, Kerenskiy did nothing to try and rescue the Tsar's family.

(Above right) Maria Stepanova and Vladimir Derevenko leaving for Tobolsk on August 18. Nikolai's diary: Thursday, August 24. *"A lovely day. Vl. Nik. Derevenko and his family have arrived, this has made up the event of the day."*

(Right) Tobolsk. Soldiers guarding the entrance of the house. The street, quite ironically was called "Liberty Street".

(Inset) Easter postcard from Olga to her father dated April 2, 1917: *"Christ Has Resurrected! My golden precious Papa. God grant you a serene and happy celebration of this luminous holiday. I kiss you awfully fondly, my dear Papa. Yours truly, Plastun [Unmounted Cossack]."*

labours by some soldiers and officers of the guard.

They were not to reap their harvest. By the end of July it had become clear to everybody in Tsarskoye that soon Nikolai Alexandrovitch, together with his family and their few servants, would be transferred to a new place; they could hardly guess where. There was a hope they might be allowed to go to England, but this never came to pass and the family's most cherished dream – to go to the Crimea, to their favourite Livadia – was also never realised. On Saturday, August 11, they were told that they should take special care and prepare more warm clothes. Colonel Kobylinskiy, who was to escort the Tsar and his family to the new place of exile, informed the Tsar secretly: "Tobolsk". It was not cheerful news, wracked as the entire family was with foreboding. At about 6 a.m. on August 14, from the small station of Alexandrovka, a special train started off and with every kilometre it covered, it took its captives further and

(Above) The Governor's House in Tobolsk where the Tsar's family was kept under arrest.

further from the possibility of a wise and humane settlement of this great human drama.

Secret negotiations with various governments about the possibility of the Family's emigration had begun back in March. But given the political situation of March-July 1917, none of the governments wished to risk their own position and safety. While the mob was screaming "Crucify him!", their so-called rulers were concerned about their own fortunes rather than those of Nikolai and his family.

"Throughout the journey the former Tsar and Tsarina, as well as their family and the persons who have volunteered to follow them, shall be treated as those under arrest", stipulated Point 1 of the instruction drawn up and handwritten by Alexander Kerenskiy, dated July 31, 1917.

On the evening of August 17, they arrived in Tyumen. There they embarked on the steamer *Rus,* bound for Tobolsk. They were installed in the governor's bleak, uncomfortable and cheerless house. Undeterred by the lack of comfort, the "prisoners" tried their best to support and encourage one another. The first period of their life in Tobolsk was rather peaceful. The children resumed their classes. Their tutors were Gilliard and Schneider, joined later by Gibbs and Bitner, a former teacher in the Tsarskoye Selo gymnasium. Nikolai became their tutor of history, and Alexandra was their religious instructor. One morning the former Tsar was to greet Gilliard: "Hello, colleague". The family were allowed to attend church. In the evenings they read to each other or played bezique. Amateur dramatics were rare entertainments to brighten up the monotony of their confinement. Their favourite pastime was chopping wood and it made for a sort of outdoor sport.

When news arrived in Tobolsk it was always late and incomplete, which depressed Nikolai. Anxiously, he followed the course of events, and the failure of Kornilov's Petrograd campaign made it clear to His Majesty that Russia was heading for disaster. Gilliard noticed that it was in Tobolsk that the Tsar began to think differently about his abdication: *"For the first time then I heard from His Majesty that he regretted his abdication. He had taken this decision hoping that those who had sought to get rid of him would be able to bring the war to a successful end and save Russia. He had feared lest his resistance should have provoked a civil war in the enemy's presence, and he hadn't wished the blood of even a single Russian to be shed for him. But hadn't his resignation been soon followed by the appearance of Lenin and his henchmen, those German mercenaries, whose criminal propaganda had disorganised the army and depraved the country? He suffered as he saw that his self-abnegation had availed Russia of nothing, for though he had sought the good of his Motherland, his exit had done Russia an ill turn. This rankling*

Nikolai continued to write his diary. Wednesday, August 23. *"Today is two years from my arrival in Mogilyov. Since then a lot of water has run under the bridge . . ."* Friday, September, 1. *"A new commissar of the Prov [isional] Govern. [ment] Pankratov arrived and settled in the suite's house with an assistant of his, a dishevelled ensign [Nikolskiy]. He looks like a worker or a poor teacher. He will be the censor of our correspondence. The day was cold and rainy."* September 8. *"For the first time [we] went to the Annunciation church . . . but the pleasure was spoilt for me by the stupid circumstances of our proceeding there. The alley of the town park, in which there was nobody, was lined by riflemen, and near the very church there was a great crowd! This exhausted me to the very depth."* Friday, September 29. *"Recently Ye. S. Botkin has received a paper from Kerenskiy, from which we've learnt that we are allowed excursions outside the town. To Botkin's question when we could start them, Pankratov the rascal replied that they were impossible for some inexplicable fear for our security. We were all filled with indignation to the extreme . . ."* Saturday, October 7. *". . . At night it was 10 degrees of frost . . . At last Mr. Gibbs arrived and told us many interesting things of life in Petrograd."*

(Top) The Tsarina enjoying the fresh air while doing needlework.
(Inset) The Tsarina's diary. There is a page with an exercise in Old Slav numbers. The ancient Slavs did not use Arabic or Latin numbers, but some letters of their alphabet denoted numbers as well. Alexandra wrote the date in Arabian numbers: 1918, and then in Old Slav. Then she drew up a table of Old Slav numbers. Then she wrote: *"January 1. Christ's Circumcision today . . . went to church . . . Olga in bed 37.3 [fever]. Tatiana too 38. German measles. Tatiana has a strong rash all over, headache and eyes bloodshot. Alexei alright again. Sat with the girls sowing. Lunched with them in their bedroom at 12. Beautiful, sunny weather, sat on the balcony for 35 m [inutes] and then with the girls till tea time . . . Played bezique with N. [ikolai], then he read to us and I knitted. We 7 [the Tsar's family], Nastinka [Anastasia Gendrikova], Trina [Catherine Schneider], Tatischev, Valya D., Mr. Gilliard, Mr. Gibbs, Dr. Botkin, Dr. Derevenko and Isa [Buxhoeveden] are here. Mother dear, Olga [Nikolai's sister], [her] husband and Tikhon [their son], Xenia [Alexandrovna] and her family are all at Ai–Todor."*
Facing page: (bottom) A photograph inscribed: *"O.N. [Olga] and A.N. [Anastasia] are in the park. A.N. is smoking. The photo was taken by M.N. [Maria]."* It was Nikolai himself who taught his daughters to smoke, and sometimes he sent cigarettes to them from the Stavka. In a letter to her father Anastasia once wrote: *"Thank you for the smokes. We are really enjoying them."*

awareness haunted him incessantly, and it grew to cause him agonies of repenting".

Could he perhaps already foresee the frightful future of Russia and fathom the yawning abyss which would soon devour millions of human beings? His predicament bore a close resemblance to that of St. Luke when he spoke to his followers, saying: *"For I know that after my departing shall grievous wolves enter in among you, not sparing the flock".* (Acts, XX, 29). And the letter Grand Duchess Olga Nikolayevna wrote in Tobolsk to their friends carried the Tsar's admonishment: *"Father asks to tell all those who are still faithful to him, and those whom they can influence that they should not revenge for Him for He has forgiven all and prays for all, that they should not revenge for themselves and they should bear it in mind that it will make the evil which has overrun the world even greater, for it is not evil to conquer evil, but love".*

The October revolution, a logical, pathetic adjunct of the February revolution, rolled over and through Russia, ensnaring the whole country. Defying massive losses, it vanquished its enemies caring little – if at all – that the opposition had comprised almost all of Russia. In the winter of 1917-18, the Tobolsk prisoners felt the approach of the revolution. First and foremost, it could be deduced from the behaviour of most of their guards who didn't hesitate to adopt the slogans of the October victors: "Liberty, Equality, Fraternity".

As the first step to implement these slogans, the Tsar's retainers, who had enjoyed relative freedom, were deprived of the privilege. Next came the abolition of rank, the commander of the detachment having thus been put on a par with his newly-made "comrades" in compliance with the decision of his former subordinates. Kobylinskiy felt power was slipping away from him. *"Your Majesty, all authority is fast slipping out of my hands,"* the Colonel admitted despondently. *"They ordered us to take off the epaulettes. I cannot be of any more use to You. If You allow me, I'd rather resign. My nerves are completely frayed. I can stand it no more".* Nikolai II and his son were also ordered to take off their epaulettes, but they refused. So they had to hide their epaulettes under their cloaks.

On April 8, the 24th anniversary of Nikolai and Alix's engagement, a humiliating telegram arrived from Moscow. It demanded that Nikolai and Alexei obey the resolution of the detachment committee and take off their epaulettes. As a compromise, it was decided between father and son that they would take off their epaulettes when they went out for a walk and wear them only at home. But the sway of vulgar soldiers' and workers' wilfulness was not to be lasting; the new power, with its rigorous decrees and severe punishments, relentlessly suppressed all local relaxations.

After the Bolsheviks' seizure of power, the "sensitive" question of the destiny of the Tsar's family became a factor in the diplomatic board-game between the new Soviet power and Germany. The position of the German government was stated by the ambassador, Count Wilhelm Mirbach, when he declared that they did not feel responsible for the destiny of the Tsar – it was a matter for the Russian people, but they were concerned for the safety of the "princesses of German blood". However, they emphasised the humanitarian significance of sparing the Tsar's life, aware of the potential public outrage his assassination would cause. The signing of the Treaty of Brest-Litovsk with Germany, so humiliating for Russia, made the subtleties of Soviet-German relations even more opaque.

On April 9/22, a commissar "extraordinaire", Vasiliy Yakovlev, a member of the Central Executive Committee, authorised with powers of "special importance", arrived in Tobolsk. For a long time Yakovlev's role has seemed obscure and mysterious. Some thought him to be a British agent; others – including the White investigator Sokolov who was the first to report on the murders of the family, and Empress Alexandra Feodorovna –

(Above) 1917–1918, Tobolsk. The guards approaching the Governor's house. (Inset) A guard on duty.

(Left) The Romanovs' ration cards for 1917, Tobolsk. It looked like a booklet, with the following text on the cover: "Surname: Romanov. Name: Nikolai. Father's name: Alexandrovitch. Occupation: Ex-Emperor. Street: Liberty. House No . . . Members of the family: 7. . . Their ration in November consisted only of: Fine wheat flour . . . – 7 1/2 pounds . . . " The co-operative from which they had to purchase the ration had the sarcastic name of "Self- Consciousness".

Nikolai wrote on December 12. *"Today there was an incident with the plank of the swing, on which there was an indecent scribble made by someone of the 2nd rifle regiment . . ."*

Thursday, December 28. *". . . We've learnt with indignation that our kind F. [ather] Alexei will be involved in the investigation, and he is under house arrest. It happened because during the service of Dec. 25 the deacon mentioned us with our titles, and in the church there were as ever many riflemen of the 2nd regiment which created a mess, probably not without the meddling of Pankratov and his gang."*

Friday, January 5, 1918. *". . . talked with the riflemen of the 1st section, 4th regiment about the removal of the epaulettes and the behaviour of the riflemen of the 2nd regiment, which they severely denounce."* Monday, January 9. *"An excellent, serene day . . . During the recent two days [I] have been reading a book from the local Gymnasium – Golodnikov's Tobolsk and its Environs – with entertaining historical notes. In the afternoon did some good works . . . helping me was a good old rifleman of the first regiment Orlov . . . "* Friday, January 26. *"Finished reading the twelve volumes by Leskov and began [reading] 'The garden of Allah' in the Russian translation . . . At the decision of the detachment's committee, Pankratov and his assistant Nikolskiy have been dismissed from their offices and have to leave Kornilov's house!"*

Thursday, February 1/14. "We have learnt that at the post-office they have received the order to change the [calendar] style and catch up with the foreign one, that since February 1, i.e. today, is February 14. There will be no end of a muddle and mishmash."

Monday, February 12/25. "Today telegrams have arrived with the news that the bolsheviks, or, as they call themselves, the Sovnarkom [abbreviation for the Soviet of People's Commissars], will have to accept the peace of humiliating conditions imposed by the German gov [ernment] in view of the fact that the enemy's troops are advancing and there is no stopping them! What a nightmare."

Wednesday, February 14/27. "We have to cut substantially our expenses for food and domestic staff, because from March 1 they close down the Hofmarshal's department and besides, our expenditure from personal funds is limited to 600 rou. [bles] a month per each one of us. We've spent the recent days calculating the minimum which will avail us to make ends meet".

Thursday, February15/28. "For this reason we shall have to dismiss many of the household because we cannot afford to support all of those who are staying with us in Tobolsk. This is, of course, hard but inevitable. At our request, Tatischev, Valya [Dolgorukov] and Mr. Gilliard have taken up the duty of running the house and the remaining household, and Volkov the valet will assist them . . ."

Wednesday, February 28/March 13 "Lately we've begun to receive butter, coffee, cookies and jam for tea from some good people who have heard about the cutting in our food expenditure. It is so touching!" Friday, March 2/15. "I remember these days last year in Pskov and in the train! [Nikolai refers to the abdication]. How long will our poor Motherland be tormented and torn apart by foreign and internal enemies? Sometimes one seems to have no strength left to bear it all, one doesn't know even what to hope, what to wish for. And yet, nobody is like God! May His Sacred will be done !"

On Thursday, April, 12 Nikolai wrote in his diary: "After lunch Yakovlev came with Kobylinskiy and informed that he had received the orders to take me away, without saying where. Alix has resolved to come with me and take Maria with us; there was no protesting. It is more than painful to leave behind the other children and Alexei – who is so sick, . . . we began to pack the most necessary things. Then Yakovlev said he would come back to bring Olga, Tatiana, Anastasia and Alexei and that probably we would see them in three weeks. [We] spent a sad evening; of course, nobody slept at night."

April 13. "At 4 a.m., said goodbye to the dear children and took the tarantasses [four-wheeled, springless carriages]: me – with Yakovlev, Alix – with Maria, Valya – with Botkin. Of the household coming with us are Nyuta Demidova, Chemodurov and Sednev, 8 riflemen and the mounted escort [of the Red Army] of 10 people. The weather was cold . . . the road was hard and awfully bumpy . . . [We] crossed the Irtysh [river] at a place where the water was rather deep. [We] had four relays having covered 130 miles during the first day. Stopped for the night in the village of Ievlevo . . . The last relay was in the v. [illage] of Borki. . ."

Saturday, April 14. "Got up at 4 a.m. . . there was a delay . . . The day was excellent and very warm, and yet it was very jolty, and I worried about Alix . . . In the v [illage] of Pokrovskoye there was a delay, and we stood long right in front of Grigoriy [Rasputin]'s house and saw all his family watching from the window . . ."

Monday, April 16. "In the morning we noticed that we are going back. It turned out that in Omsk they did not wish to let us pass! . . But instead we were given more freedom, even took a stroll twice, the first time along the train, and the second – rather far in the field together with Yakovlev himself. . ."

Tuesday, April 17: ". . . At 8.40 a.m. we arrived in Yekaterinburg . . . There were strong rumblings between the locals and our commissars. In the end the former took the upper hand, and the train moved to another station . . . freight yard. After an hour and half long stop [we] left the train. Yakovlev handed us over to the local regional commissar, with whom the three of us took a motor and drove along the deserted streets to the house prepared for us – Ipatyev's. Little by little our people joined us . . . but Valya was not allowed in. The house is big and clean. . . For a long time we could not begin unpacking . . . The examination of our trunks was like one of the customs, so thorough it was, up to the last phial of Alix's medicine chest. It made me burst out, and I curtly expressed my opinion to the commissar . . . We settled the fol. [lowing] way: the three of us – Alix, Maria and I – in the bedroom, . . . in the dining-room – N. Demidova, in the hall – Botkin, Chemodurov and Sednev. Near the entrance is the room of the guards' officer. The guards were accommodated in two rooms near the dining-room. When going to the bathroom and WC one would have to pass the sentry at the doors of the guards' room. Around the house a very high fence of planks was erected . . ., standing there was a chain of sentries, as well as in the garden.

(Top) A drawing of the time when the train carrying some members of the Imperial Family was intercepted and Yakovlev handed them over to the Ural Soviet, who took them to Yekaterinburg. (Above) The courtyard of the Governor's house in Tobolsk. (Inset) Telegram from Chelyabinsk to Tobolsk informing that the train with Nikolai and Alexandra Romanov is being detained because of sabotage. Facing page: (top) June 1917. Photograph taken by Maria of her sisters Tatiana and Anastasia bringing water for the garden. (Bottom) June 1917. Baroness Buxhoeveden and Countess Hendrikova, Alexandra Feodorovna's maids of honour. (Inset) The documents read: " Identity card No 51. The person, whose photo is on the reverse hereof, Anna Stepanova Demidova, is allowed to enter and leave the house, which by the official seal and signature is certified. Tobolsk. October 1917. Commissar of the Provisional Government Pankratov. Superintendent of the Alexander Palace Colonel Kobylinskiy."

believed him to be a German messenger. In fact, he was a true Bolshevik, one of Lenin's lieutenants, his real name being Konstantin Myachin. Before the revolution he had been a participant and organiser of the so-called "expropriations", burglaries and plunder to raise money for Bolshevik activities. Suspected by his fellow Bolsheviks of treason, he defected to the White Guards in autumn 1918. But as the accusations were discredited, he returned to the side of the Bolsheviks. There is some evidence that he worked for the Cheka. He died in Russia in 1938. From his talks with Yakovlev, Kobylinskiy inferred that the commissar intended to deport the Tsar to Moscow, and he informed the Tsar about it. *"Well, I reckon they want me to sign the Treaty of Brest-Litovsk. But I'd rather have my arm cut off than do it"*, His Majesty replied to his guard. Kobylinskiy recollected that as soon as Alexandra heard about Nikolai's ensuing departure, she demanded: *"I'm going too. If I am not there they'll force him to sign something wrong as they once made him"*. "Her Majesty must have been alluding to the Tsar's abdication act",

(Top right) Portrait of Yakovlev. (Above) Yakovlev's identity card certified by Dzerzhinskiy and another document of Yakovlev bearing the name of metal worker Ivan Klokov. Nikolai's diary entry on Good Friday, April 20. *"During the night it was much colder... I have read appropriate [parts of] Holy Gospel aloud in the bedroom... From obscure hints ... it can be inferred that poor Valya is not free and there will be an investigation, after which he will be released..."* Wednesday, April 25. *"New soldiers have arrived... the majority were Letts, ... I spoke to an ex-officer and he told me many interesting things... Ukraintsev brought us the first telegram from Olga..."* Thursday, April 26. *"... Today next to us, that is in the guard room, and with the sentries, since this morning there has been great agitation, and the telephone never stopped ringing . .. Ukraintsev has been away the whole time, though it is his duty day. Of course, they did not let us know what was happening... On duty instead of Ukraintsev was an enemy 'the pop-eyed', who had to take us out on a stroll. He kept silent all the time because nobody spoke to him. In the evening, during the bezique, he brought another queer person with him, took round of all the rooms with him and left."* Monday, April 30 *"... An old woman, and then a boy tried to get near the fence – to look at us through a slot; they were driven away by all means, but everybody made fun of them. Avdeyev the rascal came into the garden, but kept his distance..."*

Kobylinskiy concluded.

But, in this event, the mother was to leave behind her sick child, who, as Yakovlev promised, was to be brought to them later, together with all those who stayed with Alexei for the meantime. Alexandra Feodorovna had to face a pressing dilemma; forced to choose between her husband and her child. "For the first time in my life I absolutely do not know what to do. Up till now God has always shown me the right way. And today I don't know what to do, and there is no indication for me". Then suddenly she took her decision: "But it's all settled. My duty is to go with him. I can't let him go alone. And you'll be looking after Alexei here", she turned to Olga, Tatiana and Anastasia, and her eyes welled with tears. It was agreed that Grand Duchess Maria, Prince Dolgorukov, and Dr. Botkin would accompany Nikolai and Alix. They decided that Chemodurov the valet, Sednev the footman and the maid Demidova would also escort the party.

Yakovlev was noticeably nervous and he hastened the departure. On April 13, at 4 a.m., the group, escorted by ten mounted guards and eight riflemen, set out on a long, dangerous journey. Later Yakovlev described the scene as the family bade their farewells: *"The Romanov daughters and all their retainers came out onto the porch. The embarrassed Nikolai Romanov passed from one to another and with somewhat convulsive movements made the sign of the cross over his daughters. His arrogant wife held up her daughters' tears, her every gesture, every word saying that they were not to show their weakness to 'the Red Enemy'."*

The next day was marked by an event, almost mystic for its coincidence, which Nikolai noted in his diary. As they were passing the village of Pokrovskoye, Grigoriy Rasputin's birthplace, they stopped to change the horses, and it so happened that they stood right in front of Grigoriy's house and saw all his family watching them through the windows. They soon reached Tyumen where they took the train, and from the sequence of the stations they surmised they were moving towards Omsk. *"We began to conjecture where we'd be taken on reaching Omsk? To Moscow or to Vladivostok?"* Nikolai reflected in his diary. But then, suddenly, Moscow put everything into reverse. In Omsk the train was stopped and sent in the opposite direction. On the old style calendar April 17, at 8.40 a.m., the train arrived in Yekaterinburg, a "lovely warm day".

Their new place of custody was the house of the engineer Ipatyev who had been evicted from it the day before by Bolsheviks. On entering Ipatyev's house Alexandra made a mark on the post of the door to her room. She drew her Indian sign and put down the date: *"Apr. 17/30, 1918"*. Since that day, the conditions of the prisoners' confinement in the "House of Special Purpose" – as the place of their last custody was designated – became a matter of intense concern for the Council of People's Commissars and the Central Executive Committee, the supreme governmental bodies of Soviet power. Testifying to this fact are the numerous records of their sittings presided over by Lenin and Sverdlov. In one of the notes sent by Sverdlov to Yekaterinburg, to Beloborodov, Chairman of the regional Soviet, Sverdlov says: *"I suggest Nikolai be treated in the most severe manner. Yakovlev is entrusted to convey the others. Submit the estimate of all expenditures, inclusive of the guards. Inform of the details of the new confinement conditions. Chairman of the CEC Sverdlov. 3.5.18".*

In his diary, Nikolai gave his own account of some "details of the new confinement conditions", and he couldn't help lacing his commentary with irony: *"Tuesday, May 1. . . Today we were informed through Botkin that we were allowed to take only one hour walks; having been asked why, the acting superin-*

Tsarskoye Selo, 1917. (Above) Anastasia in the park of the Alexander Palace. (Left) Anastasia, Olga and Maria who is sleeping in the sun. Nikolai's diary entry:
Thursday, May 3. *"The day was grey but warm. In the rooms . . . it was very damp; the air coming through the window pane was much warmer than that in the room. I taught Maria to play backgammon. Sednev's fever abated, but he was laid up the whole day . . . In the afternoon we received coffee, Easter eggs and chocolate which Ella had sent us from Perm. The electric lights in the dining room went off and we had supper with the light of the two candles inserted in pots . . ."*
Friday, May 4. *"We have learnt that the children left Tobolsk, but Avdeyev did not mention when. In the afternoon he unlocked the door of the room which we intend for Alexei. It turned out to be larger and lighter than we had supposed as there are two windows in it; our stove makes it very warm . . ."*
Sunday, May 6. *"I have reached the age of 50, it seems so strange! . . We receive no news from the children and begin doubting if they really left Tobolsk?"*
Tuesday, May 8. *"In the morning we heard thunder, and way from the town there was [a thunder-storm], but here there were several showers. Before dinner I read the 4th part of 'War and Peace', about which I had not known before . . ."* Received a greeting telegram from Olga for May 6 [Nikolai's birth-day]."
Wednesday, May 9. *"Both Maria and I were absorbed in reading 'War and Peace'. . . We still do not know about the children . . ."*

(Right) The Ipatyev's House. (Below right) The room where the Tsar's family were murdered. (Inserts left to right) Inside the Ipatyev house, the doors leading to the basement where the Family were shot and the plan of Ipatyev's house. The inscription on the corner reads: *"The room in which Nikolai Romanov was executed. A. Beloborodov".*

When Nikolai drew a map of Ipatyev's house and tried to send it to the children still in Tobolsk, Avdeyev removed the map from Nikolai's letter informing him that this was not allowed.

Thursday, May 10. *"In the morning, within an hour, they consecutively declared that the children were several hours way off from the town, then, that they had reached the station, and finally, that they had arrived at the house, though their train had been here since 2 a.m.! What great joy it was to see them again and embrace after four weeks of separation and uncertainty. There was no end of mutual question and reply. Very few letters had reached them and us. How much moral suffering had the poor ones lived through both in Tobolsk and during the three days journey . . . Of those who had newly arrived only Kharitonov the cook and Sednev's nephew [Leonid] were allowed in. In the afternoon went out for about twenty minutes — it was cold and desperately dirty. We expected the beds and necessary things to arrive from the station before night, but in vain, and all the daughters had to sleep on the floor. Alexei spent the night in Maria's bed. In the evening he haplessly hurt his knee and all night through he suffered much and kept us awake."*

Friday, May 11. *"Since morning we've expected our people from Tobolsk to be allowed in and the remaining luggage to arrive. I decided to let my old man Chemodurov go and have a rest and instead of him to take for a while Trupp. Only in the evening they allowed him and Nagorny to come in, and for an hour and half they were interrogated and searched in the superintendent's room. Though we were all sitting in the bedroom together, I read a lot; began [reading] 'An Unfinished Story' by Apukhtin."*

Saturday, May 12. *"Everybody slept well, except Alexei . . . The weather completely matched our spirit, wet snow was falling. Through Botkin we entered in negotiations with the chairman of the regional soviet so that Mr. Gilliard be allowed to join us . . . Supper was nearly an hour late."*

Sunday, May 13. *". . . There was no mass . The weather was the same . . . As usual V.N. Derevenko came to examine Alexei; today he was accompanied by a man in black whom we took for a doctor [Yurovskiy]. After a short walk we went with superint. [endent] Avdeyev to the shed, where all our big luggage has been taken to. The inspection of some of the chests which could be opened continued. Began reading Saltykov [Schedrin], borrowed from the bookcase of the owner of the house. Played bezique in the evening."*

(Far left) Lev Davidovitch Trotskiy (1879-1940) was one of Lenin's closest comrades-in-arms. In the early 1920s his popularity in Soviet Russia was so high that there were even icon-styled pictures of him, which featured Trotskiy with legs astride, looking like St. George the Victorious, with a spear piercing a snake, which designated the world bourgeoisie. But after Stalin's succession to power he became a by-word of counter revolution, as the new Soviet leader did his best to get rid of all rivals. It is from Trotskiy's reminiscences that it is known that Lenin was fully informed about the fate of the Tsar's family, and participated in taking the fatal decision.

(Left) Yakov Mikhailovitch Yurovskiy.

(Middle) An artist's visualization of the Yekaterinburg massacre. (Bottom far left) Two handwritten copies of Yakovlev's telegrams to Moscow. The Tsar's family in them are designated as "luggage". He describes the difficulties imposed by the "left" and the "right-wingers". Yakovlev suggests he be appointed a permanent Commissar to guard the" luggage" until its liquidation. In the second one he complains that: " . . . The Yekaterinburg detachment are striving to achieve only one goal – annihilate the luggage . . . "

(Bottom left) Instructions drawn by the Superintendent Yurovskiy on the conditions of prison regime for the convicts of Ipatyev's house. The document reveals a thirst for administration which had overtaken this petty creature, making him dizzy in his new role. This one reads: "Walks. The prisoners are allowed daily walks for the term stipulated by the Reg. [ional] Soviet. Those wishing to take a walk should go out together. Before the prisoners are taken out for a walk, the superintendent gives an order to reinforce the guards at the yard where the walk will be taking place by putting the sentries there and on the balconies. The superintendent tries as far as it is possible to establish permanent time to begin the walk and appoint it within the limits from 12 till 4 p.m."

Nikolai's diary entry on Monday, May 14: "The weather was warm. Read a lot. Alexei was a bit better. In the afternoon went out for an hour. After tea Sednev and Nagorny were called out for interrogation to the reg. soviet. In the evening the inspection of the daughter's luggage continued in their presence. The sentry [who was standing on duty] under our window shot at our house because it had seemed to him that someone was moving near the window (after 10 a.m.) – I think he was playing with the rifle as sentries always do."

Tuesday, May 15. "Today it is a month since we have stayed here. Alexei's [pains] are the same. Only the periods of remission have become longer. The weather was hot and sultry, but in the rooms it was cool. Had dinner at 2 p.m. Went out and sat in the garden for an hour and 1/4. Alix cut my hair quite well."

Wednesday, May 16. "The day was excellent . . . Alexei was better. Vl. Nik. [Derevenko] put his leg in a plaster cast . . . Alix went to bed earlier because of her migraine. Nothing

Nikolai's diary entry for Sunday, May 20: "*At 11 a.m. a mass was served in the house; Alexei was present staying in bed. The weather was marvellous, hot. Went out before the mass and in the afternoon before tea. It is unbearable to be locked up like that and be unable to go out into the garden when you'd like to, and to spend a lovely evening outdoors! The prison regime!!*" Tuesday, May 21. "*. . . Went out twice. Downstairs in the guard-room there was another gun-shot; the superintendent came to find out if the bullet passed through the floor. Alexei had no pains at all . . .*" Friday, May 25. "*I spent my dear Alix's birthday in bed with strong pains in my feet and other places! The next few days I felt better and could eat sitting in the arm chair.*" After May 25, 1918, Nikolai would break his rule which he had kept for more than 37 years and interrupt the daily record of his life. There was no entry on May 26 and his diary shows many dates missing including July 1, 2, 3. With no more hope in his heart for the safety of his family, was it becoming harder for Nikolai to take pen to paper? Monday, 28 May. "*It was a very warm day. In the shed where our chests are kept someone constantly is opening the boxes and taking out various things and food stores from Tobolsk. And there is no account for that at all. All this makes us think that the things someone likes could be easily taken by them and thus be lost for us! How loathsome! The external relations have also changed during the recent weeks: the warders avoid talking to us as if they feel awkward, and one can feel some anxiety and misgiving about something in them! Inconceivable!*"

Anastasia & Maria Nikolayevna

tendent replied: '*To make it more like a prison regime . . .*" "*Wednesday, May 2. The furthering of the 'prison regime' evinced in the fact that this morning an old painter white-washed all our windows in all the rooms. Now it looks as if fog is showing through the windows.*" On May 9/22 the Tsar's children, accompanied by the faithful Pierre Gilliard, arrived in Tyumen where a special train awaited them. He recollected: "*The next morning the train arrived in Yekaterinburg. At 9 a.m. four men in grey came up to the children's carriage and entered it. A few minutes passed after which sailor Nagorny, who attended to Alexei Nikolayevitch, passed my window carrying the sick boy in his arms, behind him came the Grand Duchesses loaded with valises and small personal belongings. I tried to get out, but was roughly pushed back into the carriage by the sentry. I came back to the window. Tatiana Nikolayevna came last carrying her little dog and struggling to drag a heavy brown valise. It was raining and I saw her feet sink into the mud at every step. Nagorny tried to come to her assistance; he was roughly pushed back by one of the commissars . . . A few minutes later the carriages drove off carrying the children away downtown*". Thus Pierre Gilliard recorded the sad scene of his parting with his pupils, the last time he saw them.

The conditions of the family's confinement in Yekaterinburg were appalling. The rudeness and abuse from the new guards, often drunk and disorderly, made every day a living hell. The guards were recruited from Red Army soldiers and workers, many with criminal records. They were allowed to enter any room at anytime. The Grand Duchesses were persecuted with rough behaviour and lewd talk, both petty and vicious. Puerile porno-graphic pictures with crude captions were scribbled on the walls. Despite all this, the family maintained their courage and dignity. Among the effects found after their death were two poems, by Sergei Bekhteyev, from "Songs of Russian Grief and Tears", handwritten by Grand Duchess Olga Nikolayevna. Both poems are remarkable for their emotion and inexhaustible faith:

"BEFORE THE ICON OF OUR LADY
Of earth and heaven blessed Tsarina,
Our only source of consolation,
Lenient to every praying sinner,
Oh, heed our humble supplication.
Groping amid the dark of Spite,
Ensnared with Vice's fiendish lace,
We dare not repine at our plight,

But deign our Motherland Thy grace.
The holy land of Rus, once blessed,
Is now ordained to dire subversion,
Of all the suffering Patroness,
Oh, save our country from incursion.
Please, don't avert Thy eyes from those
Who thirst for Thy compassion,
Oh, grant us hope for repose
In our sorrow and oppression."

Olga & Tatiana Nikolayevna

"PRAYER
In time of trial and tribulation
To Thee, Lord Gracious, we appeal:
Help us to bear vilification
And to endure the ordeal.
Oh Christ Redeemer, give us force
In ghastly woe never to repine,
Help us surmount the bloodstained Way of the Cross
With meek forbearance o' Thine.
In days of outrageous tumult,
Oh Lord Creator, give us powers
To bear injury and insult
From looting enemies of ours.
Almighty Lord, Benignant Master,
Bless us with Thy divine orison,
And in the hour of dire disaster
Will give us peace Thy benison.
And at the edge of doom impending
Rid us of fear and dismay
And grant us fortitude unending
For our foes to humbly pray."

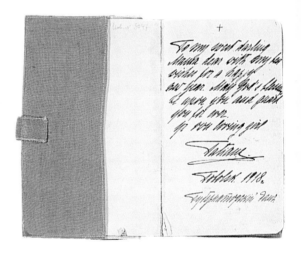

(Above) Tatiana's entry in Alexandra's diary. At that time they were still in Tobolsk. It reads: "To my sweet darling Mama dear, with my best wishes for a happy New Year. May God's blessing be upon you and guard you for ever. Your ever loving girl Tatiana. Tobolsk 1918. Governor's House"
Nikolai's diary entry on May 29: "Dear Tatiana has turned 21!... Since night a strong wind has started to blow, straight through the small opening pane in the window, owing to which the air in our bedroom was at last pure and rather cool ... For lunch Kharitonov cooked compote and it made everybody rejoice. In the evening we played bezique as usual."

The closing entry in Tatiana Nikolayevna's last surviving notebook recorded the words of the much revered preacher, who was canonized after his death, Father Ioann of Kronstadt: "*Your grief is indescribable, the Saviour's grief in the Gardens of Gethsemane for the world's sins is immeasurable, join your grief to his, in it you will find consolation*".

Soon a new superintendent of the Ipatyev's house was appointed. Nikolai's diary entry, June 21, would register the re-arrangement: "*Today there was a change of superintendents. At dinner-time came Beloborodov and others and declared that Avdeyev would*

(Below) List of "golden things" which had belonged to the Tsar's family and which Yurovskiy brought to Moscow to hand over to the Kremlin superintendent Malikov. It reads: "1/ gold watch, male – 1 Paul Bouret [Russian famous watch-makers], No 38964, 14 carat . . . 3/ lady's gold chain – 1 with 5 rubies . . . 4/ male gold chain – 1 . . . 1gold egg with a crown . . . 1 heart shaped trinket with ruby, 1 small locket with the date 1905 and initials 'O.N.' [etc]" (Right) Joy, Alexei's pet dog which survived the Yekaterinburg massacre. Facing page: The cover of Alexandra Feodorovna's diary. and the last diary record made by the Tsarina several hours before the execution. She expressed her anxiety because their kitchen-boy had been sent away. That startled her . . . on the night of July 3/16 – 4/17, 1918, the whole family, Doctor Botkin and the servants were murdered.

Cesarevitch Alexei Nikolayevitch

be replaced by the one whom we have taken for doctor Yurovskiy".

The "doctor", Yakov Mikhailovitch Yurovskiy (1878-1938), the son of a glazier and seamstress, was born in Tomsk, Siberia. He finished two classes of the Jewish-Russian school and then trained in watchmaking. At the age of twenty-two he served a sentence for manslaughter – the details of the case are unavailable because most criminal records have not been preserved "for lack of historical significance". Later he joined the Jewish socialist union "Bund" and became a professional revolutionary and a social-democrat. During World War I he worked as a medical attendant in the Yekaterinburg infirmary. He achieved his ambition after the October coup, when he became a member of the Regional Cheka Board, Deputy Commissar of Justice. As Commissar of the "House of Special Purpose", he played one of the most sinister parts in the assassination along with Philipp Goloschekin, leader of the Ural Party organization and Military Commissar of the Ural region, and Alexander Beloborodov, Chairman of the Presidium of the Ural Regional Soviet.

The scenario of the tragedy had already been written in Moscow. For days the executioner and his victims met, talked, looked each other straight in the eye. The "doctor" knew already how he would organize their murder and all he awaited was the signal from Moscow.

Alexandra Feodorovna's last diary entry was dated July 3/17, Tuesday: "Irina's 23rd BD [birthday]. 11. Grey morning, later lovely sunshine. Baby has a slight cold. All went out 1/2 hour in the morning. Olga and I arranged our medicines [a secret word for jewels]. T. [Tatiana] read. 3. Rel. [religious] readings. They went out. T. stayed with me and we read the b. [books] by pr. [preacher] Amos and pr. [preacher] Avdiy. Talked. Every morning the superint.[endent] comes to our rooms, at last after a week brought

312

Nikolay's diary entry on May 31, Ascension day: "In the morning long, but in vain, [we] were waiting for the clergymen to come for the mass: they were busy in their churches. In the afternoon we were not allowed to go out in the garden for some reason. Avdeyev came and had a long talk with Yevg. Serg. [Botkin]. According to him, he [Avdeyev] and the regional soviet fear of anarchists' actions and therefore we shall have to leave soon, probably for Moscow! He asked us to prepare for departure. We began to pack immediately, but quietly, at special Avdeyev's request, so as not to draw the attention of the guards' rank. About 11 p.m. he returned and said that we'd have to stay for several more days. So far the 1st of June we remain bivouacking, without unpacking. The weather was fine; went out for a walk, as usual, in two shifts. At last, after supper Avdeyev, slightly one over the eight, declared to Botkin that the anarchists were seized and that the danger was past and our departure cancelled! After all our preparations it became very dull! In the evening we played bezique."

Sunday, June 3. "There was no mass again. All this week I have been reading and finished today the story 'Emperor Pavel I' by Schilder — very interesting. We all are expecting Sednev and Nagorny, whom they promised to let us join today."

Tuesday, June 5. "Dear Anastasia has already turned seventeen today. . . I am reading the third volume by Saltykov: it is entertaining and clever! All the family went out before tea. Since yesterday Kharitonov cooks for us, food supplies arrive every other day. The daughters are learning to cook from him and in the evenings they knead flour, and in the morning they even bake bread! That's not bad!"

Saturday, June 9. "These recent days the weather has been lovely . . . At Botkin's written request we are allowed on hour and a half walks. Today during tea-time 6 men came in, probably – of the regional soviet, to have a look which windows to open. This question has been discussed for about two weeks! Various queer persons came and silently examined the windows in our presence. The fragrance from all the gardens of the town is wonderful."

June 10. Whitsunday. [The day] was marked with various events: in the morning they opened one of our windows, Yevg. Serg. fell ill with his kidneys and suffered much . . . a real mass was served . . . Alix and Alexei had supper with us . . . yesterday's visitors were people's commissars from Petrograd . . ."

eggs again for Baby. 8. Supper. Suddenly Leonka Sednev [the kitchen-boy] *was fetched to go and see his Uncle and flew off. Wonder whether it's true and we shall see the boy back again. Played bezique with N.* [Nikolai]. *10 1/2 to bed. 15 degrees."*

The Tsarina dated her diary up to August 31. But there were no more entries. On the night of 3/16 to 4/17 July, the former Tsar, his wife and children, together with their four retainers were executed. Ten years later Yakov Yurovskiy would write an account of the execution at the request of Pokrovskiy, a professor of history:

"On July 16, a coded telegram came from Perm which brought the order to exterminate the 'R-vs' [Romanovs]. *On the 16th, at six in the evening Philipp G-n* [Goloschekin] *organized to carry out the order. At 12 at night a car was to come to take away the corpses . . . The lorry did not come at 12, it came at half-past one. This caused delay in carrying out the order. Meanwhile, preparations were made: 12 men were selected* (inc.[luding] *6 Letts) with revolvers who were to carry out the order. Two of the Letts refused to shoot at the girls. When the automobile came everybody was asleep. We wakened Botkin, and he woke the others . . . The Romanovs did not suspect anything. The sup.*[erintendent –Yurovskiy implies himself] *went for them personally and led them down the stairs to the lower rooms. Nik.*[olai] *carried A-i* [Alexei] *in his arms, the others carried cushions and various small things. Having entered the empty room A.*[lexandra] *F.*[eodor-ovna) *asked: 'Well, isn't there a chair? Can't I have a seat?' The sup. ordered to bring two chairs. Nik. had A-i seated in one of them, and A.F. sat down on the other. The sup. ordered the others to form a line. When they did so the squad was called in. When the squad came,*

Nikolai II Tsar of Russia

(Above) A letter written by Nicky to Alix in 1894 before their engagement. At that time they were so eager to surmount the difficulties they faced, to crown their love for each other, and saw only sunshine ahead. It reads: *"Good morning my angel. I dreamt of you my sweet one & it was a comfort to be able to talk to you! The weather is fine, the sun bright – It is the 11th anniversary of Papa's Coronation. All the church-bells are ringing merrily & they cheer one up. I hope today a letter will come fr. [om] my dearest girly-darling! I must stop now Pelly-dear [this was the secret name for each other, only known to her sister Ella]. In church I am going to pray fervently for my little Alix's happiness; may our Saviour keep all griefs & sorrows away and may He bless you with any gift you ask Him for! Many tender kisses do I send you & remain my own beloved precious Alix, ever yr. truly loving & deeply devoted (unto death) old, Nicky."* Nikolai's diary entry on Thursday, June 14, is full of frustration and anxiety. *"Our dear Maria has turned nineteen today. The weather was still tropical, with 26 degrees in the shade and in the rooms 24 degrees, so hard to bear! Spent a night of anxiety and kept vigil dressed . . . All this happened because these days we have received two letters, one after the other, which informed us that we should be ready to be kidnapped by some faithful people! But the day passed, and nothing happened, and expectation and uncertainty were so tantalizing."*

the sup. told the R-vs that in view of the fact that their relations in Europe continued the intervention against the Soviet Russia, the Ural Executive Committee resolved to execute them by shooting. Nikolai turned his back upon the squad, his face to his family, then, as if having regained his senses, turned to the sup. with a question: 'What? What?' The sup. repeated quickly and ordered the squad to get ready. The squad had been instructed beforehand whom each of them was to shoot at and they were ordered to aim straight at the hearts so as to avoid too much bloodshed and finish up soon. Nikolai did not pronounce anything else, he turned to his family again, the others uttered several incoherent exclamations, all lasted a few seconds. Then the fusillade began which took two or three minutes. Nik. was killed by the sup. himself, then instantly died A.F. and the people of the R-vs. . . . A-i, three of his sisters, the maid-of-honour and Botkin were still alive and we had to finish them off. It surprised the sup. for they had aimed straight at the hearts. It was also surprising that the revolver bullets ricocheted on something and hailed thick and fast all over the room . . ."

Under the cover of night the bodies were loaded onto a lorry and driven to a forest, where they were stripped of their clothes, thrown down an old mine, and covered with earth. For the next three nights, the murderers felt restless as they continued the outrageous violation of the dead. Twice the bodies were unearthed until at last they were thrown into two specially dug graves, sulphuric acid poured over the corpses which were then covered with earth and railway sleepers so that there were no traces of the graves.

The motives behind the frenzied attempts to remove any traces of the massacre are clear: at that time Bolsheviks seemed to have little hope of holding on to power. Thus, without the last communion, in unknown graves, without even crosses to mark them, the Russian "true-believers" – the Emperor, his wife and children, and their faithful retainers who had refused to part from their Tsar – were buried. Many more secret, disguised mass burial sites would be filled with bodies of the Tsar's former subjects. Thousands of such mass graves are scattered all over the Russian land.

Tsarina Alexandra Feodorovna

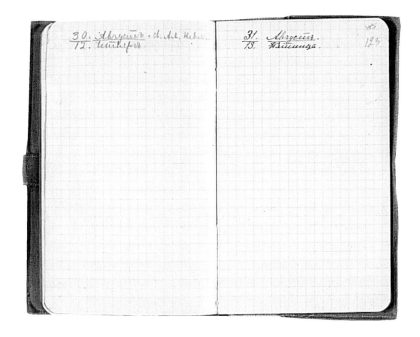

"God's Blessing And His Words Upon Us.
  Why, seeing an orthodox cemetery, do we begin to feel dull at heart?
  Because life on earth is bustle, we've never striven against the desires,
  We've served our flesh and have cared for idle comfort, in spite and slander.
  And why, standing by the shrine of pious people, do we feel contented?
  Because their life was sacrifice; as Christ suffered and after His suffering
  There was Easter.
  Thus a pious person endures spite and persecution . . ."

                                        Tatiana Romanova

Thursday, June 21. "... Today there was a change of superintendents. At dinnertime came Beloborodov and others and declared that Avdeyev would be replaced by the one whom we have taken for a doctor Yurovskiy. In the afternoon, together with his assistant, they did the inventory of the gold objects, ours and the children's, the most part of which [rings, bracelets etc.] they carried away. They explained that an unpleasant story had happened in our house and mentioned that some of our things had been lost . . . Sorry for Avdeyev, but he is to blame for not preventing his people from stealing . . ." Saturday, June 23. "Yurovskiy has brought us a box containing all our precious objects, we had to verify the contents and in front of us he sealed the box and left it with us. Yurovskiy and his assistant understood which people were guarding us and protecting us, robbing us. They were even stealing our food, now we start receiving it again."

Monday, June 25. "Our life has not changed a bit under Yu [rovskiy]. He comes into the bed-room to check the safety of the seal on the box and looks through the open window. All morning and until 4 p.m. they checked and repaired the electric lights. Keeping watch inside the house are new [ly arrived] Letts, and outside have remained the same — partly soldiers, partly workers! As rumours have it, some of Avdeyev's people are already under arrest. The door to the shed with our luggage has been sealed up. I wish it had been done a month ago! During the night there has been a thunder storm and it is fresh now."

Thursday, June 28. "This morning, at about 10.30, three workers approached the open window, lifted a heavy grating and they hanged it on the outside of the window, without us being informed by Yurovskiy. We like this man less and less every day. I have started to read the eight volumes by Saltykov."

Saturday, June 30. "Alexei has taken his first bath after Tobolsk; his knee is getting better, but he is unable to keep it completely straight. The weather is warm and pleasant. From the outside we do not hear any news."

This was the last diary entry written by the last Tsar of Russia.

(Left) The diary of the Tsarina, open on the pages in which she filled dates, for words which were never to be written.
"God's blessing And His Word Upon Us. Why, seeing an orthodox cemetery . . ." These words handwritten by Tatiana in her notebook, when in captivity, could be her own, or they could be something she had read, or a sermon she had heard. They express the nature of this very religious girl, and reflect the humility and the strength of spirit of the Tsar and his family.

Chapter Fourteen

EPILOGUE:
FAITHFUL
TO THE TSAR

" THE GREAT SOULS OF RUSSIA, SMEARED WITH THE MUD OF POLITICIANS".

The attitude of members of the Romanov House to the February revolution was varied – some hoped that the replacement of the Tsar would give Russia fresh impetus for rapid progress. Grand Duke Kirill Vladimirovitch, Nikolai II's cousin, is said to have welcomed the event with a red bow in his breast pocket; others were more discreet and preferred to lie low in their Crimean estates, far away from the centres of revolution and close enough to Russia's frontiers should flight be necessary; those who believed themselves true Russian patriots felt they had to go through these crucial days with their Motherland, sharing all hardship with the people.

All the Romanovs became ordinary citizens of the "Great Russia", and many were rather enthusiastic about it. They were alive, and full of hopes and plans. The former Tsar thought he would be able to settle in the Crimea and live the quiet family life of a country gentleman; his dreams were shared by his brother Mikhail Alexandrovitch; Grand Duke Nikolai Mikhailovitch, a noted historian, wanted devote himself solely to history and give up military service; Dmitriy Paley was a promising young poet. However, life was to show them no mercy. The fateful year of 1917 had taken away their status, property and privilege; the years of 1918-1919 took many of their lives.Twenty men, women and children were shot, bayonetted and thrown alive down mine-shafts . All these "executions" were carried out without trial or legal process, without even charges being made against the victims. Their crime was that they belonged to the Imperial family.

The first name on this list for extermination was that of the former Tsar's young brother, Grand Duke Mikhail Alexandrovitch. He was kidnapped by the Bolsheviks and shot – together with his secretary, the Englishman Brian Johnson – in Perm, on the night of June 12-13, 1918. Just over a month later came the murders in the Ipatyev House on the night of July 16-17. The next tragic chapter was staged in the small Ural town of Alapayevsk, the following night. The victims were six members of the Romanov family – the Tsarina's sister Grand Duchess Yelizaveta Feodorovna ("Ella"); Grand Duke Sergei Mikhailovitch; three of Grand Duke Konstantin Konstantinovitch' sons – Ioann, Konstantin and Igor – and Prince Vladimir Paley, son of Grand Duke Pavel Alexandrovitch by his morganatic marriage. Strictly speaking, Vladimir Paley was not a member of the Imperial House, but the fact that his father was a Grand Duke and the former Tsar his cousin, was crucial in deciding his fate. Along with Yelizaveta's "sister-nun", Varvara Yakovleva, and the Duke's secretary Feodor Mikhailovitch Remez, they were taken to an abandoned mine-shaft. They were made to stand facing the shaft as the soldiers beat them with rifle-butts. All happened so quickly that only Sergei Mikhailovitch resisted and he was shot as he tried to fight his executioners. Grenades were lobbed into the mine-shaft to complete the job. They all died immediately, as was established by Sokolov, the White Guard investigator, in 1918. In the 1920s, Sokolov would continue his investigation in Paris, and parts of his conclusions were published. After his death, the files would travel to Germany, and after the defeat of Nazi Germany, they would be found and confiscated by the Soviet KGB. For decades they were kept secret, and only recently they have become available for study by experts and historians. With a thirst for miracles, some believed in a legend that not all the Alapayevsk martyrs had died at once, that "Ella" and Ioann survived for two days; local peasants recalled that for a long time they could hear faint voices singing hymns "coming from under the earth". The facts, though, leave no grounds for substantiating this folk memory. There is no evidence about the circumstances of the death of Grand Duke Nikolai Konstantinovitch and his son Artemiy in Tashkent.

The last act took place in 1919, in the Fortress of Sts. Peter and Paul where four Romanovs were prisoners – Grand Dukes Georgiy Mikhailovitch, Nikolai Mikhailovitch, Dmitriy Konstantinovitch and Pavel Alexandrovitch. In September 1918, the Soviet Government instituted the policy of the "Red Terror" which engulfed the country and was to annihilate millions of innocent Russians. It also decided the fate of the prisoners in the Fortress. The writer Maxim Gorkiy and the Russian Academy of Sciences wrote to Lenin in an attempt to intervene on behalf of the historian Nikolai Mikhailovitch Romanov – but to no avail. The decision of the All-Russian Special Commission for Combating Counter-Revolution and Sabotage (Cheka), on January 29, 1919, meant that the Grand Dukes were executed. Many Romanovs managed to survive and escaped abroad, scattering to the four corners of the world.

Immediately after the February revolution the retinues and retainers of the Imperial Family were confronted with the dilemma – remain faithful to their deposed Tsar and Tsarina, or flight. Many were to prefer the latter. The Imperial staff was given two days to decide, and those who remained shared the lot of the Tsar and his family, and were put under house arrest. Forty-six did not abandon the Tsar; thirty-six followed him to Tobolsk.

On March 21, 1917, Anna Alexandrovna Vyrubova and Julia Alexandrovna ("Lili") Dehn, the Tsarina's maids of honour and her last close friends, were arrested and taken to the Fortress of Sts..Peter and Paul. "Lili" Dehn was set free the next day, Vyrubova was held for five months. They both managed to escape abroad. The tutors of the Tsar's children, the Swiss Pierre Gilliard and Englishman George Sydney Gibbs, followed the family to Tobolsk and later to Yekaterinburg. But when they arrived in Yekaterinburg, they were not allowed to leave the train until the Imperial children had been driven away. They did not see the family again. Gilliard stayed in Siberia while Sokolov's investigation was carried out when the White Guards recaptured Yekaterinburg. Together with the retreating White Guards units, he would escort the effects found during the investigation to Mukden in Manchuria, where they were handed over to the French Mission. Later, with his wife Alexandra Feodorovna Tegleva, who had been Anastasia's nurse, Gilliard returned to his native Switzerland where he died in 1962 at the age of 83.

General Ilya Leonidovitch Tatischev had not been a member of the Imperial retinue, but when he learned that Nikolai needed his help, he did not hesitate to join his sovereign. Later Kerenskiy characterised his action: "Tatischev always behaved with dignity, always the way one ought to – that was a rare exception among the courtiers then". He followed the Tsar to Tobolsk and Yekaterinburg, but on arrival in Yekaterinburg on May 23, 1918, Tatischev was arrested with the valets Alexander Alexandrovitch Volkov and Terentiy Ivanovitch Chemodurov; Countess Anastasia Vasilyevna Hendrikova, the Tsarina's maid of honour; and the children's tutor Catherine Schneider. Fräulein Schneider had taught the Russian language to the Tsarina and, ten years earlier, to her older sister "Ella". In exile in Tobolsk, she taught mathematics and Russian grammar to the younger Grand Duchesses and Alexei. The two women and Volkov were later taken to Perm and sentenced to death. Volkov, miraculously, managed to escape.

Prince Vasiliy Alexandrovitch Dolgorukov, the Tsar's close friend, came to Yekaterinburg together with Nikolai on April 30, only to be arrested and taken to prison the same day. He was executed together with Tatischev. Old Chemodurov was set free by the White Guards when they took Yekaterinburg after the murder of the Romanov family, but he could not survive the grief and soon died.

Only Doctor Yevgeniy Sergeyevitch Botkin; Anna Stepanovna Demidova, the maid; Alexei Yegorovitch Trupp, the footman; Ivan Mikhailovitch Kharitonov the cook; Ivan Dmitrievitch Sednev, the footman; Klementiy Grigoryevitch Nagorny, the sailor who was Cesarevitch Alexei's constant companion, and the fourteen year-old kitchen boy Leonid Sednev were admitted to the Ipatyev House. Nagorny and Sednev were later taken to prison and executed as "former sailors who had betrayed the revolution". On July 16, the kitchen-boy Sednev was sent away – the rest were murdered along with the Imperial Family. One of the soldiers later claimed that Doctor Botkin had been given a chance to save himself: "You are not responsible for anything . . . We just deem it our duty to warn you about the personal danger you are in." The doctor kept silent, then rose to his feet to say: "I am glad there are still people who care for my personal destiny. I'm thankful to you for your wish to meet my needs – but help this unfortunate family. That will be a great deed. There, in that house, blossom the great souls of Russia, smeared with the mud of politicians".

Index

In the text of this book we have used spellings for Russian names and places that give as close as possible an anglicised Russian spelling. Cross references are provided when a person is described under more than one name. This index refers only to text.